Evil and Pain

Evil and Pain

A Critique of the Materialistic Account of Evil

JOSEPH B. ONYANGO OKELLO

WIPF & STOCK · Eugene, Oregon

EVIL AND PAIN
A Critique of the Materialistic Account of Evil

Copyright © 2017 Joseph B. Onyango Okello. All rights reserved. Except for brief quotations in critical publications or reviews, no part of this book may be reproduced in any manner without prior written permission from the publisher. Write: Permissions, Wipf and Stock Publishers, 199 W. 8th Ave., Suite 3, Eugene, OR 97401.

Wipf & Stock
An Imprint of Wipf and Stock Publishers
199 W. 8th Ave., Suite 3
Eugene, OR 97401

www.wipfandstock.com

PAPERBACK ISBN: 978-1-5326-0132-3
HARDCOVER ISBN: 978-1-5326-0134-7
EBOOK ISBN: 978-1-5326-0133-0

Manufactured in the U.S.A.   JUNE 13, 2017

Dedicated to

Sophie Munyao-Okello—my dear wife who continues to bear witness to God's glory in the midst of intense suffering

Contents

Acknowledgments | *ix*

Introduction | 1
1   Pain and Pleasure | 11
2   Pain and Evil | 29
3   Pleasure and Good | 49
4   Objective Value and Relative Value | 66
5   Death and Evil | 85
6   God and Pain | 114
7   Relation of Evil to Pain | 134
8   The Problem | 152
9   The Why Question | 172

Bibliography | *191*
Index | *197*

Acknowledgments

Since my seminary days, I have spent countless hours of reflection on the question of suffering and pain. Various individuals have helped shape my view along the way. One such individual is professor Jerry Walls, who encouraged me to seek higher levels of scholarship in my academic pursuits. Several classes of philosophy with Jerry planted an intellectual seed that spurred the urge for rational inquiry into issues affecting my immediate context, one of them being the major theme of this book.

Also, various encounters with Michael Peterson, professor of philosophy at Asbury Theological Seminary, influenced my thinking in many ways, thereby giving me a road map for developing the personal philosophy represented in this work. I am deeply indebted to Mike for the materials made available by the high level of scholarship exemplified in his works. Whereas I depart, in several ways, from Mike's and Jerry's philosophical assumptions as far as this work is concerned, I still owe both of them a deep gratitude for enabling me to aspire toward higher levels of scholarship.

I am also grateful to David Bradshaw, professor of philosophy at the University of Kentucky, not only for personally guiding me through the process of rigorous thinking that has now shaped my intellectual life, but also for encouraging me, by his example, to avoid the temptation of becoming a lazy scholar. Memories of numerous classroom and office meetings with David haunt me whenever the appetitive aspects of my soul refuse to bow to the dictates of reason.

Besides these world-class scholars, I received great encouragement from faculty and students at Asbury Theological Seminary. Having taught a course on suffering, tragedy, and the Christian faith twice every three years, I am only just now beginning to understand the enormity of the subject. However, students and faculty of Asbury Seminary encouraged me to put my thoughts in writing, sensing that I might have something to say. Well, dear ones—here it is!

Within the Asbury community, I would specifically like to thank Judy Seitz who read the entire manuscript, offered invaluable suggestions for improvement as far as the language and formatting is concerned, and helped save my work from glaring and embarrassing errors. She is definitely a jewel at Asbury Seminary. I must add, however, that any conceptual or grammatical errors that might attend this work are, of course, mine.

I also thank my wonderful wife, Sophie, who always looks at me with bewilderment when I toss philosophical ideas her way. Just the same, she has always encouraged me to pursue academic excellence in spite of her suspicion that my mental faculties have quite possibly run amok. I would not trade her support and wonderful companionship for another. More importantly, Sophie does know the meaning of suffering, owing to her recent battle with cancer and subsequent treatments, which often seem as bad and, perhaps, just as dangerous as the disease itself. Countless trips to different doctors to help her with the healing process have been quite demanding, putting unimaginable strain on her. However, owing to her strong faith in Christ (much stronger than mine, of course), she continues to be an encouragement to my son and me.

The question of pain and suffering, therefore, has not been merely theoretical to my family. It has knocked at our doorstep and remains in our backyard for an indefinite period of time. The fact that it has been with us for this period of time, without question, afflicts us with great concern. Just the same, we still find hope in the one healer coming to us credentialed as the Great Physician. He alone can give us hope where none can be found.

For this reason, I thank my Savior and Redeemer Jesus Christ who conquered evil on the cross. Without him, the hope of finding release from suffering and pain is always an illusion. Without him, this book is a big lie. His promise, however, always stands, and we look forward to the day he will wipe off all our tears from our eyes and take away all the pains and sorrows from our lives.

Introduction

WHAT IS MATERIALISTIC HEDONISM? Broadly construed, it is the view in ethics that, on the one hand, finds pleasure and pain intrinsically good and intrinsically evil, respectively, while on the other, denies the metaphysical vantage point of dualism that thinks of mind as an immaterial entity substantially separate from the physical human body. Whether or not this thesis counts as a necessary truth in the logical sense will be the subject of this investigation. By "necessary truth," I refer to the kind of statements that cannot be false under any circumstances, and must, in addition, be true in all possible worlds. This hedonistic understanding of value that characterizes prominent naturalistic materialists, like that alluded to by J. L. Mackie (I describe this more fully in chapter 1), semantically seems to entail either a synonymous or a near synonymous relationship between evil and pain.

As noted, the view seems to accept the general postulates of ethical hedonism, contending that all intrinsically desirable things are what we would call *pleasure* and all intrinsically undesirable things are what we would call *pain*. More accurately, all things desirable in themselves are pleasant states of mind and all things undesirable in themselves are unpleasant states of mind. Moreover, one state of affairs remains more desirable in itself just in case that state of affairs contains more than another different state of mind. This view believes that the quantity of value in any state of affairs ought to be quantified by the amount of pleasure in it.[1]

According to Richard B. Brandt, philosophers such as Aristippus, Epicurus, Locke, Hobbes, Hume, Bentham, Mill, and Sigdwick defend ethical hedonism in their writings. Some of these philosophers, such as Epicurus, Hume, and Mill accepted the postulates of materialism. The religious suppositions of Locke, however, would have rendered him more of a

---

1. Brandt, "Hedonism," 432–34.

supernaturalist than a materialist. Additionally, whereas some philosophers made specific references to pleasure in their adumbrations of ethical hedonism, others also factored the idea of happiness into their explications as well. In their view, happiness seemed an intrinsic good. In saying that an individual is happy at any given time, the ethical hedonist really meant the individual in question was experiencing pleasure at the time. Some philosophers, however, felt that happiness was rather different from pleasure, and the debate on whether or not happiness and pleasure are essentially the same continues.[2]

According to Brandt, the hedonist would argue that the intrinsic desirability of a given state of affairs is something determined by the fact that the state of affairs is good, worthy of choice, or worthwhile when taken by itself. The hedonist does not deny that many things are desirable. Still, he or she does not find them desirable in themselves. The hedonist finds those things instrumentally desirable, but certainly not intrinsically desirable. Additionally, the hedonist observes that those things can be both instrumentally and intrinsically desirable. For the hedonist, a thing is instrumentally desirable if it results in later pleasures, and instrumentally undesirable if it yields later pain.[3]

I will show how the hedonist's thesis gained currency in the writings of major philosophers such as Epicurus, and utilitarians such as Jeremy Bentham and John Stuart Mill. According to Brandt, Bentham and Mill combined utilitarianism's generic principles with the thesis of hedonism, the generic principle being that a given course of action remains morally right if following that course of action can produce, in the agent's perspective, as much intrinsic goodness in our world as any other act the agent could perform, this goodness being understood as pleasure.[4]

Of course, in and of itself, hedonism does not entail materialism. Many hedonistic philosophers seem also to subscribe to dualistic postulates. Hence, my critique will not target these philosophers. Rather, I focus more on materialistic philosophers, whose views remain consistent with hedonism, consciously or unconsciously. Such philosophers find pain intrinsically evil and pleasure intrinsically good and, on that supposition, subscribe to a reductionism that makes one similar to the other. Given the essentialist reading of ethics, I intend to argue that this view seems rather misleading. I try to accomplish this feat, in what follows, by reorienting the contours of the debate, and suggesting that the problem of evil might, in

2. Ibid.
3. Ibid.
4. Ibid.

effect, be quite different from the problem of pain and that neither problem necessarily entails the other. Seen in this way, neither problem casts doubt on belief in God's existence.

Before embarking on a historical survey of subscribers to the hedonistic philosophy that seemed to give a nod to a materialistic understanding of evil and pain, let me describe materialism more fully than already presented. Materialists accept, as nonmaterialists do, that humans have minds. However, they begin to differ radically from nonmaterialists in their understanding of the nature of the human mind. Materialists give primary position to matter, but attribute to mind only a secondary position or no position at all. To be sure, extreme materialists, whose ethical views provide ingredients for my critique in this chapter, claim that the real world consists only of material things.[5]

Implicit in this understanding of extreme materialism is the denial of the existence of souls or spirits, a doctrine fundamental to Christian belief. According to materialism, we attribute our ability to explain anything on the basis of physical laws involving physical conditions of an antecedent nature. According to Keith Campbell, the appeal of materialism can be located in its alliance with advances in modern science. On this assumption, materialism claims that the only subject matters that can be adequately treated with a materialist methodology are those that belong to proper objects of knowledge. Whereas this claim escapes establishment by scientific experimentation, critical reflection on the range of human thought nonetheless establishes it.[6]

When materialists say humans have minds, they imply humans have sensations, emotions, beliefs, thoughts, purposes, as well as desires. D. M. Armstrong is a major thinker espousing this view. According to Armstrong, the answer to the question concerning the nature of mind can be located in the recent discoveries and hypotheses of modern science—discoveries that seem increasingly to confirm that the human mind can be accounted for in terms of purely physicochemical terms. Armstrong has in mind molecular biology and neurophysiology here. Hence, Armstrong suggests that we must try to forge our understanding of the nature of mind in purely physicochemical terms. One reason Armstrong puts great stock in science rests in his view that science is a discipline wherein individuals versed in their subject can reach substantial intellectual agreement concerning the truths they seek.[7]

5. Campbell, "Materialism," 179.
6. Ibid., 179–80.
7. Armstrong, "Nature of Mind," 209–10.

Armstrong, therefore, calls his position the materialistic view of human beings. He believes behaviorism is one account of human mental processes quite attractive to any philosopher sympathetic to the materialistic view of human beings—a view originally formulated by J. B. Watson, a psychologist. This view attracted both widespread interest and significant support from philosophers of science. Contrary to Cartesian dualism, that thought of the human mind as contained within the human body, Armstrong agrees with Watson by noting how, in his view, Descartes was mistaken for postulating this claim. For Armstrong, the mind was not an entity existing behind the behavior of the human body. Rather, it was part of that physical behavior. More correctly, Armstrong would argue, rather than believe human thought involves an inner process lying inside one's head thereby bringing about the words one speaks, Armstrong suggests we view thought as the very act of speaking or writing. The human mind, therefore, is not something internal to humans. It is external.[8]

Armstrong believes behaviorism so construed fits very well with a completely materialistic, or for that matter, physicalist view of humans. He finds the idea of drawing distinctions between mental processes and their manifestation in physical behavior quite unnecessary. For Armstrong, mental processes must be seen as identical with external expressions of physical behavior. If this claim is correct, the human mind remains consistent with the view that humans are no more than a physicochemical mechanism.[9]

The most obvious objection to this view, one Armstrong notes, is the observation that some mental processes remain unexpressed in behavior. He cites, for example, the possible fact of an individual who, though quite angry, successfully hides that feeling of anger.[10] Consider also, for example, that most humans remain relatively still while dreaming of participating in a rigorous physical activity such as running a marathon. These cases seem plausible counterexamples to materialistic behaviorism.

Armstrong tries to counter this objection by appealing to what he calls a disposition to behave. Humans do have the disposition to behave, even though at times they do not behave according to that disposition. Therefore, although an individual does not behave in any relevant way, he or she is disposed to behave in that way. Hence, suppose one could have responded angrily to an insult directed one's way through some form of physical aggression but chooses, instead, to restrain oneself. One would still be disposed to behave in that way if, say, one more relevant insult had been

8. Ibid., 211–12.
9. Ibid., 212.
10. Ibid.

hurled one's way. According to Armstrong, Gilbert Ryle defended this form of behaviorism.[11]

Although Armstrong accepts behaviorism, quite surprisingly he finds it a profoundly unnatural account of mental process. He thinks, for example, that speaking of a person's speech and action as identical with the individual's thought is quite unnatural. Rather than identifying thought with behavior, thought should be construed as lying behind behavior. For this reason, Armstrong finds behaviorism certainly wrong, though not altogether wrong. Of course, this expression sounds contradictory and Armstrong does nothing to address it. At any rate, he finds behaviorist philosophers wrong in their suppositions, quite possibly to the extent that they identify the mind with mental occurrences. But they are right to the extent that they find the human mind and its mental states logically linked to human behavior. By this expression, Armstrong means that one's mental state is such that under a suitable set of circumstances, it causes a specific range of behavior. Hence, one can define the human mind as the internal cause of a specific type of behavior rather than seeing it as the behavior itself.[12]

Behaviorism, therefore, is a version of materialism that links mental states to human behavior. It finds Cartesian dualism quite mistaken, specifically because advances in science seem to point us toward materialism or behaviorism. Gilbert Ryle, a philosopher Armstrong alludes to quite frequently in his article, also offered a philosophical critique of Cartesian dualism, a philosophical view traced back to René Descartes, as a way of defending materialism. Ryle accused Descartes of making a category mistake for postulating a mind-body dichotomy.[13]

Moreover, Roderick Chisholm summarized the materialist argument as follows: Either a human being is a physical entity or it is a nonphysical one. To the best of our knowledge, nothing seems to suggest that humans are nonphysical entities. Therefore, humans are physical things. I am a human being. This means I am a physical thing. If I am a physical thing, I must be a proper part or segment or portion of my body even if I find no way of determining, exactly, what proper part I turn out to be.[14]

Philosopher Thomas Nagel offers a powerful critique of the materialistic account of valuation, which he finds untenable specifically because of its subjectivist nature. For one, he believes we can find independent empirical reasons for rejecting the claims of the reductionism that characterizes

11. Ibid., 212–13.
12. Ibid., 213–14.
13. Ryle, "Exorcising Descartes,'" 355.
14. Chisholm, "Which Physical Thing Am I?" 295.

physicalism.[15] Second, we can find logical reasons for rejecting materialism's subjectivism about value. I wish to focus, however, on Nagel's rejection of the materialistic account of hedonistic valuation, one that might suppose pleasure is intrinsically good and pain intrinsically bad. According to Nagel, real value seems to be one of those things we find incompatible with materialism, or as Nagel labels it, evolutionary naturalism. For Nagel, the reality of value remains irreconcilable with traditional scientific and materialistic naturalism. The scientific and materialistic understanding of value seems rather subjective and depends heavily on what Nagel calls motivational dispositions and responses. This sort of subjectivism applies to the works of thinkers such as David Hume, especially because of his belief that value judgments find their expressions through the subject's sentiment.[16]

Whereas believers in realism about value can agree that pleasure and pain remain crucially linked to our responses of attraction and aversion to them, respectively, they part ways with subjectivists about value when the realists begin to determine the value of experiences removed from us—the sort of experiences whose pain or pleasure we cannot feel, including future experiences and experiences of other subjects. Subjectivists seem to suggest that determining such values remains an exercise that depends on our internal attitudes and dispositions.[17]

Nagel thinks subjectivism, in its most plausible form, relies on a variant of a Humean conception of the passions, including the moral sense we have in us. For Nagel, value judgments read in this way seem grounded in aspects of a more sophisticated and reflective motivational system than the basic appetites and instinctive emotions. This understanding suggests that moral judgments manifest an attachment to practices or frameworks that promote the general wellbeing of others. More importantly, the essential point they press is that valuations are essentially the expression of sentiment, and remain correct or incorrect in reference to sentiment.[18] By sentiment, Nagel seems to have in mind David Hume's view and contention that sentiment (or feelings) is the highest good.

According to Nagel, the realist understanding of valuation holds that the correctness of human value judgment gets determined by the fact that human dispositions and the actual structure and weight of values in a specific moral situations remain consistent with each other. The level of immediate feelings such as pleasure and pain do not determine their correctness.

---

15. Nagel, *Mind and Cosmos*, 5.
16. Ibid., 98–99.
17. Ibid., 99.
18. Ibid., 100.

INTRODUCTION

Therefore, according to Nagel, subjectivists find the ground for the truth of value judgments in psychological facts concerning our human motivational dispositions of pleasure and pain, for example.

Just the same, Nagel argues that realists about value deny this subjectivist vantage point. Realists about value do not hold that anything else, natural or supernatural, determines the truth of value judgments. Rather, it is made true by nothing but the value judgment itself. For example, consider the following claim: if you do not step on the brakes of your car, you will run over that dog. This claim confirms the moral truth that you should step on your brakes. This example allows Nagel to press his argument that the general moral truth warrants our conclusion that the moral truth in question is not affirmed by facts of any kind. The moral truth in question is intrinsic, so to speak, to the value claim. In our case, it is intrinsic to the claim that following a course of action that will alleviate the suffering of a sentient creature counts in favor of following that course of action. Hence, that truth is not based on the subjective motivational feeling of the moral agent.[19]

Nagel believes that the real badness of pain and the ability to recognize its badness seem quite superfluous in a naturalistic-cum-materialistic explanation of our aversion to pain. He holds that our tendency to avoid pain is one that enhances fitness, but only because the aversion leads us to avoid the sort of harm and injury associated with pain rather than because of the fact that pain is really bad. According to Nagel, we remain naturally blind to the fact that as far as materialistic natural selection is concerned, pain could perfectly well be in itself good, and pleasure in itself bad. The other likely alternative, however, is that both of them could be valueless in themselves. Hence, if we construe the Darwinian perspective realistically, it seems to render human impressions of value completely groundless.[20]

In spite of making this claim, Nagel does admit to thinking that pain is really bad and that pleasure is really good, and that one is not just something we hate while the other something we like. What Nagel does not seem to state, however, is whether he thinks pain is synonymous with badness and pleasure is synonymous with goodness as the hedonists do. Moreover, even though Nagel reflects some kind of realism about value, he rejects the kind of realism promoted by the supernaturalism of this work. For example, he does not find the design alternative as a real option, because he lacks the sense of divinity that compels many to see the world as the expression of

---

19. Ibid., 101–2.
20. Ibid., 109–10.

divine purpose. Nevertheless, Nagel remains grateful to the defenders of intelligent design for challenging the scientific worldview.[21]

My reason for citing Thomas Nagel in this way is to show that we do find, even among nonreligious thinkers, individuals disagreeing with materialistic ethical hedonism. I do not intend to argue here that all hedonists are materialists. Not only would such a task fall beyond my goals for this work. It seems wrong. We would not be too hard pressed to find at least one person who happens to be both a hedonist and a nonmaterialist.

What I intend to do here, therefore, is show how a specific variety of materialism, namely materialistic ethical hedonism, finds belief in God problematic based on what it adopts as an acceptable value theory on the one hand and, on the other, what it adopts as a plausible alternative to belief in God. Apparently, the claims of hedonism seemed intellectually attractive to many thinkers. Moreover, the arrival of Darwinian evolution undercut possible metaphysical presuppositions that would eventually enable them to embrace naturalism by default. Tracing a fairly thin history of this development would help shed more light on this. Notice, however, that when one adopts hedonism as a viable ethical theory on the one hand, and materialism as a viable metaphysical worldview on the other, one likely adopts a composite worldview that finds pleasure synonymous with good and pain synonymous with evil. Indeed, this process seems to play itself out when we examine individuals such as Epicurus, Bentham, Mill, and most recently, Sam Harris.

I will trace the thoughts of thinkers of this kind in chapter 1. I intend to highlight the rigors of their philosophy, while simultaneously exposing what I find conceptually misleading in their explications. This exercise will then lay the groundwork for the rest of this work, which I outline as follows. In the next chapter I contend that if the materialistic ethical hedonists such as those mentioned above use the terms *evil* and *pain* synonymously and interchangeably, then their materialist view of ethics seems fallacious. My contention is that those terms do not necessarily entail each other. Moreover, if we think they do entail each other, a logical demonstration will show the absurdities yielded by such a contention. My conclusion in this chapter is that the problem of evil is not the problem of pain. They belong to different categories.

Much like the second chapter, I contend in the third chapter, that we leave ourselves vulnerable to arguing fallaciously by using the term *pleasure* synonymously with *good*. Once again, I contend here that those terms do not necessarily imply each other. As in the previous chapter, I show how an exercise in logic reveals the absurd implications of thinking that both terms

---

21. Ibid., 12.

synonymously imply each other. I once again show that pleasure and good belong to different categories.

In the fourth chapter, I contend that objective value is a notion that makes sense only on an essentialist reading of ethics. By an essentialist reading, I refer to the view contending that morality comes from God's essentially good nature, and that since his nature is essentially good, we can trust that the standard of morality issued from him is for our own good. I conclude that the question raised by the so-called problem of evil can only be epistemologically justified under the essentialist reading of ethics rather than on a different ethical theory.

In the fifth chapter, I revisit the hitherto critiqued contention that there is such a thing as an instance of evil that is also painful. Suggesting that death is perhaps the best candidate for such an entity, I present the arguments from relevant scholars that can be given to show that death is both an instance of evil and an instance of pain. However, I also argue that if death can be seen as a good in at least one way, then it fails to satisfy conditions for which death could be strictly deemed both a pain and an evil. I proceed to point out the example in question, which shows that not even death, the highest form of human pain, can be deemed an evil in a strictly synonymous sense. I conclude that finding an instance of pain that is also an instance of evil seems extremely difficult, though perhaps possible.

In the sixth chapter, I argue that pain cannot be used as evidence against God's existence for at least the following reason: If God is a person, then God must have personalistic attributes. These include the ability to feel and express pain. Clearly, we read in Scripture that God does feel pain. He is grieved, for example, that he created us (Gen 6:6). Grieving the spirit of God is also possible. Hence, if God can experience pain in his being, pain cannot be used as evidence against God's existence.

I contend in the seventh chapter that the relationship between pain and evil is not a synonymous one. The connection should best be seen as a causal one, with evil, understood as rebellion against God, bringing about the existence of pain. This connection is what we see in the Christian doctrine of the fall of humanity. My conclusion here is that the common distinction between natural and moral evil might be misguided because it is based on the assumption that pain and evil remain synonymous, though I admit the distinction is a helpful one for purposes of clarifying our interlocutions.

In the eighth chapter I contend that the problem of evil is quite different from the problem of pain, for the simple reason that evil is not synonymous with pain. We must, therefore, restate the problem of evil differently from how we would state the problem of pain. Upon showing how we can restate these two problems differently, we will discover, in light of the frameworks presented in previous chapters, that neither problem presents severe challenges to belief in God.

In the ninth and final chapter I argue that atheists have no epistemological justification to ask why God permits the occurrence of what atheists call pointless suffering, for the atheists' epistemological framework already rules out the existence of God. They cannot meaningfully ask a being they consider nonexistent to give reasons for permitting pointless suffering. Such a question can only be asked by believers in God who, rather than believe that the suffering in question is pointless, really believe that God has reasons for such suffering, even though the reasons may be unavailable to them. Let us turn to the first chapter, which offers a brief history of how materialistic ethical hedonism might have evolved to be what it is today.

1

Pain and Pleasure

IN THIS CHAPTER, I try to locate the origin of a materialistic understanding of good and evil. I find this exercise foundational for the rest of this work for several reasons. First, a materialistic view of good and evil dominates a certain group of contemporary utilitarian thinkers who find evil and pain synonymous, or nearly synonymous. I back this claim up later in this chapter. Second, based on the assumption that these terms seem synonymous or coterminous, a certain objection (wrongheaded, I think) to believe in the existence of God ensues, based on the reality of pain, or for that matter, evil. In order to see how this fact seems to play itself out, I offer an outline of the views of the thinkers alluded to earlier. Third, if I can locate at least one area in which this view might be mistaken, the objection to theism via this materialistic front seems to lose its force.

As promised in the introduction, let me begin with a crucial allusion made by J. L. Mackie concerning a variety of thinkers subscribing to the view already mentioned. In his famous article, "Evil and Omnipotence," Mackie discusses physical evil and draws attention to a certain complaint he finds among theists. According to Mackie, theists often seize the opportunity to accuse atheistic thinkers of taking a low materialistic view of good and evil. This view equates *good* and *evil* with *pleasure* and *pain*, respectively. In other words, the view uses *evil* to denote *pain* on the one hand, and *good* to denote *pleasure*, on the other. Hence, theists find the thinkers in question, who ignore the more spiritual goods, quite capable of arising in the struggle against evils.[1] This assumption, located by Mackie, that evil and pain could be synonymous in the materialistic sense, should not strike any thinker as a recent formulation. We can locate a similar assumption among thinkers in specific eras of ancient philosophy and track a variety of

---

1. Mackie, *Miracle of Theism*, 153.

its significant adherents from that time period into modern and contemporary philosophy.

For example, from the writings of Eudoxus of Cnidus and those of Epicurus, this materialistic understanding of evil and pain finds some of its earliest adumbration. Whether or not Eudoxus was a materialist remains unclear, though Epicurus certainly subscribed to materialism. Also, a variety of modern philosophers, such as John Stuart Mill, endorse this view. In an attempt to determine how these figures develop their contentions, especially with respect to hedonism, let me begin with Eudoxus.

Eudoxus on Pain and Pleasure

In Aristotle's *Nichomachean Ethics* we find snippets of the view linking *good* with *pleasure*, and *bad*, or *evil*, with *pain*—a view Aristotle did not exactly endorse, but traces to an ancient philosopher named Eudoxus. Eudoxus found *pleasure* quite synonymous with *good*. His belief, according to Aristotle, was based on the fact that all things, whether rational or nonrational, aim at pleasure. Owing to the observation that—to use Eudoxus' words—most excellent things often constitute our object of choice, pleasure was, for all things, the chief good. Eudoxus also believes that this conclusion, that pleasure was the chief good, followed just as plainly with respect to our study of pain. He found pain contrary to pleasure. According to Aristotle's report, Eudoxus maintained that pain was an object of aversion for all things. Therefore, pleasure, its contrary, had to be an object of choice.[2]

If Aristotle cites Eudoxus correctly, Eudoxus' view seems to render pain the chief bad. Stated differently, if pleasure seems the highest good to us, and pain the contrary of pleasure, then pain, logically speaking, seems to entail the chief bad, or more accurately, the chief evil. Thus, in Eudoxus we find a conviction that comes quite close to equating feelings of pleasure with good and feelings of pain with evil.

An objector might admit that pain, in Eudoxus' view, remains the chief good. However, the objector will point out, quite correctly, how this view need not locate pain as the only evil. Some evils exist that remain quite painless. Coming solely from the objector, the objection has considerable merit. However, if taken as a possible adumbration of Eudoxus, we find no indications from Eudoxus what such evils might be. A plainer account of this view seems to find a voice in the writings of Epicurus.

---

2. Aristotle, "Nichomachean Ethics," 1153b25.

Epicurus on Pain and Pleasure

One of Epicurus' claims in his "Letter to Menoeceus" postulates that pleasure remains the starting point and goal of living blessedly. He regards pleasure as our first innate good—the starting point of every choice and avoidance. Epicurus arrives at this conclusion because he believes we judge every good by the criterion of feeling. From these words alone, one might hold, arguably, that the animalistic faculty of feeling seems the standard of determining morality. Moreover, this criterion of feeling helps the Epicurean moralists to see how they do not need to choose every pleasure because some pains remain better than pleasure if greater and longer pleasures follow those instances of pain.[3]

Thus, on the one hand, Epicurus argues that every pleasure is a good thing for the simple reason that pleasure seems to have a nature congenial to us. On the other, he thinks the moral agent ought not to choose every pleasure.[4] We find his basis for this claim in his "Principle Doctrines." In that work, Epicurus explains how things producing certain pleasures cause troubles (i.e., pain) more times than they cause pleasures.[5] Similarly, Epicurus would argue that every pain is a bad thing. However, not every pain should be avoided, for the reasons already outlined.[6] Additionally, in his "Principal Doctrines," Epicurus contends that the removal of pain sets the limit of the magnitude of pleasures, and wherever we find a pleasurable feeling, we would find no feeling of pain and no feeling of distress. He also contends that the just life (or, the moral life) is one most free from disturbance, but the unjust life is full of the greatest disturbance.[7] Disturbance, in this context, ought to be understood as a variance of pain.

From these considerations, Epicurus seems to think that feelings of pleasure and pain determine for us the nature of goodness and badness, respectively. More significantly, Epicurus seems to think that feelings remain, for us, the standard of morality. Hence, suppose a given course of action results in feelings of pleasure, or if the act is, by its very nature, a pleasurable one, then the act must be judged good. Similarly, if a given course of action results in feelings of pain, or if the act is, by its very nature, a painful one, then the action in question must be judged morally bad. Within this ethical discourse, the expression "moral badness" seems used quite interchangeably with "evil."

---

3. Epicurus, "Letter to Menoecus," 360.
4. Ibid.
5. Epicurus, "Principal Doctrines," VII.
6. Epicurus, "Letter to Menoecus," 360.
7. Epicurus, "Principal Doctrines," XVII.

As already noted, Epicurus thinks that pleasure is good without qualification. It is our first innate good. He also seems to think that pain is bad without qualification, innately bad, so to speak, because he contends that every pain is a bad thing, though, of course, he makes some concessions with respect to this intrinsic nature of pain. He does so by specifying instances where we could, appropriately, choose a painful course of action over and against a pleasurable one, on the one hand, or when we could reasonably avoid a painful course of action and choose a pleasurable one, on the other. Either way, pain is a bad thing, in his view. Hence, actions promoting pain must be considered morally bad. If they are morally bad, they must then be judged evil.

In his *Outlines of the History of Greek Philosophy*, Eduard Zeller observes that Epicurus declared the individual to be the aim of all action. Zeller's reading of Epicurus depicts a view that renders *feelings* the standard for determining good and evil, and that pleasure is the only unconditional good—the good after which all living beings strive. Zeller's interpretation of Epicurus also finds pain, in Epicurean terms, the only absolute evil—one that all beings avoid. In Zeller's view, Epicurean pleasure did not exactly mean the individual sensations of pleasure as such, but the happiness of an entire life.[8]

Zeller's reading of Epicurus might have some plausibility. However, I find his comment about individual sensations somewhat difficult to reconcile with the materialistic view upheld by Epicurus, the view that renders the human soul an entity composed of physical atoms. Epicurus reduced the human soul to a physical and material entity on the one hand, and on the other, declared it *the chief cause of sensation*. In other words, for Epicurus, the physical material soul remains the chief cause of sensation. Hence, in both instances, any state of the mind or soul must have materialistic properties irrespective of whether we speak of happiness or pleasure.

For this reason, I find Bertrand Russell's interpretation of Epicurus more correct than Zeller's when Russell portrays the Epicurean view upholding the claim that mental pleasures involve the contemplation of pleasures of the body, and that the only advantage mental pleasures have over bodily pleasures seems to include the fact that we can learn to contemplate pleasures rather than pain, thereby having more control over mental pleasures than we do over physical pleasures. Moreover, Russell adds, unless virtue means prudence in pursuit of pleasure, it remains a name without a referent; it remains empty.[9]

A significant number of contemporary philosophers believe Epicurean hedonism does, in fact, reduce *bad* to *pain* and *good* to *pleasure*. In other words, this view endorses a materialistic bias of the sort alluded to at the

---

8. Zeller, *Outlines of the History of Greek Philosophy*, 257.
9. Russell, *History of Western Philosophy*, 243–44.

beginning of this chapter. For example, Steven Luper recapitulates this very notion by noting that in the Epicurean view, something can be bad only if it causes pain in us. Similarly, something can be good only if it causes pleasure in us. Moreover, Luper ties this materialistic understanding of pleasure and pain to the Epicurean doctrine of annihilation. For example, Luper notes that given this hedonistic criterion, Epicurus could claim that dying is nothing to us for the simple reason that it causes us neither pain nor pleasure.[10]

Fred Feldman, without necessarily adopting the Epicurean position, finds no hesitation in branding Epicurus a hedonist. In order to show how Epicurean hedonism would spell itself out with respect to pain and pleasure, Feldman begins with the following consideration. Suppose that the simplest form of hedonism strikes us as true. According to this view, pleasure will be found intrinsically good and pain intrinsically bad. Moreover, nothing else would have any intrinsic value in this kind of a world. Thus, if we find a way to measure the amount of pleasure contained in an episode of pleasure and a way to measure the amount of pain contained in an episode of pain, and that both ways of measuring remain commensurate, the intrinsic value of that world can be determined in some definite sort of way, as follows: it is determined by considering how much pleasure is experienced throughout the history of that world and how much pain is also experienced throughout that same history. One then proceeds by subtracting the latter from the former, and the result is the hedonistic value of that world. Thus, the simplest form of hedonism says that the intrinsic value of that world remains identical to the hedonic value of that world.[11]

As already noted, Feldman does not think that a person's real welfare level ought to be determined in the simple-minded hedonistic manner sketched out in this way. He believes, quite correctly, that several other factors seem to contribute to determining how good a world is for a person. Just the same, Feldman, for purposes of his work, proceeds on the assumption that hedonism is true.[12]

The Epicurean view provides a basis for various versions of ethics in contemporary philosophy, especially with respect to discussions concerning the philosophy of death and dying. For example, Stephen E. Rosenbaum acknowledges that Epicurus offers a remedy for our attitude toward death. According to Rosenbaum, Epicurus seemed to claim that since death is neither good nor bad for the dead person, and since fearing something lacking some form of badness remains groundless at best, fearing death must strike

10. Luper, "Annihilation," 203.
11. Feldman, "Some Puzzles," 224.
12. Ibid., 225.

us as an unreasonable disposition. For this reason, no one should fear death. Hence, if Epicurus were correct in his supposition, we should, perhaps, try to revise our attitude toward our own deaths.[13]

By making this claim, Rosenbaum seemed to find the Epicurean view of death quite attractive. Notice that the Epicurean view of death was based on the contention that the soul, being made up of atoms, remains the chief cause of sensation of pleasure and pain. Stated differently, atoms make up the soul. The soul is the chief cause of sensation. Therefore, the atoms of the soul remain the chief cause of sensation. Moreover, human sensations of pleasure and pain become fundamentally materialistic. Conclusively, if Rosenbaum found Epicurean hedonism attractive to the extent of meriting Rosenbaum's approval, he had to have embraced the materialistic ethics that seemed to reduce *good* and *evil* to *pleasure* and *pain*, respectively.

Let me pursue this line of thought further by focusing on the materialistic nature of Epicurean ethics. My aim here will be to show why Epicurean ethics, as construed in the utilitarian-cum-Epicurean tradition, seems necessary to find pain synonymous with evil and, by the same token, good synonymous with pleasure. A fundamental assumption of this tradition contends not only that material atoms remain the only building blocks of the human soul, but also that all forms of sensation find their origin in the soul. Therefore, the absence of the soul necessarily implies the absence of sensation. Besides the usual features ordinarily attributed to sensation (sight, sound, smell, taste, and touch) all of them can, ultimately, be reduced to two principle types of feeling: pain and pleasure. More accurately, therefore, the absence of the soul from the human body must, of necessity, imply in the Epicurean sense, the absence of the sensations of pleasure and pain. Moreover, since, according to Epicurus, the soul separates from the human body at death, Epicurus finds death neither pleasurable nor painful. Death must be seen as nothing to the person who dies. Death necessarily implies the absence of sensation. This state of affairs must also be seen as neither good nor evil; it cannot be, given that the sensation of pleasure and pain, the only available standard for good and evil, dissipate at the soul's departure from the body at death.

Modern Epicureans embracing the view that death must be viewed as neither good nor evil must also be seen as endorsing an Epicurean ethic. Thus, Frederik Kaufman, for example, agrees with Epicurus that death cannot be experienced as bad specifically because it annihilates the person. Kaufman, however, seems prepared to accept as plausible the view that death is evil because of what death keeps us from getting, namely, the goods

---

13. Rosenbaum, "How to Be Dead," 173.

we would have enjoyed had we not died. Death must not be seen as an evil we can experience as such.[14]

By a similar vein, David B. Suits argues that death must be a very peculiar kind of misfortune indeed if we find it bad for the one who died. This misfortune must certainly not be the kind of misfortune the victim could complain about specifically because a dead person does not know, does not appreciate, and does not, in any possible way, experience any effects of death.[15] By making this contention, of course, Suits demonstrates his agreement with the Epicurean contention that death is nothing to us. Suits then proceeds to affirm, in a manner consistent with the Epicurean view, that pain remains intrinsically bad, and that considered in itself, we find pain as something we wish to avoid.[16]

My contention, therefore, can be captured as follows: Thinkers accepting the Epicurean account of death as entailing annihilation of the person must also be prepared to accept Epicurus' view that death implies a lack of sensation of pleasure and pain. More accurately, it implies that death is neither good nor evil. This entailment, however, seems to rest on the assumption that pain and evil entail each other, and that good and pleasure also entail each other. This materialistic understanding of evil seems the sort of understanding Christian theists find problematic—one alluded to by J. L. Mackie as noted at the beginning of this chapter. Let me now turn to Cicero's account of pain and pleasure to see how other ancients interpreted Epicurus.

Torquartus' Defense of Epicurus

In his book, *On Moral Ends*, Cicero records a conversation between him and Torquartus, a defender of Epicurus. After stating his rejection of Epicurus' view on pain and pleasure, Cicero gives Torquartus the opportunity to defend Epicurus. Torquartus begins his defense by stating his understanding of what the Ultimate Good entails—an understanding he finds acceptable to all philosophers; namely, it must be the end and all other things must be a means to it, and second, it must not, itself, be a means to anything else. According to Torquartus, Epicurus believed pleasure was this Chief Good, and its opposite, pain, the Chief Evil.[17]

Torquartus then recapitulates Epicurus' proof of this contention as follows: every animal, immediately after birth, seeks pleasure, delighting in it

14. Kaufman, "Pre-Vital and Post-Mortem Non-Existence," 242.
15. Suits, "Why Death is Not Bad," 265–66.
16. Ibid., 266.
17. Cicero, *On Moral Ends*, I.IX.

as the Chief Good, and recoils as far as it possibly can from pain, avoiding it as the Chief Evil. According to Torquartus, Epicurus finds this observation obvious enough as to require no argument in its defense, specifically because he found the facts quite perceptible by the senses. All that was needed was merely for him to draw attention to the facts. Thus, if humans were to be stripped of sensation of pleasure and pain, nothing would remain.[18]

Torquartus, however, presented a further refinement of the argument, a refinement he claims gained currency in the Epicurean school. The argument, according to Torquartus, maintains that for the judgment of good and evil to rest with the senses is not enough. The fact that pleasure is intrinsically desirable and pain intrinsically undesirable remains graspable by the intellect and reason. Therefore, the view that we should seek one and avoid the other continues to be a fact naturally implanted in our minds.[19]

Torquartus also reminds Cicero that no one rejects, dislikes or avoids pleasure itself simply because it is pleasure. Rather, individuals who do not know how to pursue pleasure rationally experience extremely painful consequences. Similarly, no one loves or pursues pain itself specifically because it is pain. Rather, they pursue pain because, occasionally, circumstances occur in which toil and pain can procure those individuals some great pleasure, as we find among athletes engaging in rigorous physical exercise. Overall, Torquartus argues, no one has the right to find fault with anyone who chooses to enjoy pleasure that lacks annoying consequences. Similarly, no one has the right to find fault with anyone who avoids a pain that produces no resultant pleasure.[20]

However, Torquartus would argue, we would denounce with righteous indignation individuals who remain beguiled by the charms of the pleasure of the moment and blinded by the painful consequences of those kinds of pleasures. Still, when nothing prevents us from doing what we like best, Torquartus argues, we must welcome every pleasure and avoid every pain. For this reason, the wise individual adheres to the following principle of selection: reject every pleasure in order to secure other greater pleasures or endure pains in order to avoid worse pains.[21]

Moreover, according to Torquartus, humans pursue not only the kinds of pleasures directly affecting the body with a delightful feeling, but also the kind of pleasure resulting from the complete removal of pain, which, in his view, is the greatest pleasure. For Torquartus, release from pain is, in

18. Ibid.
19. Ibid.
20. Ibid., I.X.
21. Ibid.

itself, a source of gratification. However, whatever causes gratification is a pleasure, just as whatever causes annoyance is pain. This observation leads Torquartus to conclude that the complete removal of pain must, for this reason, be termed "pleasure."[22]

In order to understand the argument further, Torquartus asks Cicero to consider the states of hunger and thirst. When food and drink eliminate both states, the absence of their uneasiness results in pleasure. Torquartus also notes, from this observation, that a neutral state of feeling intermediate between pleasure and pain does not exist. The neutral state, as supposed by some thinkers, remains characterized by the entire absence of pain, and this complete absence of pain is really "a pleasure of the highest order."[23]

In order to show that pleasure is the chief good and pain is the chief evil, Torquartus argues the following: Consider a person living, on the one hand, in the continuous enjoyment of numerous and vivid pleasures of body and mind, and on the other, undisturbed by the presence of pain. Such an individual must possess, in the first place, mental strength that stands as proof against all fear of death or of pain, specifically because such a person will know that death means complete unconsciousness. This state of existence, then, is most excellent and most desirable. It is a state of the ultimate good. Such an individual lacks any dread of a supernatural power and does not allow the pleasures of the past to fade away; rather, he constantly renews their enjoyment in recollection.[24]

According to Torquartus, a person experiencing both mental and bodily anguish, with no hope of ultimate relief in view must, apparently, be in a state of ultimate evil. A life full of pain is the thing most to be avoided. Hence, such a life is the highest evil. This view implies that a life of pleasure must be seen as the ultimate good. Every sorrow and fear can be traced back to pain. No other thing, besides pain, because of its own nature, remains capable of causing either anxiety or distress.[25]

Torquartus, additionally, seems to categorize pleasures as either mentally or bodily. However, he contends that mental pleasures arise from bodily ones, despite the fact that we experience annoying mental pleasures. Mental pleasures and pains seem more intense than bodily pleasures specifically because we experience bodily pleasures at the time our senses get activated to experience them. The mind, though, remains capable of remembering past pleasures and can anticipate future pleasures. Thus, granting that bodily

22. Ibid., I.XI.
23. Ibid.
24. Ibid., I.XII.
25. Ibid.

pain is equally painful, sensations of pain seem greatly increased by the belief that a future evil of unlimited magnitude and duration could befall us. Analogous remarks can be made with regard to pleasure. This observation leads Torquartus to conclude that intense mental pleasure or distress contributes more to happiness or misery than bodily pleasure or pain of equal duration.[26]

In their interpretation of Cicero, contemporary philosophers A. A. Long and D. N. Sedley affirm how the Epicurean view, as interpreted by Torquartus, confirmed the truth of the commonest claim that all living creatures pursue pleasure and avoid pain. This observation, in Long and Sedley's view, demonstrates the naturalness of judging pleasure to be good and pain bad. Moreover, everyone's feelings indicate the self-evident desirability of pleasure and undesirability of pain. Long and Sedley find Epicurus, as Torquartus reports him, inviting us to consider ourselves as nothing if not sentient beings, with pain and pleasure as irreducible objectives of our pursuits and avoidances. Thus, Long and Sedley find themselves stating the Epicurean doctrine as follows: every pleasure *qua* pleasure is good, and every pain *qua* pain is bad.[27]

From these findings, we conclude that given the Epicurean view, whether from Torquartus or from Epicurus himself, good and evil seem reduced to sensations of pleasure and pain in an Epicurean understanding. The Epicurean understanding of pleasure and pain is fundamentally materialistic. Hence, this understanding of good and evil seems materialistic as well. Also, pain directs us to the sorts of actions to avoid, and pleasure points us to the sorts of actions to embrace. Stated differently, a course of action is good to the extent that following it produces pleasurable feelings, and an action is bad to the extent that following it produces painful consequences. In other words, Epicurus and his counterparts seem to equate, almost synonymously, pleasure with good and pain with evil. This sort of assumption seems to underlie utilitarianism, which readily accepts the conclusions of Epicureanism. Before examining the utilitarian view, let me turn to the views of David Hume, specifically because Hume seemed to uphold a materialistic view of ethics by contending that morality finds its basis on feelings. I call this view materialistic because Hume's philosophy of mind seemed to prefer a materialistic understanding of human persons to a dualistic one.

---

26. Ibid., I.XVII.

27. Long and Sedley, *Hellenistic Philosophers*, 112.

David Hume on Feelings

In his *Treatise of Human Nature*, David Hume claims that humans know moral good and moral evil by specific distinguishing impressions, which he calls pain or pleasure.[28] In other words, Hume finds a direct and almost synonymous (if not fully synonymous) relationship between *good* and *pleasure* on the one hand, and *pain* and *evil* on the other. This observation finds further confirmation when one considers Hume's contention that morality comes from feelings. He argues that all decisions concerning moral rectitude and depravity find their basis on perceptions. Perceptions, however, can be located in only one of two sources: impressions or ideas. Hume does not think that perceptions belong to ideas. Impressions, therefore, remain as the only alternative source. This observation, Hume thinks, allows him to further conclude that we more properly feel morality rather than judge it.[29] In order to clarify his contention, Hume asks: Of what nature are these impressions, and after what manner do they operate upon us? The agreeable impressions are those arising from virtue, while the uneasy ones are those arising from vice. Thus, Hume contends that noble and generous actions strike us as fair and beautiful while cruel and treacherous ones strike us as abhorrent.[30]

In other words, Hume reduces morality to feelings of pleasure and pain. One of Hume's plainest accounts of reducing *good* to *pleasure* and *evil* to *pain* arises from his contention that the distinguishing impressions, out of which we know moral good and moral evil, should be regarded as nothing but particular pains and pleasures. Thus, we find a certain action virtuous or vicious because the action in question causes pleasure or uneasiness of a certain kind, and by giving a reason for pleasure or uneasiness, Hume argues, virtue and vice find a sufficient explanation. According to Hume, having a sense of virtue is nothing but to feel some sort of satisfaction of a particular kind from the contemplation of character. This feeling, according to Hume, constitutes our praise and admiration.[31]

Additionally, Hume argues that merely because a certain character pleases us does not make us *infer* the character as virtuous. In other words, conclusions about character do not find their basis on some kind of logical inference. Rather, upon feeling that the character pleases us after a certain manner, we *feel* that the character is virtuous. Hence, for Hume, morality cannot

---

28. Hume, *Treatise of Human Nature*, II.1.II.
29. Ibid., III.1.II.
30. Ibid.
31. Ibid.

be an inferred thing. Morality remains confined to feelings. This conclusion applies to judgments concerning all kinds of beauty, tastes, and sensations.

In a later work entitled *An Enquiry Concerning the Principles of Morals*, Hume continues to uphold his doctrines about pain and evil on the one hand, and pleasure and good on the other. He suggests, for example, that the final sentence pronouncing characters amiable or odious, and praiseworthy or blamable, depends on feelings internal to ourselves—feeling universalized in all of us by nature. For Hume, this sentence renders morality an active principle. On this sentence, virtue is our happiness and vice is our misery. Notice, here, that the term has changed from pleasure to happiness. Seemingly, Hume uses both terms interchangeably.

David Hume carried this view throughout his discussion of the problem of evil in his posthumous work, *Dialogues Concerning Natural Religion* (henceforth referred to as *Dialogues*). A majority of Hume's interpreters maintain that Philo, one of the interlocutors in that dialogue, ought to be regarded as Hume's mouthpiece. In the *Dialogues*, Philo seems to use *evil* interchangeably with *pain*.

Nelson Pike, in an article entitled "Hume and Evil," agrees. According to Pike, Philo quite clearly uses the term *evil* as a tag containing all instances of suffering and pain. Pike correctly notes that Philo offers no analysis of the term "evil." Moreover, Philo's challenge to Cleanthes, another interlocutor in the debate, does not in the least find its basis on the particularities of the logic of the term. At one stage of the argument, for example, Philo presents his challenge to Cleanthes without employing the term "evil," and merely speaks of misery.[32]

In order to see, then, how Philo develops his argument, wherein he challenges the moral aspects of God based on the reality of evil, let me present a brief outline of his argument. He begins, in Part X of the *Dialogues*, by postulating how just representations of human misery and wickedness seem the best and, indeed, the only method of bringing everyone to a due sense of religion. Philo aims, in this approach, not so much to prove what he believes everyone feels within themselves; rather, he aims to make his audience feel, presumably, the fact of human and animal misery more intimately and sensibly.[33]

Philo finds no problem believing that God's power is infinite, noting that God executes whatever he wills. However, neither humans nor animals seem happy. For this reason, Philo concludes, God does not will their happiness. Moreover, given that God never makes mistakes in choosing the

---

32. Pike, "Hume on Evil," 86.
33. Hume, *Dialogues*, 61.

means to any end, and given that the course of human nature tends not toward human or animal felicity, Philo concludes that humans and animals were not designed for the purpose of felicity.

To bolster his case, Philo appeals to the Epicurean challenge that the question raised by the problem of evil, or for that matter, pain, remains unanswered, namely: "Is God willing to prevent evil but unable to do so? Then he is impotent. Is he able but not willing? Then he is malevolent. Is he both able and willing? Whence, then, is evil?"[34]

More importantly, however, Philo identifies four circumstances upon which he thinks all the greatest ills tormenting sensible creatures actually depend.[35] Notice how all four circumstances portray pleasure and pain as the only factors involved in determining good and evil respectively. Let me begin with the first one below.

According to Philo, the first circumstance introducing evil displays the sort of economy by which both pain and pleasure motivate all creatures to action, thereby making them vigilant in the work of self-preservation. Under this circumstance, pain and pleasure seem designed to achieve the goal of self-preservation in the animal kingdom. However, the use of pain and pleasure in this way comes with a specific sort of economy. Philo believes that pleasure, by itself, seems sufficient to attain this goal, given, for example, that humans pursue pleasure just as eagerly as they avoid pain. Therefore, carrying on the business of life without any pain seems possible, quite clearly, and Philo finds no reason why any animal should be rendered susceptible to the sensation of pain.[36]

Philo locates the second circumstance in the process by which general laws conduct the world. According to him, had the second circumstance not been obtained, the capacity of pain would not produce any pain by itself. Thus, God could have eliminated all evil (i.e., pain) in all its possible locations and produced all good (i.e., pleasure) without creating a long process of cause and effect of the sort we find in the outworking of natural law. Consider, for example, that although considered exactly regular, the present economy of nature seems irregular to us, and its events uncertain, thereby disappointing expectations. In order to illustrate this observation, Philo points to instances of health and sickness, natural disasters, and what he calls "an infinite number of accidents whose causes are unknown and invariable." He notes that they afflict sentient beings, and their reality wields a great influence both on the fortunes of particular persons as well as on the

---

34. Ibid., 66.
35. Ibid.
36. Ibid.

prosperity of public societies. Notice that Philo calls them "accidents," and he believes that all human life, in a certain sense, depends on them.[37]

The third aspect, in Philo's view, comes from his observation that nature seems quite rigid by giving, in restricted measures, powers or endowments to supply us with certain necessities. Seemingly, this restriction has resulted in much pain and unhappiness in sentient beings. Philo believes that an indulgent parent would demonstrate more generosity by bestowing a large stock sufficient to forestall possible accidents and to secure the happiness and welfare of its creatures, even in the most unfortunate circumstances. This state of affairs would, then, ensure that every course of life would not be surrounded by situations where, to use Philo's words, "the least departures from the true path by mistake or necessity" results in misery and ruin.[38]

Philo believes the fourth circumstance finds its source in the inaccurate workmanship of the principles of nature. He admits that the irregularity of nature is perhaps not significant enough to destroy any species. However, that irregularity seems sufficient to involve the individual in ruin and misery. In other words, the irregularity seems sufficient to cause pain in sentient creatures.[39]

The important thing to note, from Philo's consideration above, seems to be Hume's use of the terms "evil" and "pain" as if, or almost as if, both enjoy some kind of synonymy. Just as significant is Philo's use of "pleasure" and "good." These findings should not strike us as surprising. They seem to be the logical outworking of Hume's ethical convictions already considered, and we have already noted that many thinkers regard Philo as Hume's main mouthpiece in the *Dialogues*. For these reasons, Nelson Pike seems quite right in his conclusion about David Hume's use of the terms. Moreover, the complaint, alluded to by Mackie, that theists charge the atheists for reducing the problem of evil to a materialistic view of pleasure and pain, seems well founded.

These considerations, though not exhaustive, should suffice as representative of the materialistic nature of Hume's view on ethics as well as his view on the problem of evil. To be sure, if he makes any departures in those areas from what we have already considered, they seem inconsequential. Let me turn, now, to another major philosopher whose view on morality, though certainly not Humean, seems a reinvention of Epicurean ethics; namely, John Stuart Mill.

---

37. Ibid.
38. Ibid.
39. Ibid.

John Stuart Mill on Happiness

In his view on pain and pleasure, John Stuart Mill seems to follow not only in the footsteps of Epicurus, but, more immediately, in those of Jeremy Bentham. According to Russell, Bentham thinks that the good ought to be seen as pleasure or happiness. Moreover, Russell notes, quite correctly, that Bentham uses pleasure and happiness quite synonymously. Additionally, badness involves pain. This consideration leads Russell to conclude about Bentham that one state of affairs remains better than another if that state involves a greater balance of pleasure over pain, or a smaller balance of pain over pleasure. The best of all possible states of affairs, however, involves the greatest balance of pleasure over pain.[40]

Also, according to Russell, James Mill, the father of John Stuart Mill, considers pleasure the only good and pain the only evil, but values moderate pleasure most. James Mill finds intellectual enjoyments the best, and temperance the chief virtue. Recall, though, that intellectual pleasure, whether in Epicurean terms or in utilitarian terms, must be considered physical and material owing to the fact that both views subscribed to some form of materialism with respect to their philosophy of mind. Hence, the sort of immaterialism characterized by, say, Cartesian dualism, does not factor in this view of ethics.[41]

This short background allows us to consider the views of John Stuart Mill. A chief defender of utilitarianism, Mill holds that the theory of utility implies pleasure itself rather than something we must contradistinguish from pleasure. The theory must also imply exemption from pain.[42] Therefore, according to the morals of utility, which Epicurus calls "the greatest happiness principle," actions are right to the extent that they promote happiness, and wrong if they produce the reverse of happiness.

In what ways, exactly, does Mill define happiness and unhappiness? According to him, happiness implies intended pleasure and the absence of pain. Unhappiness, by contrast, implies the privation of pleasure. In Mill's view, pleasure and freedom from pain remain the only things desirable as ends. All desirable things remain desirable either for the sort of pleasure intrinsic to them or as instruments of promoting pleasure and preventing pain.[43]

Mill seems aware of possible objections to his view, suspecting that his opponents will find the principle of utility quite swinish given its emphasis

---

40. Russell, *History of Western Philosophy*, 775.
41. Ibid., 776–77.
42. Mill, *Utilitarianism*, 6.
43. Ibid., 7.

on pleasure as the highest goal. He notes how Epicurus endured similar oppositions in his adumbration of the Epicurean doctrine.[44] Still, Mill finds the comparison of the Epicurean life to that of beasts quite degrading for at least one reason: the pleasures of a beast fail to satisfy a human being's understanding of happiness. They fail specifically because humans have faculties more elevated than the appetites of animals. Once one becomes conscious of them, one fails to regard anything as happiness that does not include the gratification of the higher consciousness. Moreover, Mill argues that utilitarian writers, in general, find mental pleasures superior to bodily pleasures, and they base this superiority in the greater permanency, safety, and uncostliness of mental pleasures. In Mill's view, the utilitarians have fully proven their case on all these points.[45] The important thing to note is that the utilitarianism of Mill and Bentham, as well as the hedonism of Epicurus, seem quite unashamedly materialistic, providing an understanding of good and evil that seem synonymous, or almost synonymous, with pleasure. Let me now turn to the work of Sam Harris.

Sam Harris and the Well-Being Doctrine

In his work, *The Moral Landscape*, Sam Harris undertakes an ambitious project—attempting to show how science can determine human values. He intends to argue, in that work, that questions about values must be seen as questions about the well-being of conscious creatures.[46] He believes that human well-being entirely depends on worldly events, and more so, on the human brain. For this reason, scientific truths to be known about human well-being really do exist.[47] Of course, by this conclusion, Harris assumes that morality must be seen as a branch of science, though an undeveloped one.[48] At any rate, Harris takes pains to underscore his contention that meaning, values, morality, and the good life relate to facts about the well-being of conscious creatures.[49]

Harris does not locate the exact nature of the well-being he discusses. However, he gives us a clue when he describes his version of the moral landscape. According to him, the moral landscape constitutes a space of real and potential outcomes. The peaks of these outcomes correspond to the zeniths of

44. Ibid.
45. Ibid., 8.
46. Harris, *Moral Landscape*, 1.
47. Ibid., 2.
48. Ibid., 4.
49. Ibid., 6.

potential well-being. But the valleys represent the deepest possible suffering.[50] Harris does admit that the concept of well-being is quite difficult to define, but this should present little difficulty to the imagination given that the concept of health is just as difficult to define, yet we find it indispensable.[51]

Notice, in this description, that even though we may not have a clue as to what well-being does entail given Sam Harris' description, we certainly have a clearer idea of what the opposite entails—the deepest possible suffering. In other words, if well-being, whatever it is in Harris' terms, represents our understanding of good,[52] the opposite of well-being, namely, evil, entails the deepest form of suffering. To be sure, Harris notes that anyone truly interested in morality should remain open to new evidence that bear upon issues of happiness and suffering.[53] Stated differently, Sam Harris seems to understand intrinsic badness as a state of affairs synonymous with pain.

This understanding of ethics seems quite materialistic in approach, analogous to Epicurean hedonism, for at least one reason: it presents itself as empirically testable, at least, in theory. Owing to the fact Harris' methodological naturalism uses observable physical and material objects as ingredients for epistemology, this reason seems necessary. Whereas Harris believes he has made a case for science as the basis of ethics, he has merely succeeded in rehashing the Epicurean argument. His use of happiness and suffering as representing good and evil, respectively, bear close resemblance to the Epicurean version of ethics. If so, then Harris offers nothing new in his work. What we find in his work is the assumption that formed the basis of the complaint mentioned at the beginning of this chapter, a complaint J. L. Mackie alluded to as originating from theists.

Harris, along with Epicurus, Hume, and versions of utilitarianism sympathetic to Mill and Bentham seem vulnerable to this complaint. The complaint remains the focus of this work more importantly because the problem of evil was initially formed in a logical fashion by the Epicurean quadrilemma as follows: either God is willing or unable to eliminate evil. If he is willing but not able, he is impotent. If he is able but not willing, he is malevolent. If he is both willing and able, he is both impotent and malevolent. If he is neither willing nor able, whence, then, is evil? If Epicurus finds pain synonymous with evil, then his quadrilemma's reference to evil is, very plausibly, a reference to pain. Of course, if the critical reader can locate the flaw in my reading of Epicurus, then this work will, largely, be wrongheaded.

50. Ibid., 7.
51. Ibid., 11–12.
52. Ibid., 12.
53. Ibid., 22.

The evidence, however, seems overwhelming that my reading of Epicurus is right. At any rate, I turn to a critique of the materialist contention cited by Mackie at the very beginning of this chapter, a contention that seems to find pain intrinsically evil, thereby rendering its thesis a necessary truth whose terms imply each other synonymously or almost synonymously.

2

Pain and Evil

IN THE LAST CHAPTER, I highlighted a variety of philosophers who I found subscribe to a materialistic description of good and evil, and most notably, an understanding that seems to find evil fully or nearly synonymous with pain. In dealing with the problem of evil, those thinkers have, over the years, used the term "evil" synonymously with "pain," in a manner suggesting a symmetrical implication between both terms. In this chapter I will demonstrate the extreme difficulty of showing that evil is always identical with pain. More accurately, I will argue that philosophers of religion who subscribe to the materialistic view that *evil*, as an entity, remains synonymous with *pain*, base their arguments on an erroneous understanding of the postulates of Christian doctrine. Philosophers have, for decades, been content to distinguish between moral evil and natural evil, the former referring to evil brought about by actions of free-willed agents, and the latter referring to evil caused by processes of nature. Most theists and atheists seem to agree on this distinction.

What has not been exhaustively explored, however, is just what the term "evil" denotes. As noted by J. L. Mackie, a cursory glance at the literature on the problem of evil seems to indicate that, by and large, materialist philosophers use the term *evil* synonymously or nearly synonymously with *pain*. Put differently, they seem to assume that both terms logically imply each other. In other words, a certain instance of evil (E) does not merely imply the occurrence of pain (P). Additionally, P also implies E. More accurately, where E occurs, P will also occur, and vice versa. Or stated differently, every instance of E is also an instance of P, and every instance of P is also an instance of E. My intention is to show that this sort of characterization seems based on a misconception of the nature of the terms, specifically because if, in fact, this characterization is correct, then the following statement must hold true:

1. For any entity E, if E is evil then E is pain.

The implication here is simply that the class of things we call evil belongs to the class of things we call pain. Thus, if E does not belong to the class of things called pain, E itself cannot possibly belong to the class of things called evil. Notice also, that if evil and pain are to be used synonymously, that is, in a way that assumes one logically entails the other, then the converse of the statement ought to be accepted:

2. For all entities E, if E is pain then E is evil.

Hence, the implication here is that the class of things we call pain belongs to the class of things we call evil.

However, basic logic instructs us that the converse of these kinds of categorical propositions cannot be legitimately inferred from their original standard forms. Following Aristotelian logic, I use the phrase "categorical propositions" to refer to statements that speak of relationships that can be seen to hold between two or more classes (hence the term "categories") of things. For example, the standard form claim, "All cats are animals," is a categorical proposition stating that the class of things called cats belongs to the class of things called animals. Suppose we accept the claim, "All cats are animals." We would be erroneous to infer "all animals are cats" from this claim. Whereas the premise, "All cats are animals," is true so far as we can tell, the conclusion, "All animals are cats," is of course false. Hence, the argument is invalid, for cats are not the only animals we know about. Similarly, the claim, "All instances of pain are things we call evil," is a statement that cannot be legitimately inferred from the statement, "All instances of evil are things we call pain."

Nevertheless, following the law of identity, the converse inference would have been legitimate if the subject term was exactly identical to the predicate term. In other words, the converse inference would have been allowed if pain and evil were synonymous, such that we could have inferred, "All instances of pain are things we call evil," from, "All things we call evil are instances of pain."

To see this logic, consider two finite sets, A and B, each with the following members: $A=\{2,3,4\}$ and $B=\{2,3,4\}$. Following Leibniz's Law, set theory reminds us that set A is identical to set B if and only if every member of A is a member of B and every member of B is a member of A. Focusing only on these two sets, and with respect to them, we can correctly say, "All members of A are members of B." The converse of this claim is also true, namely, "All members of B are members of A." This example proves that the converse inference of a categorical proposition is legitimate if and only if the subject term is exactly identical to the predicate term. In fact, we are no longer speaking about two different entities; rather, we speak about one and the same entity irrespective of whether their names vary.

Can we do the same thing with evil and pain? In other words, can we show or establish or prove, as we did with sets *A* and *B* above, that evil has properties exactly identical to pain? One way to try and establish this premise is to use immediate inferences of the sort used in basic logic, namely, those of the Modern Square of Opposition. This logical function tells us, for example, that we contradict ourselves when we simultaneously affirm claims such as, "All cats are animals" with claims such as, "Some cats are not animals." To be sure, we do not need the Modern Square of Opposition to see the contradiction. If all cats are animals, then surely the claim, "Some cats are not animals," is false. If all cats are animals, as indeed they are, then we cannot find an instance where a certain cat is not an animal. Thus, if statement 1 is true (namely, for any entity *E*, if *E* is evil then *E* is pain), we must infer the following:

3. It is not the case that there is an entity *E* such that *E* is evil and *E* is not pain.

And from 2 we also infer the following:

4. It is not the case that there is an entity *E* such that *E* is pain and *E* is not evil.

A simpler way of understanding claims 3 through 4 is to restate them in standard form categorical propositions. Thus, without losing its original meaning, claim 3 could read as follows: it is not the case that some things we call evil are not things we call pain. Claim 4 would also read: it is not the case that some things we call pain are not things we call evil. Once again, let us remind ourselves that 1 through 4 are true claims if and only if the term evil is synonymous with pain.

However, establishing through direct proof the veracity of propositions 1 through 4 would be a long and tedious process. It would require that we verify that all instances of pain occurring in the world are also instances of evil. It would also require that all thinkers agree on conditions that must be satisfied in order for a given entity *E* to be classified as evil. A quicker and shorter way would be through some form of *reductio ad absurdum*, in which we establish the falsity of at least one of the claims. In other words, we would need to specify conditions under which any of claims 1 through 4 could be false. The condition would involve finding at least one example of evil that is also not an instance of pain and an example of pain that is not an instance of evil. If we can find at least one example of evil unattended by pain and an example of pain unattended by evil, these propositions will turn out false. These examples would then further confirm the error of always using the term evil interchangeably with pain.

As we shall see later, finding an example that could confirm this error for us can also be a matter of contention because not all thinkers, modern or otherwise, subscribe to the same ethical theory or standard by which to judge one thing good and another thing evil. Some take the Aristotelian approach, others take the utilitarian approach, others the Kantian approach, and so on. However, I believe we can provisionally find a working example that is not only unanimously accepted but also religiously neutral—one to which perhaps a majority of ethical theorists would quite possibly subscribe.

Before going too far, though, let me address the issue of religious neutrality with regard to such an example. First, most atheologians wrestling with the problem of evil raise their objections to belief in God because they have difficulty believing that the existence of the Christian God can be reconciled with the facts of evil. In other words, the problem of evil is a problem precisely because the Christian God is presented as one who must, as a matter of necessity, eliminate evil. Second, the problem of evil is just *that* because the term evil gets its definition from classical Christian doctrine, which already presupposes the existence of God. Put differently, if we accept the definition of evil offered to us by Christian theology, as well as the claim that God exists, then according to the atheologian, we at once encounter a logical oddity of some kind. This observation is precisely the one that leads me to think, with regard to the problem of evil, the interlocutors in the debate will have difficulty remaining religiously neutral about the ethical theory to be adopted. If we have to cite examples of evil, such examples will either have to be those identified as such by Christian theology or, at the very least, be consistent with the idea of evil as understood by Christian theology. As one might suspect, some aspects of evil, as defined by Christian theology, fail to meet the ethical standards of some non-Christian rival theories. For example, on a utilitarian reading of ethics, adultery may be permissible if it promotes more pleasure and eliminates pain for the majority of people. From a Christian reading of ethics, adultery remains sinful whether or not it promotes pleasure or eliminates pain.

Quite significantly, some thinkers, whom I cite below, seem to presuppose that one need not subscribe to the tenets of Christian theology to know what evil is. To be sure, some atheists hold that one could quite easily locate instances of evil independent of religious overtones afforded by Christian theology. One could then use those instances of evil as ingredients for formulating arguments against the plausibility of Christian doctrine. However, theistic thinkers such as Richard Swinburne argue that such occurrences of evil do not decisively undercut theistic belief. Following Swinburne, they proceed to contend that intrinsic good can actually exist without God. Swinburne's interpretation of the first chapter of the book of Genesis leads him to conclude that God caused the inanimate world for the simple reason that its existence was an intrinsically good thing. According to Swinburne, this view remains a constant motif of Christian doctrine. Moreover, he thinks that the medieval philosophers, such as Augustine, subscribed to the view that God created concrete things, such as stones, because their existence is intrinsically good.[1]

Michael Martin, an atheist, has tried to defend this very claim, namely, that objective good can exist independently of God. Martin thinks that Swinburne is perhaps the most famous contemporary Christian thinker. He therefore appeals to Swinburne's argument to underscore the significance of the existence of his nontheistic objective morality. For example, he notes Swinburne's contention that irrespective of the commands one promulgated, genocide and torturing children are morally wrong acts and would always remain so. Moreover, Swinburne adds that adjudicating moral conflicts would still be possible even if God did not exist.[2]

Indeed, Martin's overall objective is to challenge the view that atheism implies nonobjective ethics. He tries to do at least two things in his work: first, he tries to demonstrate that one can quite reasonably subscribe to nontheistic objective ethics as well as live a meaningful life without God; and second, he tries to demonstrate that serious obstacles face the ethicist who tries to develop a religious-based objective ethics, or one who tries to have a meaningful life based on the dominant religious point of view.[3]

Whereas I remain sympathetic to Swinburne's theism (and of course reject Martin's atheism), I find both Swinburne and Martin mistaken as far as their view of objective morality is concerned. Let me simply note in passing, though, that one would be hard-pressed to demonstrate that objective good is possible without God. For one, moral goodness is informational in nature, hence intelligible. One can reasonably suppose that moral goodness must have an intelligent source rather than a nonintelligent one. A nonintelligent source cannot, in principle, bring about intelligible entities such as moral laws. Martin seems to believe that this is possible, which I think is mistaken. Whereas Swinburne believes that morality need not have an intelligent source, such as a divine Mind, as its promulgator, I would imagine that he would be open to the possibility that such a Mind could promulgate moral laws. The contention that such a state of affairs is even possible is a

---

1. Swinburne, *Providence and the Problem of Evil*, 51–52.
2. Martin, *Atheism, Morality, and Meaning*, 14.
3. Ibid., 12.

discussion that requires a fuller treatment, and will therefore be dealt with more comprehensively (though perhaps not decisively) in chapter 4.

Meanwhile, let me revisit my attempt to cite the example I alluded to previously, one that I believe is religiously neutral, such as the case of students cheating on an exam. Generally, a majority of institutions of learning believe cheating is wrong. Cheating or plagiarism, some of them contend in their handbooks, is an offense punishable by suspension from school. Logically, a student can possibly cheat and get away with it but experience no instance of pain.

Suppose a student, named Adam, cheats just once in his lifetime and gets away with it. He thereby earns a good grade from that act of cheating—a grade that he would otherwise not have earned. Suppose also that Adam feels no immediate or long-term remorse from that very act of cheating. We can correctly say that Adam did an evil thing by engaging in that act of cheating. However, no painful consequences followed that act of cheating. This thought experiment illustrates the logical possibility that not all instances of evil are instances of pain.

Notice also that ethical theorists differ concerning what about cheating makes it evil. For example, do the consequences of cheating make it evil, or the very act of cheating itself? However, appealing to virtue ethics, some theorists would seem to agree that an act of cheating exhibits some flaw of character in the person actually cheating, and this evil is not desirable in students.

In some instances, one makes false promises or tells lies without painful consequences arising from these acts. But notice that for the most part, most of us agree that telling lies or making false promises constitute aspects of evil at the very least. Going by Immanuel Kant's deontological ethics, his categorical imperatives use reason to show that lying is morally wrong, hence evil.[4] This case in point illustrates the following truth: some evils occur unattended by pain. In other words, we may infer the following:

5. An entity E exists such that E is evil and E is not pain.

But notice that this claim contradicts 3 above, for claim 3 contends, "It is not the case that an entity E exists such that E is evil and E is not pain." In other words, claim 5 assumes that some of the things we call evil are not things we call pain. Notice, though, that according to 3 we make a false claim when we say that some things called evil are not things called pain. Thus, claim 3 denies what claim 5 affirms. However, as we have discovered about claim 5, our intuition seems to tell us that we have the possibility of envisioning a situation in which an evil act may not be deemed painful, after all. Thus, 5 proves the wrongness of assuming that evil is always synonymous with pain.

4. Kant, "Grounding for the Metaphysics of Morals," 847.

In all fairness, this sort of evil is perhaps not the kind that would lead the atheologian to abandon belief in God. Here's why. Suppose an individual, call her Sue, happens to be both a philosopher and, sadly, a liar. Assume that Sue refuses to subscribe to theism precisely because of what she takes to be a logical oddity attended by simultaneously positing the existence of God with the reality of evil. Would Sue include her traits of lying among the sorts of evil she would cite as evidence against God's existence? I doubt it, for it would seem quite odd for Sue to blame God for creating liars such as she. On the assumption that Sue is a glad atheist, she would have to be glad on the whole (using William Hasker's phraseology to be more fully expounded in the next section) that she exists, whether she is a liar or not. This state of affairs would have to be the case if individuals such as Sue wish to be consistent. Evidence against God's existence with regard to the problem of evil must, therefore, be looked for elsewhere instead of citing the moral problem of lying.

One might object that the example of cheating, raised above, is a classic illustration of lawbreaking, but it is not a classic illustration of evil. In other words, a law or a rule being broken in no way implies that some act of evil has occurred. In order for the lawbreaking act to be an example of evil, the objection continues, it must be attended by pain. By way of reply, the objector must show that what is painful is also what is evil and vice versa. This demonstration would be extremely difficult to illustrate in the absence of an objective frame of reference agreeable to all or most ethical theorists. In addition, as a separate example, I submit that the moral problem of lying seems to be a classic example of evil that can occur unattended by pain. This view seems to be universal. Unless one's psychological disposition is malfunctioning, I know of no one who seriously delights in being deceived or, for that matter, lied to.

We turn to a different situation where our intuition could lead us to envision a situation in which a painful act may not be deemed evil. Once again, finding a religiously neutral example as an illustration would be helpful. If we do, then claim 4 would be contradicted. One such example is in the area of physical fitness. To be fit one must endure instances of considerable physical pain. Athletes know the pains that follow moments of intense workouts. Whereas not everybody finds such moments enjoyable, a considerable number of people do, in fact, embrace them. They also admit that those physical activities are painful and challenging. As painful as those physical activities are, associating them with evil does not seem correct, or much less, calling them such. For one, intense activities of this sort have physical health benefits for the athlete, benefits we would properly call good. In other words, in one sense, some given types of pain contribute to the overall good of the person. Hence, we could put this claim in the following format:

6. An entity E exists such that E is pain and E is not evil.

In other words, at the very least, some things exist, things that we would call pain that, in fact, are not things we would call evil. Once again, notice that claim 6 contradicts claim 4.

One should also note that some form of this truth has been adumbrated in Plato's "Gorgias." Socrates contends that using the term *evil* synonymously with *pain* and using the term *good* synonymously with *pleasure* is erroneous. Socrates' argument is a simple one. He contends that good and evil are contraries, and cannot inhere in the same entity. However, Socrates continues, pain and pleasure are not contraries and can be experienced simultaneously by the same person. For example, a person quenching his thirst with water simultaneously experiences the pain of the thirst itself and the pleasure of quenching the thirst. The person at the same time experiences both sensations, according to Socrates. From Socrates' perspective, evil is entirely distinct from pain; hence, the two terms should not be used simultaneously.[5]

Where, then, do these findings lead us? The facts of experience seem to suggest that 5 and 6 do correspond with reality, in light of the intuitive examples I have suggested. If this supposition is correct, then propositions 3 and 4 are false. If they are false, we must conclude that always using the terms evil and pain interchangeably, such as we find among the materialist philosophers already examined, is incorrect, considering the fact that claims 3 and 4 are the converse results of using the terms evil and pain simultaneously. Hence, it would seem that the class of things called evil belongs to an entirely distinct category from the class of things called pain. Always lumping these two terms together puts one at risk of committing the fallacy of equivocation, which involves a shift in meaning of a given term T while retaining the use of T.

So far our study has revealed two important truths. First, it has revealed that some things we would normally call pain are not things we would call evil. Second, it has revealed that some things we would normally call evil are not things we would call pain. A third possibility also needs some attention. Some things we would call pain are things we would also call evil, and this possibility is formally stated as follows:

7. An entity E exists such that E is pain and E is evil.

The converse of this statement would read as follows:

8. An entity E exists such that E is evil and E is painful.

5. Plato, "Gorgias," 557.

One way of simplifying this claim is to call it painful evil. Hence, the sort of evil described by statement 5 is what I would call painless evil, and that described by statement 6 is what I would call nonmoral pain. Painful evil is the sort of evil in which pain and evil coincide in such a way that one is really the other.

As already noted, painless evil does not seem to be a cause of the atheist's unbelief. Similarly, the atheist would be hard-pressed to use nonmoral pain, as previously described, as evidence against God's existence because this sort of pain has been considered beneficial by a good number of those very atheists. However, if painful evil exists, it should be high on the atheist's list of evidence against God.

How, then, do we go about locating an instance of painful evil? An act of murder is perhaps a fitting example with which many thinkers would, quite possibly, agree. On the surface, the evil in murder consists in the fact that a life, which is essentially irreplaceable, is taken away prematurely. Notice also that the murderous act is itself a painful one; otherwise, the result it brings would not be the kind of thing we find ourselves naturally inclined to avoid.

However, we at once encounter a problem. Is murder evil because it is painful, or is murder painful because it is evil? If we say, "Murder is evil; therefore, it is painful," we immediately beg the question, for we have not yet demonstrated, as a necessary truth, that whatever is evil is also painful. On the other hand, if we say, "Murder is painful; therefore, it is evil," we still beg the question, for once again we have failed to demonstrate, as a necessary truth, that whatever is painful is also evil. Therefore, we would have extreme difficulty finding a description of evil that is also necessarily a description of pain, especially if we do so on a religiously neutral reading of ethics.

A more promising example is the question of death. That all living things have a natural instinct or desire for survival is itself a fact that would categorize as evil anything that takes away their existence, namely, death. Once again we are faced with a dilemma similar to the one previously alluded to. Is death evil because it is painful, or is death painful because it is evil? Neither this question, nor its answer, will provide us with useful insights, for each disjunct of the question assumes that evil and pain do imply each other. In other words, the question assumes a curious form of false dichotomy. Why not, as a way out of the dilemma, contend that death is both an evil and a pain?

Epicureans, as we have already noted in the first chapter, would say that death is neither an evil nor a pain. Their contention is that death is literally nothing because when a person dies, all sensation is gone. Hence, the person does not experience any pain.[6] The only ones feeling pain at death are the bereaved survivors of the deceased. We must bear in mind, though, that most atheists subscribe to Epicureanism when the subject turns to the question of death, thus Epicurean atheologians would be hard placed to think of death as involving both evil and pain. Still, as we shall see in chapter 5, some thinkers argue that Epicureans was mistaken, and that death is really evil. If they are right, then painful evil might as well be a reality humans routinely face. The chapter will also highlight the Psalmist's contention that death might actually be a good thing. Hence, the verdict might still be a long way coming.

Arguably, rape seems to be the prime example of painful evil, wherein the aggressive nature of the act inflicts pain in the life of its victims. This example could then be used to indicate that at least one instance of evil exists that also counts as evil, and vice versa. The question still remains: what aspect of rape makes it an evil? If we say the pain involved is what makes rape evil, are we implying that if rape was not painful it would, for that reason, cease to be evil? This conclusion would sound woefully misguided because quite intuitively, rape is still evil whether painful or not. To be sure, for the case of rape and many more, we are left with the following question: What makes rape, cheating, lying, or murder the sort of evils we think they are? As noted earlier, not all thinkers agree on what makes a given act evil and on what makes another good. Consider the following brief history of the major philosophers regarding the source of good as well as what they took to be the highest good.

Plato, for example, maintains that the highest good is the Good Itself and that the proper use of reason could lead one not only to know this Good Itself, but also to do it. For Plato, one does the good if and only if one knows the good. Seemingly, Plato comes quite close to equating the Good Itself with deity.[7] But Aristotle objects to this Platonic idea of the good by suggesting that the highest good is happiness. He defined happiness as the activity of the soul in accordance with reason. In other words, when one lives a life consistent with reason, one becomes a moral person.[8]

Epicurus, on the other hand, equivocates happiness with pleasure, a position that was later endorsed by Jeremy Bentham and more fully developed by John Stuart Mill. Epicurus contends that morality comes from pleasure[9] and that the highest good is a life of *ataraxia*, translated as tranquility,

---

6. Epicurus, "Principal Doctrines," 362.
7. Plato, "Republic," 770.
8. Aristotle, "Nichomachean Ethics," 1104.
9. Epicurus, "Letter to Menoeceus," 360.

in which the soul is free from disturbance and the body is free from pain.[10] But Augustine criticizes the Epicurean notion of *ataraxia*, observing that attaining this kind of tranquility in a true sense is impossible in this world. Augustine suggests, instead, that the highest good is eternal life in heaven, which, in his opinion, is true *ataraxia*.[11]

Thomas Hobbes does not think that the Good Itself exists. He does not think the Bad Itself exists either. In his opinion, good and evil are always used in relation to the person who uses those terms.[12] For Hobbes, humans have a tendency to act in their own self-interest, so they have to use reason, in a collective sense, to determine through some kind of a social contract among themselves what will be good for them as a society, that is, as they live together in some kind of a commonwealth.[13]

David Hume, as we noted in the first chapter, believes not only that morality comes from sentiment but also that the highest good is sentiment itself. From Hume, for example, we know that a certain course of action A is bad because we express sentiments of disapproval regarding A. We also know that another course of action, call it not-A, is good because we express sentiments of approval regarding not-A.[14] Kant, though, insists that morality comes from reason, and reason has the production of the good will as its highest goal.[15]

The thinkers hitherto mentioned are only a handful of those who contributed to the debate. Hence, the dispute has a long and distinguished career, namely, the dispute between ethical theorists concerning the source of morality and the meaning of being moral. The significance of this realization can be located as follows: with such disputes already in place, moralists can quite easily talk past each other when they engage in debates about the problem of evil.

Fortunately, though, the problem of evil is not quite a dispute about philosophers disagreeing among themselves as to what constitutes the highest good. It seems to come from their feeling that what has often been presented as the goodness of God is in some way contradictory to some facts of the universe. More pointedly, it seems to arise from the fact that the postulates of Scripture affirming the goodness of God, on the one hand, seem inconsistent with its numerous accounts, on the other, that present a God who seems to allow his creatures to experience pain and suffering. To be sure, if any meaningful debate about the problem of evil is to take place,

10. Ibid.
11. Augustine, *Concerning the City of God*, 852.
12. Hobbes, *Leviathan*, 33.
13. Ibid., 104.
14. Hume, *Enquiry Concerning the Principles of Morals*, 127–29.
15. Kant, "Grounding for the Metaphysics of Morals," 837.

the participants of the debate must appeal to some form of Christian ethics, whether they subscribe to it or not, as a basis for launching their various attacks. Launching their critiques from a secular consequentialist, virtue-based, or even deontological reading of ethics would be out of place, for they would be operating on the false assumption that the Christian doctrine they are attacking is sympathetic to their ethical theories.

Some agnostics and atheists, therefore, contend that the existence of God—as presented by classical Christian doctrine—is logically incompatible with the existence of evil. J. L. Mackie's forcefully argued essay, "Evil and Omnipotence," is a classic example. Mackie argues that some three classical doctrines of theology, "God is all good," "God is all powerful," and "Evil exists"—are positively irrational when taken together. But Mackie notes that the contradiction is not immediately apparent. He believes that in order to expose the inconsistency one must add a fourth claim: "A good thing always eliminates evil as far as it can." Mackie then suggests, as a solution to the problem, that the theologian must deny the truths of at least one of the first three claims in order to avoid the contradiction; but the theologian cannot consistently adhere to all three claims.[16]

In his response to Mackie, Alvin Plantinga's "Free Will Defense" demonstrated quite convincingly, I think, that there exists no logical contradiction between the existence of evil and the existence of God. In a widely quoted segment of his defense, Plantinga contends that a world with significantly free creatures is more valuable than one without any free creatures at all. He notes that an omnipotent being can make such creatures. However, omnipotence would not determine such creatures to do only what is right, for doing so would preempt their freedom. In order to create beings with the capacity for moral good, God must design them with the capacity for moral evil. God is unable to endow them with freedom to perform evil and simultaneously prevent them from doing so. It turns out, Plantinga continues, that some of God's created free creatures used their freedom to perform evil acts, and this explains the existence of moral evil. Nevertheless, this fact neither undercuts God's omnipotence nor his omnibenevolence. To be sure, God can forestall the possibility of moral evil. To do so, however, he must also remove the possibility of moral good.[17]

Owing to the success of Plantinga's argument, other agnostics and atheists more recently abandoned their attack from the deductive front used by Mackie. Instead, they pressed their attacks from a more inductive, or for that matter, probabilistic front. Some have argued, for example, that the

16. Mackie, "Evil and Omnipotence," 47.
17. Plantinga, *God, Freedom, and Evil*, 30.

existence of evil makes God's existence unlikely, or improbable or implausible. Despite the various attacks from these renewed efforts, Plantinga once again shows that the attacks themselves are not as forceful as the above-mentioned scholars would want us to believe.

At this stage, it would be a distraction on my part to try and locate the very nature of the exchange between theistic and atheistic thinkers on this issue. I will postpone a review of the exchange to a later chapter. Just the same, notice that even with such powerful responses from Plantinga, the mistaken assumption of deeming evil synonymous with pain lingers in the debate, especially from those subscribing to the atheistic-materialistic perspective. Interestingly, Plantinga makes some attempts to draw the distinction. He does say, for example, that quite possibly, what we call natural evil is really moral evil brought about by nonhuman free-willed agents.[18]

However, some aspects of the debate would have to change quite considerably once such distinctions are drawn. Then one can easily see why classical Christian doctrine finds no contradiction between the existence of God and the existence of evil and why they also see no contradiction between the existence of God and the existence of pain.

To accomplish the task of this distinction, I draw attention, as a preliminary step, to what it is that thinkers find problematic with respect to the scriptural teaching that God is good and its affirmation that evil exists. Thinkers wrestling with belief in God in light of the existence of evil assume that something about the very nature of suffering, which they believe is some kind of evil, negates the very existence of God. As already noted above, the thinkers seem to assume that the sort of all-powerful, wholly good God posited by Christianity would not allow his creatures to suffer. They seem to assume that evil is synonymous with pain. I have already shown that equating evil with pain is erroneous, at least in the manner that such thinkers allow.

I propose, instead, an understanding of evil that may or may not include the sorts of pain-reflecting qualities found in atheistic literature. This exercise is necessary for several reasons: First, the problem of evil is an ethical issue. Second, and as a consequence of the first reason, before we begin to understand what makes evil problematic, we must also understand that the underlying ethical theory presupposed by both sides of the debate must, of necessity, be some form of Christian ethics rather than an alternative theory.

Therefore, I suggest that an essentialist view of Christian ethics is the ethical theory that the theistic philosopher must adopt in order to engage in any meaningful debate about the problem of evil. An essentialist view of

---

18. Ibid., 58.

Christian ethics contends that whatever God commands is good specifically because that command is issued from God's nature, the sort of nature that Christianity holds is essentially good. The essentialist view of ethics is different from the divine command theory, which basically contends that "something is good because it is commanded by deity." The divine command theory does not specify the sort of deity in question, for all we know, the deity could be some idol sanctioning evil acts. By contrast, the essentialist view of Christian ethics is specifically Christian and is, therefore, confined to the God of the Bible. The essentialist's view of Christian ethics can be seen to run as follows:

9. God's nature is essentially good.
10. Hence, anything issued out of God's nature will also be essentially good.

Because, in the problem of evil debate, the materialistic hedonist calls God's existence to question based on the postulates of Christian doctrine, defending this essentialist view of Christian ethics will not be necessary at this point. For this reason, I will merely assume that this is the position that atheists and agnostics find problematic in their rejection of God's existence in light of the existence of evil. Put differently, the materialist in question turns Christian theology on its own head by suggesting that taken on its own terms, the dictates of Christian theology yield a contradiction of whatever nature by suggesting, on the one hand, that God is good, and on the other, that evil exists. More accurately, the argument suggests that if God is as good as Christians say he truly is, it must be concluded that this claim is irreconcilable with the facts of evil in the universe.

Implicit in this objection is the assumption that evil is contrary to the goodness of God. If we take the essentialist view of Christian ethics, a more accurate definition of evil emerges, namely, evil is anything contrary to God's essentially good nature. But I take this definition one step further and suggest that it is also a reflexive definition: anything contrary to God's essentially good nature is evil. A more formal delineation of evil would thus run as follows:

11. For all evil entities E, E is evil if and only if E is contrary to God's essentially good nature.

I use the term *nature* synonymously with *character* or *attributes*. Hence, the essentialist view of Christian ethics is a divine form of virtue ethics specifically because it lays emphasis on the goodness of God's being and character. With these stipulations about essentialism in mind, notice that the rules of basic logic allow us to restate claim 11 in the following way: if E is evil, then E is contrary to God's essentially good nature and if E is contrary to God's essentially good nature then E is evil. In other words, all that is needed for something to qualify as evil is for the thing in question to exhibit qualities that run contrary to God's essentially good nature. Thus, if God issues a command, which, on the essentialist's reading, is understood as good, then going contrary to that command must necessarily qualify as evil.

With this stipulation in place, we can now make some interesting discoveries previously invisible in this debate. Let's revisit our restatement of claim 11: if E is evil, then E is contrary to God's essentially good nature, and if E is contrary to God's essentially good nature then E is evil. We at once discover that if E is not contrary to God's essentially good nature, then E is not evil. We also discover that if E is not evil then E is not contrary to God's essentially good nature.

We then ask ourselves the following questions: Can we find an instance of E that is painful but not evil? Or can we find an instance of E that is evil but not painful? More accurately for our purposes, can we locate or identify an instance of E that is painful but not contrary to God's character? Or can we locate or identify an instance of E that is contrary to God's character but not painful? If we can answer at least one of these questions in the affirmative, then we will have demonstrated that not all instances of pain are contrary to God's character; hence, we will show that not all instances of pain are evil.

In view of these possibilities, I contend that one can find an instance of pain not synonymous with evil but quite compatible with the existence and character of God. I refer here, for example, to the question of discipline for the sake of character building. Christian Scripture teaches, for example, that God disciplines his children in the same manner that any father disciplines his children.[19] This sort of discipline is not only necessary, but desirable. Quite often the discipline in question involves some level of pain. According to Christian theology, such discipline is the sort of pain that God would put his children through. The aim of such discipline, the theologians tell us, is to shape the believer's character with a view to making it more consistent with God's character.

Moreover, the Bible teaches that God's very being can suffer pain. For example, Gen 6:5–6 reads,

> The Lord saw how great man's wickedness on the earth had become, and that every inclination of the thoughts of his heart was only evil all the time. The Lord was grieved that he had made man on the earth, and his heart was filled with pain.

---

19. For example, see Heb 12:8–11.

This text presents God as grieving over the fact that the humans he had created were routinely evil-hearted, and that this fact filled his heart with pain. In short, God suffered emotional pain. As an example of God suffering physical pain, we only need to refer to Christ's death on the cross, assuming of course that we accept the contention of Christian theology that Jesus was God incarnate. The implication, then, is that if God can suffer pain, pain is not contrary to his character. I note that this view is also endorsed by Plantinga.[20] Thus, from an essentialist's reading of Christian ethics, the following claim holds:

12. An entity E exists such that E is painful but E is not contrary to God's character.

If 12 is true, then we must infer that the entity denoted by E in claim 12 is not evil since it is not contrary to God's character. We can still push this finding even further. We can locate an instance of E that is evil, on the one hand, but not painful, on the other, at least not initially anyway. (I note here that according to Christian teaching, some evil will initially be attended by immediate pleasure, only to be followed by pain as a consequence much, much later.) We can, for example, argue that on the essentialist's view of Christian ethics, sex outside of marriage is an evil act. In spite of this possible state of affairs, sexual activity in and of itself is pleasurable rather than painful. Thus, an activity of this sort could be recapitulated as follows:

13. An entity E exists such that E is contrary to God's character and E is not painful.

Of course some non-Christian ethical theorists could argue that sex outside of marriage is not evil provided those performing the act are consenting adults. Given the trend that Western culture is taking, the virtue of abstinence with respect to sex is widely disregarded among the unmarried; thus, anticipating such an objection is not far-fetched.

This objection is unfair and wrongheaded for one reason: it is trying to woo the essentialist to a theory to which the essentialist does not subscribe. If the essentialist accepts this objection, he or she will have abandoned the underlying ethical theory. Hence, for the objection to have any force at all, both the essentialist and nonessentialist must argue on the basis of the same underlying ethical theory. Second, the objector is not warranted in raising this objection if his or her aim is to undercut belief in the existence of God via the problem of evil. In order for his or her objection to have any force at all, he or she must do so on the basis of the essentialist's reading of ethics. The objector

---

20. Plantinga, *Warranted Christian Belief*, 319.

must show how, on the essentialist's reading, sex outside of marriage should be permitted—a very difficult thing to do in light of scriptural teaching.

Alternatively, the objector will have to show, based on some form of nonessentialist ethical theory, that sex outside of marriage is permissible. Whereas the nonessentialist might formulate a forceful argument toward this end, the argument must be rejected from the essentialist's viewpoint specifically because the argument, however well formed, would be advocating for acts that run contrary to God's character, a view that the essentialist would understandably reject.

We now come to the following important findings: The essentialist's view of God contends that some acts that go contrary to God's character are not painful. It also contends that some painful acts are not acts that go contrary to God's character. In fact, it teaches that such acts (that is, those that do not go contrary to God's character) ought to be desired for the purpose of character building. It is, therefore, wrongheaded for the atheist to suggest that Christian doctrine postulates a God that contradicts his own character by teaching that God is depicted as putting his creatures through suffering and pain. Nothing is inconsistent with God's character and his act of disciplining his children, sometimes with pain, for the purpose of making them morally like him. C. S. Lewis seems to endorse this observation by postulating that God made us primarily so that he may love us and that we would be objects in which God's love may rest well-pleased. According to Lewis, if we asked God to be content with us as we are, we are really requesting that God should cease to be God. For the simple reason that God is God, it must follow that his love is somewhat hindered and repelled by specific blemishes in our character. However, Lewis insists that God must labor to make us lovable specifically because he already loves us. Therefore, we must not wish, even in our better times, that God should reconcile himself to the infirmities we currently have in us. [21]

We must now ask, "What exactly do we mean when we say that a certain entity E is contrary to God's character or nature or attributes?" It appears that a proper answer to this question would involve appealing to something that violates God's will or law, or more accurately, his own nature (God's law is an expression of his nature). I doubt that there is an alternative way of seeing the answer to this question. If something stands or acts in violation of God's law, then the entity in question must be something capable of understanding what that law is. In short, the entity in question must be a rational creature capable of exercising free will. Thus, when such rational creatures violate God's law, logically, one thinks of them as capable

---

21. Lewis, *Problem of Pain*, 41.

of being punished by God. Once again, I will postpone a fuller treatment of this motif for a later chapter and proceed to address possible objections.

One might object, for example, that the Christian doctrine of hell is both a description of evil and necessarily a description of pain. In other words, a description of hell necessarily involves a description of pain. A description of hell also necessarily involves a description of evil. Whereas these two contentions might be true, they do not imply that a description of pain necessarily involves a description of evil. A counter example should immediately reveal the fallacy. This objection seems to argue as follows: A description of a man necessarily involves a description of a mammal. A description of a man necessarily involves a description of a rational animal. Therefore, the description of a mammal necessarily involves a description of a rational animal. Of course, this type of argument is misleading. Just because one describes a mammal does not necessarily involve describing a rational animal. One might as well be describing a cow.

The only way we can make a legitimate inference from the statements on hell is if we have every reason to believe that hell is synonymous with both pain and evil. We do not question that, on the essentialist reading, hell is called by that name specifically because of the pain experienced by those who will finally end up there. Indeed, this teaching is endorsed by Scripture.

What might need to be settled, though, is whether we have reason to believe that hell is also an evil place. One could object, for example, that by creating hell, an evil place, God created something contrary to his character. This objection is easily answered by considering a human analogy. Human systems of justice find it morally logical to put institutions in place that address instances of law-breaking. Without such institutions and the principles underlying them, societies break down. Hence, lawbreakers, so we argue, must be punished if social order is to be maintained. We then find ourselves establishing frameworks that help to deal with crime as a matter of morally logical necessity. We find that the existence of such frameworks is a good thing.

By analogy, the divine system of justice is such that the existence of hell addresses instances of deliberate and determined rebellion against God's laws. If the essentialist doctrine of Christian ethics is correct, hell exists as a matter of morally logical necessity—a demonstration of God's respect for human choices. Seen in this way, the existence of hell must be a good thing, for it serves as a place of divine justice for those who willfully choose to live contrary to God's character. To be sure, God's essentially good character demands that free-willed entities who deliberately and intentionally violate God's will are respected for the choices they make. The doctrine of hell serves this precise purpose. God's character makes provisions for such choices. If viewed in this way, then the existence of hell is a good thing.

To see the goodness of the existence of hell further, from this perspective, consider that many guilty people seem to go unpunished in this life. We have, for example, the sorts of crimes and atrocities committed by dictators, mass murderers, and rebel soldiers in war-torn countries. A number of these have died without any form of punishment meted out against them here on earth. The assumption (and indeed the teaching) of Christian doctrine is that such individuals will face the justice of God. The Christian is thus thankful that God has put frameworks in place that deal with just such unfortunate situations. The Christian, therefore, knows that it is a good thing that hell exists because it is a place meant for evil people—people who have chosen to conduct their lives deliberately in a manner contrary to God's character. On this reading, then, hell is a place for evil characters. Its existence is a good thing.

In the meantime, the upshot of the entire argument in this chapter can now be captured as follows: If evil and pain are synonymous, then the materialist atheologian must accept claims 1 and 2, namely that the class of things we call evil properly belongs to the class of things we call pain, and vice versa. However, we have also shown that the materialist atheologian would perhaps be hard placed to reject claims 5 and 6, which hold that some things we call evil do not properly belong to the class of things we call pain, and vice versa. Thus, the materialist atheologian must not only adhere to 1 and 2 but must also, presumably, adhere to 5 and 6. This adherence yields a contradiction resulting from immediate inferences entailed by 1 and 2, as captured by the following argument:

1. For any entity E, if E is evil then E is what we would properly call pain.

2. For any entity E, if E is what we would properly call pain then E is evil.

3. It is not the case that there exists an entity E such that E is evil and E is not what we would properly call pain (entailed by immediately inferring 01).

4. Also, it is not the case that an entity E exists such that E is what we would properly call pain and E is not evil (entailed by immediately inferring 02).

5. But we do know that an entity E exists such that E is evil and E is not what we would properly call pain.

6. We also know that an entity E exists such that E is what we would properly call pain and E is not evil.

7. However, claim 05 contradicts claim 03, and claim 06 contradicts claim 04.

8. Ergo, we entail a logical contradiction when we insist that evil and pain strictly imply each other.

9. This strict implication is the sort assumed by the materialist atheologian in his or her objection to theistic belief via the problem of evil.

By way of summary, then, we discover the following: some things we consider evil are not necessarily things we would call pain and some things we would call pain are not necessarily the sorts of things we would call evil. Similarly, we have discovered that since good is what flows out of God's essentially good nature, evil must be that which runs contrary to God's nature or character. Given these findings, one could possibly think of something that is both painful but quite consistent with God's character, showing that always using the term evil synonymously with pain is a mistake. Conclusively, it is not always the case that the existence of pain calls God's existence into question, since pain is consistent with God's character.

If these findings are correct, not only are we on the verge of redefining the problem of evil, but also seeing that it might not pose as much intellectual difficulties as initially thought. Moreover, if these findings are correct, likely analogous remarks could be made about the relationship between the terms *pleasure* and *good*, and making these analogous remarks will be the task of the next chapter. I intend to ask whether atheistic materialist philosophers of religion are correct in their philosophical enterprise to proceed with the debate on the problem of evil on the assumption that *pleasure* and *good* are synonymous terms. I now turn to this task.

3

Pleasure and Good

I ARGUED IN THE last chapter how showing that evil is always identical to pain is extremely difficult. I tried to indicate that the claim, "All instances of pain are instances of things we call evil," is not a necessary truth. I noted that in spite of this demonstration, thinkers of the materialist persuasion, with respect to value, use the term evil synonymously or nearly synonymously with pain in attempting to deal with the problem of evil. In this chapter I turn to what I consider "the other side of the same coin." I note, analogously to the last chapter, that in dealing with the problem of evil, thinkers of the materialist persuasion about value have used the term good synonymously with pleasure, or for that matter, synonymously with the absence of pain.

Thinkers of the materialist persuasion about evil often consider pleasure and pain to be some kind of opposites, perhaps in the same way that good and evil are. Additionally, just as they find pain synonymous, or somewhat synonymous, with evil, they also find pleasure analogously synonymous with good. If I have successfully demonstrated in the previous chapter that pain is not always a synonym of evil, I can also demonstrate by the same token, and with a reasonable degree of success, that pleasure is not always synonymous with good. In other words, I will argue how showing that good is always identical with pleasure is extremely difficult and that the materialists who think that good and pleasure are always synonymous base their arguments not only on an incorrect understanding of Christian doctrine, but also on an erroneous understanding of the nature of the moral world. This way of thinking is especially true of objectors who point to the problem of evil as an objection to positive claims about God's existence.

The question to ask is whether this sort of characterization is correct. At first glance, this view appears to be correct. In fact, in many instances, we avoid the sort of actions that bear painful consequences, and we follow courses of actions that bear resultant pleasures, though our lives do not seem to be guided solely by pleasure. To be sure, we have different ways of showing that this manner of looking at morality is flawed. One way would be to draw attention to the fact that sources of pleasure are different for many people. In other words, if pleasure is indeed the standard of right action, following a certain course of action for one individual could be right for that individual and wrong for another, especially if that other individual finds the action painful. For example, a variety of individuals find pleasure in smoking, others find it deeply offensive. Some people find pleasure in drinking alcohol; others find its taste repulsive. If pleasure is the standard of morality, then we find ourselves introducing into our ethical system a highly relativistic way of viewing ethics.

Moreover, if this sort of characterization of good and pleasure is correct, and if good is indeed always synonymous with pleasure, then the following statement must hold true:

1. For any course of action *P* that one ought to follow, if *P* is good then *P* is pleasurable.

The implication here is simply that the class of things we call *good* belongs to the class of things we call *pleasure*. Thus if *P* does not belong to the class of things called *pleasure*, then *P* cannot belong to the class of things called good. Notice also, that if good and pleasure are to be used synonymously, then by the law of identity adumbrated in the last chapter, the converse (in the deductive logic sense) of the statement should hold true:

2. For any course of action *P* that one ought to follow, if *P* is pleasurable then *P* is good.

Hence, the implication here is that the class of things we call *pleasure* or *pleasurable* belongs to the class of things we call *good*. As with the last chapter, we draw some insights from basic logic, insights that remind us that statement 2 cannot be legitimately inferred from statement 1 unless the terms involved are synonymous. This insight would of course be incorrect if we can find a counterexample that makes just this inference from antonymous terms. Our task, then, is to establish whether good and pleasure are synonymous. More exactly, we must try to establish whether good is an entity exactly identical to pleasure so that if 1 above is true, then the following must also be true:

3. It is not the case that a course of action *P* exists such that *P* is good and *P* is not pleasurable.

Similarly, from 2 we also infer the following claim:

4. It is not the case that a course of action *P* exists such that *P* is pleasurable and *P* is not good.

Or, put differently, claim 3 could read as follows: The claim that some *good* are not things we would call *pleasure* is a false claim. Also, claim 4 could read as follows: It is false that some things we would call *pleasure* are not *good*. Once again, claims 1 through 4 are true if and only if *good* is synonymous with *pleasure* or *things that we call pleasurable* or merely *pleasurable*. Thus, claims 3 and 4 are immediate inferences that one must make if one believes that pleasure and good strictly imply each other in a manner that obeys the law of identity.

We must now ask whether these claims obtain. In other words, is the premise really false that some *good* are not things we would properly call *pleasure*? Or is it really false that some things we would properly call *pleasure* are not *good*? As we noted with pain and evil, it would perhaps take a long time to verify that all instances of good are identical to all instances of pleasure. Hence, we must take a shorter route, namely, by way of a *reductio* of sorts. Here, we must show that if we find at least one instance where both 1 and 2 do not hold, then we can conclude that they are false, including the immediate inferences that could be drawn from them.

Let's take the first one. We must cite an example that locates an instance of good that would not be considered pleasure. Once accomplished, the task will show that claims 1 and 3 do not obtain. I note here, as I did in the last chapter, the importance of finding an example that is theologically neutral—at least one agreeable to most thinkers—to avoid early disagreements before the terms of engagement are put in place in this chapter.

To begin, let me revisit our example of Adam, the cheating student. Assume, for the sake of argument, that Adam is deeply troubled by the fact that he cheated in his first exam in college. He feels remorse for his action and is indeed agonized by the fact that he attained a good grade through what he becomes convinced were illegitimate means. Thus, Adam decides to confess this act of wrongdoing to his professor. He also vows to resist the temptation of cheating in future exams, even if this action would entail getting a bad grade on his part. His decision to confess his wrongdoing to his professor is no doubt a good thing, but it is not pleasant, even though it has the benefit of releasing his conscience from guilt.

At any rate, Adam's professor forgives him for his violation of school policy and decides to give him a second chance. Not long afterwards, Adam finds himself faced with another exam. He prepares for it as diligently as he can. However, as he begins to write the exam, he discovers that he has no clue about the answers to the questions. He knows he will fail the exam if he does not cheat. Just the same, owing to his determination to be morally upright, he successfully resists the temptation. He feels he would rather fail an exam, despite his valiant efforts in preparing for the exam, than earn a good grade through dishonest means. Clearly, Adam's refusal to cheat is laudable. It seems to be a good thing, though not pleasant. Adam's confession of his wrong act and his vow to earn his grades honestly are instances of good, but they are also instances of pain.

Many thinkers, I presume, would neither doubt the logical possibility of this state of affairs nor find it too farfetched to obtain in the actual world. This observation, therefore, illustrates the following truth: Some good things are not what we would properly call pleasure. In other words, given the truth of this example, we may rightly infer the following:

> 5. At least one course of action P exists such that P is good and P is not what we would properly call pleasure.

We would not call P a pleasurable act specifically because P remains essentially non-pleasurable. The interesting thing about this claim is that it contradicts 3. Claim 3 says, "It is not the case that a course of action P exists such that P is good and P is not pleasurable." In other words, claim 3 contends that the claim is false that holds that some instances of good are not what we would properly call pleasure. Contrary to what claim 3 says, our intuition seems to tell us that we have at least the possibility of envisioning a situation in which a good act does not belong to the class of things we would call pleasure. To be sure, claim 5 yields some surprising results, for it implies that some good things are painful. Formally put, this result would read as follows:

> a. At least one course of action P exists such that P is good and P is what we would properly call pain.

This result is certainly not trivial. A key assumption in the debate on the problem of evil, especially those made by philosophers of religion of the materialist persuasion, is that evil and pain are synonymous or nearly synonymous terms. In other words, such thinkers seem to believe that all instances of pain are instances of evil, and vice versa. Thus, formally put, the statement would read:

> b. For any instance of pain P, P is evil if and only if P is what we would properly call pain.

Notice that since P in claim 5(a) has been identified as pain, it is also identified as evil in claim 5(b), that is, on the erroneous reading I am trying to criticize. If we follow the rules of existential instantiation[1] and universal instantiation, both 5(a) and 5(b) would finally have to entail the claim that some evil things are good things, which should strike one as rather odd. Thus, by existential instantiation and the rule of simplification, 5(a) would have to yield the following 5(c) and 5(d) claims:

    c. P is good, and

    d. P is what we would properly call pain.

Consider also that by universal instantiation and simplification rules, statement 5(b) would yield the following 5(e) and 5(f) claims respectively:

    e. If P is evil, then P is what we would properly call pain, and

    f. If P is what we would properly call pain, then P is evil.

Let us now look at claims 5(d) and 5(f). These two claims can be legitimately combined as follows: If P is pain, then P is evil (claim [f]). P is pain (claim [d]). Therefore, P is evil. We have also noted, following claim 5(c) that P is good. Notice what this observation enables us to conclude in a perfectly logical manner. It allows us to conclude that P is both evil and good! This surprising result is what I warned the reader about, which now allows us to state the claim more formally as follows:

    g. P is evil and P is good.

Finally, by the rule of existential generalization,[2] 5(g) would eventually yield the odd claim that I mentioned previously:

    h. At least one course of action P exists such that P is evil and P is good.

That is, 5(h) implies that some things are both good and evil. If something is evil, surely it cannot be good. Also, if something is good, it cannot be evil. To say that something is both evil and good is to imply that something is

---

1. Roughly speaking, a rule of instantiation is a rule of logic that allows us, in one or more steps, to move logically from a general statement about a certain entity to a particular example that illustrates that entity. Thus, if we have a general statement such as, "All men are mortal," we can infer a particular example such as, "If Socrates is a man then Socrates is mortal." Also, a rule of generalization is a rule of logic that allows us to make a general statement by observing particular examples. Thus, from a particular statement such as, "Kitty is both a cat and an animal," we can make a general statement such as, "At least one thing is both a cat and an animal."

2. See my remarks in footnote 1 of this chapter.

both good and not good. It also implies that something is both evil and not evil. Both implications are, of course, nonsensical. To make these claims is to assert nothing meaningful. The paradox of the sort endorsed by claim 5(h) is the result of erroneously contending that evil is a term synonymous with pain while at the same time conceding that good is a term synonymous with pleasure. Some materialist philosophers, such as those alluded to in the first chapter, embrace assumptions that ultimately result in this paradox. Thus, even if the problem of evil is a reason for the materialistic naturalist to abandon belief in God, he or she seems to be doing so on an assumption that eventually results in absurdities.

I now turn to a different situation where our intuition could lead us to envision a situation in which a pleasant act may not be deemed good. Once again, we need to find an example that would be religiously neutral, for the sake of simplicity. If we do, then statement 4 would be contradicted in much the same way that statement 3 was. To refresh our memories, statement 4 contends, "It is not the case that some things we would properly call pleasure are things that are also not good." More formally put, it reads, "It is not the case that a thing P exists such that P is what we would properly call pleasure and P is not good." What we need is a realistic example that illustrates just the opposite.

Here we go. Many materialistic naturalists, I think, would agree that pedophiles derive a lot of pleasure from molesting children. To be sure, the reason pedophiles cannot help molesting young ones is precisely because they seem unable to resist the pleasure that follows such acts. We may wonder why pedophiles seem unable to resist their pedophilic urges. Possibly they were involved, initially, with a choice to resist the urge, which they could have and should have taken. However, after nursing the urge, molestation became a habit they found difficult to resist. Thus, they not only develop the urge to molest children, they also try their best to keep their actions a secret. Nevertheless, a most intuitive reason why pedophiles keep their behavior a secret, or for that matter, wish to be anonymous, is precisely because they know, quite intuitively, that the act is wrong.

At the risk of making a sweeping statement, no materialistic naturalist I know will admit that a pedophilic act is a good one. Besides appealing to the essentialist version of ethics mentioned in the last chapter, our intuitions seem to tell us immediately that such an act is wrong. Even the ethical relativist will have to abandon a relativistic stance on this count. Thus, in spite of the fact that pedophiles derive some pleasure from their behavior, without question their acts cannot be classified as good. In other words, some given types of pleasure can quite properly be called *not good*. Putting this claim in some logical format would read as follows:

6. A course of action P exists such that P is what we would properly call pleasure but P is not good.

In other words, some things that we would call pleasure, are things that we would call *not good*. Once again, notice that proposition 6 contradicts proposition 4. As with claim 5, notice that claim 6 yields some surprising results as well. Put differently, the claim would read as follows:

   a. A course of action P exists such that P is what we would properly call pleasure and P is evil.

This statement may not be as surprising as 5(a) above and it is perhaps almost trivial. The materialistic naturalist surely accepts the truth of 6(a). If he or she does, and maintains that evil is synonymous with pain, then the following interesting results will have to hold. For one, if we apply the existential instantiation and simplification rules on 6(a), the following 6(b) and 6(c) propositions will hold:

   b. P is what we would properly call pleasure, and

   c. P is evil.

Second, the conjunction rule between 5(f) and 6(b) will of necessity yield the following:

   d. P is what we would properly call pain and P is what we would properly call pleasure.

Or more briefly, P is both pain and pleasure. The result in 6(a) is not exactly as surprising as 5(a). As noted in the previous chapter, in Plato's "Gorgias," Socrates did believe that something can be both painful and pleasurable. However, Socrates seems to be referring to an *is* of predication rather than an *is* of identity. In other words, Socrates did not mean that an entity P exists that is identical to pain as it is identical to pleasure. Rather, he seemed to imply that an identity P exists that had the property of a painful sensation as well as a pleasurable sensation simultaneously. For example, one experience can involve the pain of thirst and the pleasure of quenching the thirst.

However, what 5(d) implies is that an entity exists that is identical to pain as it is identical to pleasure, which is clearly absurd. What turns out to be even more nonsensical, however, is the fact that we can both logically and legitimately lump 5(h) and 6(d) together by the rule of conjunction. Such a statement would turn out as follows:

   e. P is evil, P is good, P is pleasure, and P is pain.

This claim, of course, is nonsense. We are claiming here that a certain entity or course of action has evil, good, pleasure, and pain as its attributes. In other words, the entity in question has *evil, not evil, pleasure,* and *not-pleasure* as its attributes. These attributes seem to form an inconsistent set, taken as a whole. We have not communicated anything meaningful by arriving at such a conclusion. Indeed, the laws of logic allow us to make just this inference quite legitimately from earlier assumptions, but we make these absurd derivations because we started off with erroneous assumptions at the very beginning, namely, contending that good is synonymous with pleasure and evil is synonymous with pain. I contend that if we started off with correct assumptions, we would perhaps avoid just these kinds of absurdities.

Of course, the materialistic naturalist will deny that he or she endorses 6(e). What I mean to press, though, is the fact that he or she assumes a vantage point such that if pressed to its logical conclusion, not only do we arrive at the absurdity expressed by 5(h) (i.e., that a thing is both evil and good simultaneously), but we also arrive at a further absurdity, namely, pain is evil, evil is good, good is pleasure, and pleasure is pain—a conclusion suggesting that all these terms strictly imply each other. No right-thinking individual would endorse this contention. To avoid these sorts of absurdities, then, the materialistic naturalist must abandon the claim, the one to which J. L. Mackie alluded, that *good* is strictly synonymous with *pleasure* and that *evil* is strictly synonymous with *pain*.

Once again we ask, "Where does this lead us?" The facts of experience seem to suggest that we should abandon claims 1 through 4 and accept 5 and 6 (of course, without the small letters [a] through [h]) as the sort of claims that correspond with reality, for as we have seen, if 5 and 6 are true, 1 through 4 cannot be true. We seem to accept 5 and 6, minus the small letters. Thus, 1 through 4 cannot be true. If our first four claims are false, we must conclude that we cannot use the terms *good* and *pleasure* synonymously.

Thus, our study in this section reveals two important truths. First, some things we would legitimately call pleasure are not things we would call good. Second, some things we would call good are not things we would call pleasure. Also, as we did with the previous section, we note that a third possibility worth our consideration exists, namely, some things we would call pleasure are things we would also call good. Formally put, it could be articulated as follows:

7. An entity (or course of action) P exists such that P is pleasurable and P is good.

The converse of this statement could also be legitimately derived from it as follows:

8. An entity (or course of action) *P* exists such that *P* is good and *P* is pleasurable.

I will call this sort of good *pleasurable good*. How do we go about locating it? The holy act of sexual intimacy in marriage seems to count as a good example, for it is both a form of pleasure as well as a form of good, and the good mentioned here is religiously neutral—one that ethical theorists would accept without much controversy, irrespective of the ethical theory they adopt. Locating this example in this way, however, seems to be as far as we can go. If we try to justify just what about an example of such a good makes it a good, we hit controversies at many junctions. The controversies arise because such justifications must necessarily depend on a given ethical theory, and we learned from the previous section that ethical theorists do not quite agree as to what truly counts as the standard of morality or what truly counts as the highest good.

We need to now ask what implications these findings have for the problem of evil. Plenty, I should suppose. Take our findings in 5(a) and 5(b). We arrived at one interesting claim, namely, "An entity *P* exists such that *P* is good and *P* is not what we would properly call pleasure," and its semantic entailment, namely, "An entity *P* exists such that *P* is good and *P* is not what we would properly call pain." Suppose then we revisit the Mackiean triad discussed in Mackie's famous article, "Evil and Omnipotence." Recall his contention that some key doctrines of Christianity—God is good, God is all-powerful, and evil exists—are positively irrational. If the materialistic naturalist erroneously uses the term evil synonymously with pain, the use of evil in the Mackiean triad could quite easily be substituted with the word *pain* as follows: God is good, God is all-powerful, and pain exists.

We immediately see that the contradiction Mackie discusses here, even if it was there at all, is already diffused. As we saw in the previous chapter, pain is not contrary to God's character, for even God himself is capable of suffering. What must be contrary to God's character is that which, of necessity, attempts to violate his nature or attributes. Moreover, as 5(a) and 5(b) have already shown, some good can be what we would properly call pain. Thus, we arrive at the conclusion that good and pleasure are semantic terms that do not imply each other, though in some sense they might not be mutually exclusive. I intend to revisit this argument in greater detail in chapter 8.

Meanwhile, one might object that this formulation does not in any way settle the issue. For example, what the materialistic naturalist finds inadmissible regarding Christian postulates on suffering is precisely the fact that God seems to violate his own moral nature by remaining passive at the suffering of his people. An analogy should suffice. Suppose your loved one finds himself or herself in a state of significant pain, one that you know you would alleviate if you had the power to do so. If your love for that person is genuine, would you not do the best you can in order to alleviate your loved one's suffering?

I believe that something like this objection captures what is precisely at the heart of the materialistic naturalist's objection. God is presented as loving to all he has made. Unfortunately, his children seem to experience moments of intense suffering, some of them quite horrific. If he is loving in the manner depicted by theologians of classical Christianity, his failure to act to alleviate such pain is, in itself, a contradiction of God's character. If so, then we have here a classic instance of evil that satisfies the definition presented by classical Christianity. Recall that our definition of evil was presented in statement 11 in our previous chapter as follows: E is evil if and only if E is contrary to God's essentially good nature. God's failure to act to alleviate pain goes contrary to his essentially good nature. Hence, God's failure to act to alleviate pain is essentially evil.

Notice that this objection has been raised in a way that avoids the error of using the term evil synonymously with pain. It is raised in a way that allows pain to be in a category quite different and distinct from evil. It is also raised on the presupposition that God's apparent passiveness in the face of suffering and pain is what appears to be a disposition contrary to his own character. Thus, the unbelieving objector will contend that my distinction between evil and pain still fails to absolve God from blame. To be sure, Anthony Flew raises this objection. According to Flew, the nonreligious people often find that sophisticated religious people never seem to concede that a certain event or series of events would count as sufficient reasons for them to abandon belief in God's existence or to abandon belief in God's love. The religious people often remark with assurance that God loves the people he has created in much the same way that a father loves his children. Evidently, however, children have died of incurable illnesses such as inoperable cancer of the throat. The father of a child who suffers in this way frantically tries to help his son, but God, the heavenly father, shows no obvious signs of concern.[3] The objection hinges on God's passiveness. He does not seem to act, according to the materialistic naturalist, when, intuitively, he should be acting to save the lives of his suffering creation.

I believe, however, that the objection still misses an important point of the formulation. Christian theology teaches, with regard to the issue of pain and suffering, that in certain cases God's purposes are best fulfilled precisely by his not acting in the way humans expect him to. Suppose, for example, that God intends to build a person's character through the very act

---

3. Flew, Hare, and Mitchell, "Falsification Debate," 348.

of suffering and he knows how weak of character the sufferer would be in the absence of just this kind of suffering. Clearly, the person's best interests are served by going through that period of pain, as unpleasant as the experience might be. An intervention on God's part, under these circumstances, would be bad for the individual, as our illustration leading to claims 5 and 6 has shown. That God chooses not to intervene in such situations in no way violates God's character. Such a state of affairs is well illustrated by Paul's thorn in the flesh.

> I know a man in Christ who fourteen years ago was caught up to the third heaven. Whether it was in the body or out of the body I do not know—God knows. And I know that this man—whether in the body or apart from the body I do not know, but God knows—was caught up to paradise. He heard inexpressible things, things that man is not permitted to tell. I will boast about a man like that, but I will not boast about myself, except about my weaknesses. . . . To keep me from becoming conceited because of these surpassingly great revelations, there was given me a thorn in the flesh, a messenger of Satan, to torment me. Three times I pleaded with the Lord to take it away from me. But he said to me, "My grace is sufficient for you, for my power is made perfect in weakness."[4]

We also find a similar teaching in the book of Hebrews, as follows:

> Endure hardship as discipline; God is treating you as sons. For what son is not disciplined by his father? If you are not disciplined (and everyone undergoes discipline), then you are illegitimate children and not true sons. Moreover, we have all had human fathers who disciplined us and we respected them for it. How much more should we submit to the Father of our spirits and live! Our fathers disciplined us for a little while as they thought best; but God disciplines us for our good, that we may share in his holiness.[5]

The main emphasis from the writings of Paul and the author of Hebrews is simply that in some cases, God has very good reasons for refraining from alleviating pain. He allows pain as a form of discipline or character building. However, in chapter 9 we will examine the contention that not even the sort of character-building goals that are supposedly achieved by God are the sort of goals that warrant the occurrences of some instances of pain. In the view

---

4. 2 Cor 12:2–9.
5. Heb 12:7–10.

of these contenders, the argument goes, some instances of evil are clearly pointless. I will then offer a response to this contention.

The view that evil has character-building goals is somewhat endorsed by philosopher John Hick in what he terms "God's process of soul-making." Let me note here that Hick's view took a different turn from Irenaeus, its original formulator, for Hick believes that since God disciplines all his people, they will finally attain the desired level of maturity such that none will be condemned to eternal damnation. Thus, Hick's pluralistic account radically deviates from the classical Christian account. Whether or not he is right (I believe he is wrong) is not the issue at this point.

Fyodor Dostoyevsky takes the objection to a deeper level in a way that the believer in God should find troubling. Presented in dialogue format between Ivan Karamazov and his brother Alyosha, Ivan asks Alyosha whether, if he were God, he would have designed the present cosmos provided that its creation entailed the suffering of even one innocent child. After a moment of thoughtful silence, Alyosha answers that he would not consent to create such a world.[6]

Another way to state this objection is as follows: God knows the future, presumably. He knows the sort of world he would create. Suppose he knows that one of the inhabitants of that world is a child who, at one stage in its tender life, will be tortured mercilessly, and that he will hear the child's cry but will not respond. If God knows that in order to create such a world he must bring it about that at least one child should suffer in this way, then God would surely be morally blameworthy for creating a world of this kind. Ivan's apparent implication was that this is just such a world. According to Ivan, a morally good person would not consent to creating such a world. Thus, God violated his own nature by not coming to the rescue of such dying children.

Admittedly, the occurrence of horrendous pain of the sort mentioned by Ivan is perhaps one of the most troubling realities for the Christian believer. On the surface, there appears to be no solutions in sight for the occurrence of suffering that strike us as meaningless. What purpose, for example, can God be attempting to accomplish, not only by allowing innocent birds to die in a forest fire, but also by allowing innocent children to be molested? To use an Alvin Plantinga line, would the existence of a world bedeviled with numerous evils of the sort we see in this world convincingly count as a defeater for Christian belief? Presumably not.

Stephen Wykstra, William Alston, and William Hasker present different ways of dealing with this issue. I believe their arguments succeed in

---

6. Dostoyevsky, "Rebellion," 65.

answering this objection. However, my intention will not be to state the entire formulations of their arguments. Instead, I will focus on the broader picture adumbrated by their postulations.

Wykstra and Alston bring it to our attention that an epistemic distance between God and us exists. Given that God is omniscient and that we are substantially limited in knowledge by comparison, we should not be surprised that his reasons for some of the things he permits completely escape us. Following Wykstra and Alston, Plantinga would seem to argue as follows: Suppose I look inside my tent (perhaps I am camping out in the woods) and fail to see a St. Bernard. Probably, then, no such dog is inside my tent. Avoiding detection in a small tent would not be easy for a St. Bernard. However, suppose I look inside my tent and fail to see *noseeums*—very small midges with enormously painful bites. Concluding that the midges are not in my tent could very well be false. Even if they really were in my tent, I would not see them specifically because they are too small to see. The reader is then left with the following question: are God's reasons, if any, for allowing such evils analogous to the St. Bernard scenario or to the midges scenario?[7]

Going by the context in which Plantinga makes this claim, the inference seems easy to see. God's reasons for permitting evils such as the rape and murder of a five-year-old girl or the lingering and painful death of a fawn in a forest fire are hidden, like the *noseeum* illustration above. Plantinga's argument will receive a deeper treatment in chapter 9, which focuses on the why question. I will, therefore, simply move on to William Hasker's treatment of the subject.

William Hasker takes a different approach to the problem. Generally speaking, he notes, most human beings would be glad for their existence despite their share of pain, which they experienced during their lifetime. In addition, such individuals would also be glad for the existence of their significant others. Hasker notes that if, for example, the mother of one of the individuals had married someone else, then the individual would not be one of the offspring from that union. Moreover, had significant events in the history of the world been different, then quite likely, the individual in question, including his or her relatives, would not have existed. Given these considerations, most individuals would be glad that they exist.[8]

If one is glad that a certain circumstance P obtains, one cannot be sorry that P obtains. Also, if one is glad that P obtains, and that P's obtaining entails Q, then one must in addition be glad that Q follows P. This gladness of P is on the supposition that one knows that Q is a consequence of P, for

---

7. Plantinga, *Warranted Christian Belief*, 466.
8. Hasker, "On Regretting the Evils," 155–56.

one cannot be expected to extend one's gladness to Q if one is unaware that P entails Q.

To see just how this works, consider the following example. Suppose the Florida Gators won the NCAA basketball championship in 2015 (of course they did not). Their victory entails the existence of the NCAA. One could possibly believe that the NCAA's existence is a bad thing. Thus, Tom, a fan of the Florida Gators, could regret the existence of the NCAA. Notice that Tom could still be in this state of regret even if the Gators had lost. Just the same, it is still true that Tom is glad the Gators won.

This example enables Hasker to distinguish between what he calls circumstantial gladness and gladness on the whole. Tom has circumstantial gladness, for example, if and only if he is glad that the Gators won, but he regrets the existence of the NCAA. By contrast, Jill, another fan of the Gators, is glad on the whole just as she is less concerned about the undesirable aspects of the NCAA. Notice the difference between Tom's gladness and Jill's gladness. Tom is glad about the Gators' victory under the circumstances. Jill, however, is simply glad on the whole that the Gators won.

Circumstantial gladness can be illustrated as follows: Tom knows that the Gators won. He knows that the Gators' existence implies the existence of the NCAA. Nevertheless, he regrets the existence of the NCAA. Still, he knows that without the existence of the NCAA, the Gators would perhaps not exist either. Thus, with regard to circumstantial gladness, according to Hasker, one is glad that P. One knows that P entails Q. Still, one regrets that Q and one knows that if Q does not obtain, then P will not obtain either.[9]

Gladness on the whole can also be illustrated as follows: Jill knows that the Gators won. She knows that the Gators' existence implies the existence of the NCAA. However, she is glad that the NCAA exists. She knows that without the existence of the NCAA, the Gators would not exist either. Thus, one knows that P. One knows that P entails Q. One is glad that Q exists and that without Q, P would not exist.[10]

The point of this formulation is to show the following: Suppose an individual is glad on the whole that P and that one knows that P entails Q. Then rationally, the individual must be glad on the whole that Q. In other words, suppose one is glad on the whole that one exists, and that one's existence entails the existence of those whom one loves. Then rationally one must be glad on the whole that those whom one loves do exist. Further, suppose one knows that one's existence entails the existence of world history.

---

9. Ibid., 158–59.
10. Ibid., 159.

Then one must be glad that the history of the world has been as it is in its major aspects.[11]

Hasker also notes that in order to state the problem of evil, one must positively regret that one exists, one's friends and family exist, and that all the rest of us have lived. In fact, one must truly favor some different world without the inhabitants of this world. The other option is to prefer the existence of no world at all. Thus, in Hasker's view, this argument would not engage the regretting materialistic naturalist since it assumes that one is glad on the whole about one's existence.[12]

But the glad materialistic naturalist may not get off the hook that easily. He or she may state the famous Mackiean triad we alluded to earlier, namely, God is all-powerful, God is good, and evil exists. He or she may then conclude that these three claims imply a contradiction. Whereas the materialistic naturalist could make this claim without committing himself or herself to the truths of the premises, Hasker notes that this problem is normally presented to convey a strong sense that something is drastically wrong with the world from a moral point of view. If God existed, he would be morally at fault for causing the world to be as it is, and believers in God are illogical and immoral for failing to recognize this.[13]

According to Hasker, the "gladness on the whole" argument has an effective answer to this kind of presentation. On the one hand, materialistic naturalists, of the sort alluded to by Mackie, make the moral protest that the world is morally objectionable. On the other, they admit they are glad for their own existence. Hence, they are glad that the world exists. In fact, they are glad that the main features of the world's history have been as they have. Hasker believes that this admission on the part of the materialistic naturalist cancels out their moral protest. They cannot consistently press the complaint on the one hand and make the admission on the other; for if they are glad on the whole about their own existence, including the existence of loved ones, they lack the moral basis for reproaching God for the major events of the world's past history. Blaming God for creating such a morally objectionable world means sincerely regretting that they exist in such a world. Nevertheless, as Hasker already notes, the glad materialistic naturalist raises this objection (Hasker calls them *the glad atheists*) rather than one who sincerely regrets that the world is morally objectionable. Hence, the objection the materialistic naturalist raises is both irrational and insincere.[14]

---

11. Ibid.
12. Ibid., 162.
13. Ibid., 162–63.
14. Ibid., 163–64.

If we were to apply Hasker's argument to Ivan's challenge, then if Ivan is a glad atheist, his claim that this world is morally objectionable is insincere and perhaps irrational. If Ivan is expressing regret for his existence, then he will surely desire a better world with no evils. The other option is for Ivan to regret his existence, preferring nonexistence to it. If Ivan is an atheist, his claim that God is morally objectionable in creating such a world is one that self-destructs, for if God does not exist, he cannot legitimately blame a nonexistent entity for creating such a world. However if, in Ivan's view, God exists and is of the sort that Christian theism talks about, then Ivan may not have legitimate reasons for blaming God for creating a world that he finds morally objectionable. Consider, for example, that God might have reasons beyond our cognitive grasp for allowing the occurrence of horrendous evils, given that God is omniscient. Indeed, given the limitations of our cognitive capacities, we would be in error to assume that we have exhausted all possible explanations for evils that, in our view, strike us as horrendous and pointless.

One might further object that whereas Hasker's answer correctly faults the happy atheist for raising the existential objection to the problem of suffering, it does not quite answer the question posited, namely, that God seems to violate his own nature or character for not acting to prevent horrendous sufferings experienced by his sentient creatures. Following Plantinga, the objection can be captured as follows: The person properly sensitive to and aware of the sheer horror of suffering experienced in our cruel world will simply see that no being of the sort God is alleged to be could possibly permit it. Such an objection is raised, not through some form of argumentation, but through enabling the interlocutors in the conversation to see how the full horror of the world's suffering clearly stands out in its loathsomeness. If God exists, he would be morally reprehensible in allowing this kind of suffering to occur.

One thing needs to be said in response to this objection: Christians fully convinced of God's active presence in their lives will undoubtedly be troubled by the reality of this sort of suffering. They will perhaps go as far as protesting against the existence of this kind of evil. In spite of this state of affairs, they will still not think of God as morally reprehensible in light of the larger context in which their religious experience as well as their scriptural knowledge furnishes them with further information about God. The believer will not think of God as morally reprehensible for allowing specific instances of horrendous suffering to occur, in light of her religious experiences as well as personal knowledge about God derived from Scripture and the internal witness of the Holy Spirit. An omniscient God of the sort revealed in Scripture has reasons beyond our cognitive reach.

Consider, for example, that God had reasons for allowing Job to suffer. God wanted to make it plain to the devil that Job would remain loyal to his faith in God in spite of the suffering and pain the devil would eventually inflict on him. Notice, however, that Job seems completely unaware of this fact, as evidenced by his constant demand for an explanation from God for his suffering. In spite of the suffering, Job's faith remained steadfast.

Hence, the following findings provide us with a conclusive response to the objections I have presented. First, the glad materialistic naturalist is inconsistent when he objects, on the one hand, that God is morally at fault for allowing evil in our world, while implicitly conceding, on the other hand, that he is glad that the history of the world has been as it is.

Second, the materialistic naturalist is unwarranted in claiming that God is morally reprehensible for allowing the occurrence of horrendous kinds of evil. That is, God is not justified in allowing the existence of pointless suffering. However, the naturalist in question fails to consider that given God's omniscience and given the limitations of our cognitive abilities as humans, God may have reasons beyond our cognitive reach for allowing the occurrence of suffering. We cannot, therefore, conclude that God has no possible reasons for allowing pointless suffering. If so, we cannot conclude that God is morally at fault in allowing the occurrence of what we think is pointless suffering. That is, we would be in error to conclude that God violates his own nature for allowing instances of pointless suffering to occur.

As with evil and pain, which I discussed in the previous chapter, I have tried to show in this chapter that the terms *good* and *pleasure* do not strictly imply each other. I have also tried to show that a major objection one would raise against my formulation could be met quite significantly when considering other factors relevant to the discussion—factors I have outlined. If my findings in both chapters are correct, then perhaps what we traditionally think of as the problem of evil needs to be reviewed differently. We need to know, for example, what exactly the terms *good* and *evil* semantically entail. We also need to figure out what the terms *pleasure* and *pain* imply, and in what way all four terms could be factored into the problem of evil. I defer this task to chapter 8 of this work. I now turn to the next chapter in which I try to determine whether objective morality, if it exists, emanates from God's essentially good nature rather than from a different source.

4

Objective Value and Relative Value

IN THE PREVIOUS CHAPTERS, we examined the logical error involved in contending that pain strictly and always implies evil. More specifically, I contended that one encounters interesting absurdities and logical contradictions by contending that pain does imply evil. Similarly, good and pleasure cannot be strictly taken to imply each other—at least not always. Once again, I showed that one encounters surprising contradictions not only by maintaining that pain and evil strictly imply each other, but also by maintaining that good and pleasure strictly imply each other. If pain and evil are not identical, and if pleasure and good are not identical either, what philosophers have hitherto characterized as the problem of evil perhaps needs to be redefined. That is, the problem of evil is quite likely of a different sort than what materialistic naturalists think they are familiar with.

In order to redefine the problem of evil, we would need to locate the precise nature of evil. If pain is not necessarily an evil, or if evil does not strictly imply pain, what, then, is evil? In other words, when we talk of evil, how exactly should we understand it? How should we characterize it? In claim 11 of chapter 2, I proposed a definition, or for that matter, a characterization of evil, which I will state differently as claim 1 in this chapter:

1. For any course of action A, A is evil if and only if A is contrary to God's essentially good nature.

We have different ways of making this claim. For example, one could say, following the Aristotelian way of categorizing statements of this sort, that all evil entities run contrary to God's essentially good nature, and vice versa. Alternatively, one could say that all evil courses of action are of the sort that directly contradict God's essentially good nature, and vice versa. In light of these considerations, one would be erroneous to contend that some evil entities are not contrary to God's essentially good nature or that some entities contrary to God's essentially good nature are not evil. Thus, following some rules of logic, we can derive the following from claim 1:

2. It is not the case that a course of action A exists such that A is evil and A is not contrary to God's essentially good nature.

Indeed, this statement is the thesis I wish to defend in this chapter. That is, an evil act is the sort that must, of necessity, violate, contradict, or run contrary to God's character, and one would be hard-pressed to find even one instance of evil that does not violate God's essentially good character. Of course, this contention follows on an understanding of God as an all-wise, all-powerful, and omni-benevolent being—an understanding of God as presented in classical Christian doctrine. The contention is that if such a God exists, then evil must be understood in the manner stipulated above: If a certain act violates God's character, it is evil. Otherwise, it is not. These considerations then define the parameters of the thesis to be defended in this section.

What I hope to achieve at the end of this chapter is to show how a certain aspect of Christian belief, originally taken to be irrational, can overcome certain objections raised against it. The aspect I have in mind here, of course, is the contention that the existence of evil casts doubt on the existence of God. I want to show that the assumptions made by interlocutors in this debate arise from a confusion of the terms of engagement involved. If we can clarify the assumptions, I believe the problem of evil could be redefined in a manner that would enable the Christian believer to overcome it.

What I do not intend to do in this chapter is defend the claim that God exists. I do not intend to defend the claim that *all* of Christian belief is rational either, though such a position will be assumed throughout this work. I believe other thinkers have done a better job with regard to formulating arguments for the existence of God. I refer, for example, to thinkers such as David Basinger's contemporary formulation of the cosmological argument, William Lane Craig's defense of the Kalam cosmological argument, and Alvin Plantinga's restatement of Anselm's ontological argument.

Also, Plantinga's defense of the claim that belief in God is properly basic has enormous promise. He takes trouble to contend, however, that proper basicality is itself not an argument for the existence of God, any more than the belief that one is seeing a chair, for example, is an argument for the existence of a chair. Rather, Plantinga contends, following Aquinas and Calvin, that all human beings have a sense of divinity (what he terms *sensus divinitatis*) in them such that belief in God arises naturally among them when this sense of divinity does its work.[1]

1. Plantinga, *Warranted Christian Belief,* 179.

In light of what I take to be the cogency of these recent and powerful defenses, I will simply assume that an omniscient, omnipotent, wholly good and perfect being exists—a being of the sort discussed in classical Christian theology. By classical Christian theology, I refer to a view of God endorsed by prominent medieval theologians such as Augustine, Anselm, and Aquinas as well as modern theologians such as John Wesley, contemporary believers such as Mother Teresa and Billy Graham, and a host of other believing philosophers and theologians such as Alvin Plantinga, William Alston, and Nicholas Wolterstorf.

Several considerations underscore the importance of this thesis. First, as already noted in chapter 2, only within this formulation can the problem of evil be legitimately raised. In other words, since the debate on the problem focuses squarely on theological postulates, the interlocutors of the debate must, of necessity, assume that evil is the sort of thing or entity or action defined by some form of Christian theological literature, which, of course, is purported to be revelatory in nature. Outside this epistemological framework, as we shall see in our second reason, we immediately lack a common understanding of evil. Thus, for classical Christianity, evil must be the sort of thing defined as such by the Bible as well as by subsequent pieces of literature that build their understanding of evil from the Bible. Such pieces of literature seem to present evil as something that runs contrary to God's nature or, for that matter, attributes. Therefore, the task of the materialistic naturalist would entail turning this understanding of evil—along with its presentation of good as emanating from God's nature—on its own head by showing that evil construed in this way presents a problem for the theistic view. Of course, the theologian would try to show, by way of rebuttal, that the materialistic naturalist is mistaken.

For example, as noted toward the end of chapter 3, one could contend that God violates his own essentially good nature by permitting the occurrence of horrendous and pointless suffering. In other words, by not acting to alleviate the intense and agonizing suffering of his creatures, God not only flouts his own rules, but contradicts his own personhood or essence as a wholly good, loving, and divine omnipotent being. The theologian committed to biblical postulates must, therefore, show that in allowing such instances of suffering to occur, God is not violating his own nature but, on the contrary, is acting consistently with it. He must show, for example, that God must allow some instances of pain in order to accomplish his own good purposes. Something like this is what I attempted to do, though quite briefly, in the previous chapter.

Second, as alluded to earlier, one questions whether, outside the essentialist reading of ethics, the problem of evil can be legitimately raised. To be sure, outside of this essentialist reading, all objections to the problem posed by God's apparent passivity in the midst of suffering seem to lose their force. Thus, one cannot legitimately draw attention to this problem on a purely eudaimonistic, subjectivist, utilitarian, relativistic, or even egoistic reading of ethics, specifically because modern thinkers committed to these positions routinely betray a materialistic naturalist perspective. I have highlighted a variety of thinkers representative of these views in chapter 1.

I see the possibility of raising such a problem from the Kantian deontological perspective. However, even here, the prospect of a forceful formulation of the problem of evil on a deontological reading seems rather dim. For example, suppose one contends that objective morality, binding on all people, exists independently of God. One must then show why an omnipotent, omniscient, wholly good God ought to bow to the dictates of just this morality. Indeed, one must begin to wonder whether God is, after all, omnipotent, if he has to bow to some power external to himself. Once one begins to question God's omnipotence in this way, one will perhaps begin to think that God is, after all, impotent in his dealing with evil, for he has at least one power to which he must bow, namely, some objective standard of morality existing independently of him. To be sure, one could begin questioning whether the entity under consideration is the sort of God discussed in theological circles.

Neither could one raise the problem of evil on utilitarian grounds, because the principle of utility uses the terms *happiness* and *pleasure* synonymously with *good*, and *pain* synonymously with *evil*. Pleasure and pain remain at the heart of a materialist understanding of ethics for the utilitarian rejecting positive claims about the existence of God. I have already shown in the previous chapters the error involved in making this claim. For our purposes here, though, we see at once that some instances of pain could be beneficial and therefore good, and this observation seems consistent with some aspects of utilitarianism. Consider, for example, the utilitarian claim that sometimes living through or experiencing some pain is important in order to attain some greater pleasures or, for that matter, some greater good. If utilitarians can accept this view, they have no reason to deny the claim that God can sometimes use pain to accomplish his purposes, which ought to be taken as a greater good for the majority of his creation.

Suppose we try to raise the problem from Humean subjectivist grounds. One will recall Hume's contention that morality is based on sentiments, that is, feelings of approval or disapproval. Thus, Hume would say, for example, that a given course of action A is virtuous just in case A is such that we express feelings of approval toward it, and vicious if and only if we express feelings of disapproval toward it. We might ask whether God experiences feelings of approval in remaining seemingly passive about the suffering of his sentient creatures. On this subjectivist reading, we have to conclude that if God does experience such feelings of approval, then he is morally justified in remaining passive while his sentient creatures suffer. Hence, the problem of evil cannot be legitimately raised from a Humean subjectivist perspective.

Here is how it might work. Imagine that some child of God (*C*) is stricken with cancer. The cancerous tumors invade *C* to the extent that *C* finally succumbs to the advance of the disease. *C* eventually dies. At the period of time in which *C* was going through chemotherapy to combat the disease, God remained excruciatingly passive, at least in the opinion of *C*'s significant others. Moreover, the view presented by one of *C*'s significant others turns out to be the sort of Humean subjectivism previously explicated; namely, God was not only passive, but he had feelings of approval over his passivity. In other words, God believed that his passivity was a good thing, that his failure to alleviate *C*'s cancer from spreading was something praiseworthy for himself. Though quite odd, nothing about this view conflicts with Hume's subjectivism. Once we see that this state of affairs is possible under a subjectivist reading of ethics, the problem of evil ceases to be a problem on subjectivist grounds; rather, it turns out to be consistent on just those grounds.

Similar claims can be made on a relativistic reading of ethics. Recall that ethical relativism states that an individual's moral law is binding only for that individual. A more widely accepted view of ethical relativism contends that the ethical laws of a given culture are binding only for that culture; for that reason, those laws are not universally binding on all cultures or on all people. If an individual's moral law is binding only for that individual, then we can easily say that God's moral laws are binding only for God. If God's moral laws are binding only for God, then God can arbitrarily choose to remain passive while his sentient creatures suffer. After all, such passivity is what God would take to be a morally good option for him. We cannot blame him for choosing to remain passive if we accept moral relativism as an ethical option.

Earlier, I did suggest that a more forceful objection to the problem of evil could be raised from a Kantian deontological perspective. Kant believes that we could arrive at some form of objective morality by positing what he calls a universal law formulation: act in such a way that you can at the same time desire that the action in question becomes a universal law. Another way to look at this idea is to consider the following scenario: Suppose I am faced with a course of action *A*. In deciding whether I should or should not pursue that course of action, I must ask myself whether I can envision a world in which everyone performed *A*, or whether I would like to live in a world where everyone performed A. If my answer is in the negative, then I should refrain from pursuing that course of action.

Thus, with regard to the problem of evil, one must ask whether I can envision a world in which everyone allowed sentient creatures to suffer, or whether one would like to live in a world where everyone allowed all instances of suffering to occur. Presumably, one would want to answer in the negative here. If such is the case, then a Kantian deontologist could quite conceivably raise the objection posed by the problem of evil. If God exists, he is morally at fault in remaining passive at the suffering of his creatures, for no one, not even God, would want to inhabit a world or to be a part of a world in which all sentient beings remain passive at the intense suffering of others. Hence, God should not be passive at the intense suffering of his creatures.

Another way in which a Kantian objection could be raised is to consider his second law, which he calls the law of humanity. "Always act, whether in your own person, or in the person of another, in a manner that treats people as ends, and not merely as means." In other words, treat people as ends and not as tools to achieve certain ends. Hence, the Kantian deontologist could say that if God indeed permits his sentient creatures to suffer (especially humans) for his own purposes, then he is treating them as tools rather than as ends.

Quite interestingly, however, Kant admits that his view is perhaps morally impotent unless the fear of God is somewhat instilled in the moral agent. In other words, he seems to admit that morality of the sort he endorses is quite useless unless one is motivated to act in the way that he suggests. Such motivation, Kant admits, needs some form of fear of God in order for one to be moral. Essentially, Kant seems to say objective morality remains quite powerless with regard to motivating sentient beings to act. Something more than knowing that "doing A is the right thing to do" is needed in order to do A. That thing, argues Kant, is the fear of God.

However, from the classical Christian perspective, Kant's view is unacceptable, at least for the reason explicated by my consideration of a God-independent objective morality, for if objective morality exists independently of God, and if God must bow to just this type of morality in order for him to be considered moral, then God must obey at least one law, leaving the Christian essentialist to wonder whether God is omnipotent after all. For God to be the proper object of worship, every good thing must be seen to emanate from his essentially good nature, including objective morality. I will return to a more elaborate explication later. Let me now focus on another issue of importance.

Third, my thesis in this chapter underscores not only the important claim that morality is objective but also the fact that such objectivity can only be located in the person of God rather than in some other entity or location outside of God. Such morality can be trusted to work because it is seen to emanate from a perfectly moral God. It can be trusted as a safe guide for the moral agent to live a moral life. Consider, therefore, the contention that morality is relative. My thesis rejects the notion that moral relativism is an adequate position with regard to morality. Moral relativism cannot be an adequate view of morality, for it would seem that a proper definition of moral relativism immediately becomes objective. In other words, the relativistic contention that the moral claims of a given individual are true and binding only for that individual is a contention that presents itself as an objective claim. However, if the claim is objective, then it must be binding on all individuals. Put differently, although moral relativism argues that moral rules of a given individual are true and binding only for the individual in question, its definition is formulated in a way intended to apply to all individuals. Thus, moral relativism destroys itself before it takes off the ground. As such, it cannot be used as a platform for drawing our attention to the problem of evil.

Louis Pojman offers a different version of this critique of relativism. He finds at least two problems with relativism. First, they fail to provide any grounds for criticisms against the individuals that strike them as intolerant. Second, they are unable to offer a rational critique of individuals that espouse what relativists might regard as a monstrous view. According to Pojman, valid criticism seems to presuppose some form of objective standard. If so, then relativists fail to offer a moral criticism of anyone outside the moral relativist's culture. It turns out, then, that under moral relativism, Adolf Hitler's genocide is as morally legitimate as Mother Teresa's altruism. Under moral relativism, then, racism, genocide, oppression, slavery, and unjust war are as moral as their opposites. Moreover, if some culture started a nuclear war with their own moral justification, the moral relativist would not be able to criticize members of that culture.[2]

This objection is not the only doubt Pojman raises against moral relativism. He notes that if ethical relativism is a correct view, then reformers would be considered morally at fault, for they seem to violate cultural standards. For example, the moral or ethical relativist will have to conclude that William Wilberforce was wrong to fight against slavery; the British government was wrong to oppose the burning of widows in India, an act that is now illegal there; the early Christians were wrong to refuse to enlist in the Roman army or to bow to Caesar as if in worship of him in light of the fact that the Romans believed that both acts were moral duties; and Jesus was wrong to break the law of his day by healing on a Sabbath day. However,

2. Pojman, *Ethics*, 33.

notes Pojman, we normally feel the exact opposite. For example, we feel that the reformer exemplifies courage, which is a good thing.[3]

I believe Pojman's consideration, as well as my take on moral relativism, is sufficient to demonstrate the implausibility of this theory. Since, broadly speaking, morality is either objective, absolute, or subjective, hence, relative, we are left with the former option if moral objectivism is shown to be a failure.

Fourth, my thesis avoids the weaknesses attended by the divine command theory. The divine command theory seems to imply that something is good because it is commanded by a divine being of some sort. The divine being, however, could quite conceivably be some entity that may not be properly construed as morally perfect, and, for this reason, could be vulnerable to moral weaknesses of the sort witnessed by human beings. Thus, we find the problem presented by the morality of the different Greek gods. To what extent their promulgations of divine law should be trusted is a question whose answer is not clear. My thesis assumes that if God is perfect both in attributes and in his morals, he can be trusted to promulgate laws and rules beneficial for his rational creatures.

I foresee an objection to this consideration: God's goodness is what is already at issue, yet that premise is what I am assuming in order to prove it. In other words, one might accuse me of begging the question by assuming that God is perfect both in attributes and in character, and that whatever he commands, as a consequence, will be good for his children. The objector might proceed to point out, subsequently, that God's perfection is what we are trying to establish rather than to assume.

This objection, however, is easily answered when we make the following consideration: If morality comes from a source external to God such that God must be seen to bow before the promulgations of the source in question, then God is no longer the omnipotent being considered as such by theologians and philosophers of religion. In other words, God would no longer be God. In order for God to be the sort of being worthy of our worship, he must be seen not only to be the source of morality but also the source and standard of good upon whom creatures must base their lives. Put differently, by definition, God is both a substantially and morally perfect being, and his creatures expect that perfection of him in his governance of the universe. If God's creatures expect perfection from him as he governs and rules the universe, assuming that God is perfect both in attributes and character involves no circularity. Consequently, the objection loses its force.

3. Ibid.

Fifth, this thesis assumes that one cannot have an adequate conception of good without positing or presupposing the existence of God. More importantly, it maintains that a nontheistic view of ethics is quite incapable of explaining or delineating or defining the conditions that must be met in order for a given act to count as evil. It holds that since the moral law is informational in nature, one cannot have information without a mind. Therefore, whatever objective morality that exists, it cannot exist independently of a Mind, making the following claim about an essentialist reading of ethics:

3. An objective moral law L exists.

Claim 3 is arrived at upon eliminating the only rival alternative, namely, the claim that morality is relative. We have already seen the fatal flaw attending the claim that morality is relative: it is self-defeating. We now proceed to consider the sorts of implications that follow from accepting the claim that morality is objective, which I have briefly alluded to already. It reads as follows:

4. For any moral law L, if L is objective and we know that L exists, then L is intelligible (or understandable).

Claim 4 is not difficult to see. Clearly, when we are aware of the existence of a moral law in the world external to us, then our grasp of that law implies that the law itself possesses an essential quality that must be understandable. More accurately, one of its essential qualities must be of the sort that we can make sense of; it must be intelligible. It should be obvious that an unintelligible law is nonsensical, and, if nonsensical, it might as well be discarded as impractical. If in fact it turns out to be useless, nonsensical, and impractical, we would most likely ignore it. Obviously, however, we have noticed it for the simple reason that it makes sense to us; it is understandable. Thus, if objective moral law is understandable, then we have the following claim as a consequence:

5. For any moral law L, if L is understandable, then L has informational attributes.

The claim that something is informational if it is understandable seems so fundamentally intuitive such that few thinking people would deny it. However, claim 5 seems to suggest that when a certain law is issued, the agent in question will understand the dictates of the law in question. Such an understanding may be partial or complete, but it would follow, just the same. In addition, such an understanding is possible because the law in question is laden with information, information deemed intelligible. In other words, when the law is promulgated, some form of communication is presupposed, assumed, and achieved. Once we admit these entailments, the next possibility is easy to see:

6. For any moral law L, if L has informational attributes, then L originates from Mind.

Claim 6 thus reminds us that law originates from Mind, since it is understandable and informational. To see that a certain course of action A ought to be followed implies the occurrence of some information that originates from some kind of intelligence, or Mind, for that matter. Notice, however, that the nontheistic objectivists are reluctant to arrive at claim 6. They are willing to contend that information has always existed, and have not in any way originated from a mental source. I contend here one would have extreme difficulty, bordering on impossibility, thinking of a way in which information can be issued without a mental source of some kind, especially when we consider how behind every bit of information we know, the intention to convey something always, or nearly always, arises.

Hence, the nontheistic objectivist must be faced with three different alternatives: to contend that the pieces of information in question were issued by material physical entities that we properly call matter, or contend that such pieces of information have eternally existed with matter, or admit that such information did in fact come from an intelligent source that we call Mind, which classical Christianity identifies as God.

The first option sounds absurd, for it essentially suggests, as Lewis would say, that matter issues commands.[4] To what extent, one would ask, would we trust a moral law issued by the physical and material aspects of our world? Stated differently, can we legitimately and confidently trust unconscious and nonrational matter to provide reliable guidance on how best to conduct our lives? Suppose, for example, I follow a certain course of action A, and you, my observer, demand specific reasons for my choice to follow A. Assume, for the sake of argument, that A was one horn of an ethical dilemma, or even a trilemma, presented to me such that whatever course of action I would follow, some law would have to be broken by my choice of A. Upon asking me to justify my selection of A as a course of action, I respond by telling you that I was instructed by physical matter to follow just that very course of action. As the observer in question, you will rightfully conclude that I am in error, or that I have acted unwisely, or that I have lost my mind. This conclusion is essentially what the first option entails. When pressed to its logical conclusion, that option must eventually admit that on

---

4. Lewis, *Mere Christianity*, 34.

its reading, matter promulgates moral law, which of course is absurd, and for this reason, it must be rejected.

To such musings, one might object by contending that a purely naturalistic account of morality can be given. For example, one could argue that the desire for survival is just as good a naturalistic account of the origin of morality as any. In addition, following Occam's razor, the objector can state that a given phenomenon is needlessly explained supernaturally if, in fact, it can be explained naturalistically. He or she can then observe that the desire for survival is a naturalistic explanation for the origin of morality. We do not need a supernatural explanation for the origin of morality.

Prima facie, this objection may sound forceful. I think, however, that it is merely a cover-up of the fatal flaw attending the naturalistic account of the origin of morality. When pushed to the limits, we at once see that it does very little, if any, to alleviate the concern I explicated. Whether morality originates from the desire for survival or not, given a naturalistic reading, one of the options will have to be that morality originates from matter. If it does originate from matter, then the plausibility of its dictates are highly questionable, for it does not seem prudent to trust commands issued by material entities bereft of an intelligent antecedent Mind. More accurately, matter is no promulgator of morality. Hence, the objection makes little progress and we are back to where we began.

The second option, whereas not quite as absurd as the first one, seems extremely improbable with respect to the claims of the Big Bang. Let us assume, for example, that the Big Bang occurred unguided by some intelligent mind behind it. Indeed, we must make this assumption in our second option if we are to make this argument because it is an assumption adopted by the God-independent ethical objectivist. How a random event triggered by the Big Bang can bring about an organized series of information that we now call the moral code is an extremely improbable event. In other words, the probability that an intelligible moral code organized itself in an intelligible order with respect to the highly randomized process of nature triggered by a nonintelligent explosion is extremely low. The question with which we are left is whether an intelligible moral code can be logically traced to an intelligent source or not. The former option seems to be more likely with respect to our knowledge of how such laws are issued and this leads me to the following conclusion:

7. Therefore, for any moral law L, L originates from Mind.

If L originates from Mind, this Mind has to be distinct and apart from the human mind. If the Big Bang theory is true, the essentialist reading could quite conceivably contend that some divine Mind must have triggered the event and with it, the formulation of a moral code accessible by human reason, and this reason is also a faculty that can be traced back to this divine Mind. Scientists such as Francis Collins have tried to show that the Big Bang theory is consistent with Genesis 1 and that God could quite properly be seen as the causal Mind of the Big Bang.[5] Of course, the onus is on the theist to show that this Mind is divine and identical to the being called God in classical Christianity. I believe that such a demonstration can be made. However, such is not the goal of this chapter; neither is it the goal of this work. The goal of this chapter is to show that objective morality is incomplete when we fail to trace it back to some mental origin.

Having underscored the importance of this thesis, we might now ask ourselves the question, "What reason do we have to think that this thesis is true?" In other words, what reasons do we have for contending that the claim is true that contends all evil actions are those that run contrary to God's character? First, the very nature of God, if he exists, gives us a reason to think the claim is true. That is, if God exists, defining evil as an act that runs contrary to the very character of God would be true and correct. A moment's reflection leads us to suspect that this claim is at least plausible because God is the sort of being, according to Anselm, for which a greater cannot be thought. He is infinitely superior to us in every way—being substantially perfect as well as morally perfect. By God's substantial perfection, I refer to the faultless aspect of his necessary attributes, without which he cannot be God. Indeed, to be a being worthy of our worship, God cannot be anything else but perfect in this way. By God's moral perfection, I refer to his impeccability. That is, I refer to the notion that he cannot violate his own nature.

Famous philosophers such as Descartes and Leibniz endorsed the view that God must be a perfect being. For example, speaking of God in his third meditation, Descartes demonstrates his understanding that an infinite substance has more reality than a finite one. He believes that the perception of the infinite was somehow prior in him to the perception of the finite. In other words, he holds that his perception of God was prior to the perception he had of himself. Descartes believes that unless he has some idea of a more perfect being for comparison by which he can recognize his own defects, he is incapable of understanding that he is not wholly perfect. He goes on to contend that the idea of this supremely perfect and infinite being is true to the highest degree. Thus, for Descartes, the idea of God presents him with a perfect standard by which he can adjudicate between different values.[6]

5. Collins, *Language of God*, 67.
6. Descartes, "Meditations on First Philosophy," 361.

Leibniz also expresses his view that God is perfect in a manner quite similar to Descartes. Leibniz believes that a fairly sure test for being "a perfection" is this: any form or nature incapable of a highest degree is itself not a perfection, including entities such as numbers or figures. In Leibniz's view, the greatest of all number implies a contradiction. However, the greatest knowledge and omnipotence does not involve any impossibility. The results of this test lead him to conclude that power and knowledge are perfections, and insofar as they belong to God, they do not have limits.[7]

This consideration, in Leibniz's view, leads Leibniz to the following conclusion: God possesses supreme and infinite wisdom. He acts in the most perfect manner, both metaphysically and morally. The more we are enlightened and informed about God's works, the more we are in a position to see their perfection—and in full agreement with what our desires might have been.[8]

The contention among both of these philosophers, and many more not mentioned here, is that if God exists, he must be a perfect being, both morally and structurally. Without this sort of divine perfection, humans must forget about believing in a being that impeccably superintends over the affairs of the universe. He must be the sort of being that humans can absolutely trust with their whole lives. They must think of him as the sort of being capable of morally guiding their lives with impeccable reliability. Therefore, with regard to morality, a morally perfect being, of the sort God is claimed to be, must, of necessity, be our standard of morality such that anything that fails to meet that standard is considered morally imperfect. Thus, the following claim would have to be true of God, as differently stated in claim 9 of chapter 2:

8. God is the sort of being whose nature is essentially perfect both structurally and morally.

Claim 9 of chapter 2 simply stated this claim as follows: "God's nature is essentially good." Here, however, we come to a fuller adumbration of the claim, given our ongoing considerations. Once we see that 8 is true if God exists, we begin at once to see the relevance of claims 1 and 2. Moreover, we see that a definition of evil must be implied by claim 8.

9. If God is the sort of being whose nature is essentially perfect both structurally and morally, then for any course of action *A*, if *A* is evil, then *A* runs contrary to God's essentially good nature.

Thus claims 8 and 9 would logically entail claim 1, or for that matter, claim 2. Notice that this claim proceeds on the assumption that God exists. In

7. Leibniz, "Discourse on Metaphysics," 463.
8. Ibid.

other words, it contends that if God exists, then he should be the sort of being that provides us with our standard of morality such that anything that violates that standard performs an action we would properly call evil.

Notice that the contrapositive of a specific derivation of claim 1 is also true. A contrapositive claim (also called a transposition in some logic texts) is one that transposes a conditional claim by stating the negation of the conditional's consequence as an antecedent and the negation of its antecedent as a consequence. Thus, the contrapositive of the claim, "If *A*, then *B*," is really, "If not-*B*, then not-*A*." Suppose a derivation from claim 1 runs as follows: for any course of action *A*, if *A* is evil then *A* runs contrary to God's character. We infer the contrapositive of this claim as follows:

10. For any course of action *A*, if *A* does not run contrary to God's essentially good nature, then *A* is not evil.

A different way of stating the claim is to say that if *A* is consistent with God's essentially good nature, then *A* is good. This result, of course, implies that the claim is false which contends that an action *A* exists such that *A* is consistent with God's essentially good nature and *A* is not good. Consequently, if God is the sort of being whose nature is both structurally and morally perfect, then a given course of action is good if that action is consistent with God's good nature. It being good is derived from the fact that it is consistent with what God has defined as good.

At this point we should ask the following questions: What exactly is implied by the claim that an action runs contrary to God's good nature? How do we know that a given action does exactly that? The other side of the question can also be asked. What is implied by the claim that an action is consistent with God's good nature? Moreover, how do we know that a given course of action is, in fact, consistent with God's good nature?

The answer to this question would provide a second reason why I believe my thesis is correct. Augustine tries to answer this question in an interesting way. He contends that evil is the absence of the good, in much the same way, for example, that sickness is the absence of health. Lewis seems to pick up on this Augustinian understanding of evil in his book *Mere Christianity*. Whereas both Augustine and Lewis uphold a view that has some promise, I would like to answer the given questions from a different perspective.

If God indeed is the standard of good, or for that matter, morality, and if morality emanates from God's own nature, God seemingly cannot violate his own nature, for to violate his own nature would imply that God violates himself. This important theological postulate is what many Christian philosophers of religion uphold when they assume or argue that God does not commit evil. What they imply is that God does not sin against himself. Put differently, the claim would read as follows:

11. If an action A runs contrary to God's essentially good nature, then God cannot follow the course of action entailed by A.

The implication of claim 11 is that if God follows the course of action entailed by A, then A would not be the sort of action that runs contrary to God's essentially good nature. Put differently, if God follows A, then one must conclude that A is not the sort of action that one would think violates God's nature. Both logically and morally speaking, God's violation of himself would be an action external and contrary to God's self-interest, unless, perhaps, such violation would be of the sort that brings about what he believes would be a greater good, in which case the violation in question would be seen to promote his interest.

For example, one could argue with some justification that the death of Jesus Christ on the cross is an example of God violating himself. In other words, theologians tell us that in the person of Christ, God violated himself by taking the sins of the world upon himself. Put differently, he found himself having to put upon himself the very thing he hated most (our sins) in order to promote a greater good—eternal salvation of all humankind. The fact that a being of Absolute Holiness took upon himself the sins of the world, which bear the exact opposite of his attributes, is itself a clear example of God violating his very own nature. Whereas this violation was bad when seen in isolation, it turned out to be of eternal benefit for the salvation of those human beings who would willingly accept it.

Additionally, God violated himself when, through Christ, he decided to take a nature contrary to his own, namely, death. If life is in every way consistent with God's attributes, then nonlife, logically speaking, is inconsistent and indeed contrary to God's attributes. If God is a metaphysically necessary being, as theistic cosmologists correctly argue, then we at once encounter an oddity of sorts when something such as death seemingly overrides his metaphysical necessity. That is, we at once encounter a contradiction, or a violation of sorts with respect to God's nature, when that very necessity is not only threatened by death, but violated by it.

We are thus reminded that on the cross, Jesus died, thereby assuming a nature contrary to his very own. However, as already noted, he did not die pointlessly. He did so to achieve a greater good. In other words, whereas such a scenario can be envisioned in this kind of framework, it would perhaps be illogical to assume that God would or could violate himself pointlessly. Perhaps then we could modify claim 11 as follows:

12. If an action *A* runs contrary to God's essentially good nature, then God cannot follow the course of action entailed by *A* unless *A* is of such a kind that pursuing it would promote God's interest and not pursuing it would fail to promote God's interest.

The assumption made by claim 12 is that God would not violate himself unless such violation has some purpose or some greater good to be achieved. A different way of seeing this assumption is to state that if the action in question appears to violate God's nature, then God would abstain from following that course of action unless failure to follow it would hurt God's interests. One way in which such failure would hurt God's interest is if the action in question is pointless from God's perspective.

Seemingly, however, the claim, "God can follow a pointless course of action," is itself an odd one. It suggests, for example, that perhaps an aspect of God's character exists that is not only pointless, but also brings about, or is the explanation for, pointless courses of actions. He would then no longer be the being who possesses what we would consider Ultimate Meaning for our lives. Ultimate Meaning would seem to imply that the being and nature of God is such that it is entirely meaningful rather than partially meaningful. Moreover, if we subscribe to the view, contended by Anselm, that God's reason for his very being is in himself rather than outside of himself, it would seem that God's purpose for his own existence is within the God-self. In other words, he is the ultimate source of his own meaning, significance, purpose, or goals. To think, therefore, that meaninglessness, or pointless activity would emanate from God, seems rather paradoxical. If a course of action *A* that God chooses to follow appears meaningless, I would argue, given our considerations, that such meaninglessness can only seem to be so from our perspective rather than from God's. Thus, God would not violate himself pointlessly or purposelessly anymore than a given sentient rational creature of his, call her *P*, would violate herself purposelessly. We assume, by logical induction, that if rational sentient creatures like ourselves can be seen to refrain, for moral reasons, from acts such as suicide, for example, God would reasonably be seen to refrain from similar acts. Following Jerry Walls, such a state of affairs is entailed by the logical consideration that if we were indeed created by God, he would not create us with the sort of moral convictions we have if God himself were not moral.[9]

Before we go further, several assumptions need to be introduced, or for that matter, added in order for claim 12 to work. Many classical and orthodox theologians assume (correctly, I believe) that being omniscient, God knows the course of action that would produce the greatest benefits when eventually

9. Walls, *Heaven*, 23.

followed. They further assume that God knows the course of action that would produce the worst consequences when followed. Because God has all these pieces of information at his disposal, he is best placed to decide the course of action to take and the course of action to avoid. Thus, when he pursues a given course of action, we must assume that he knows why he chose it.

The upshot of this brief consideration is that if God exists, then the essentialist reading of morality is quite likely the best candidate for thinking of morality with regard to its bearing on the problem of evil. We do not seem to find good reasons for believing that rival moral theories will suffice in our attempts at being clear about the issues when trying to understand what has, over the years, become a troubling issue for philosophers and theologians. Moreover, if we adopt those rival moral theories, the problem of evil, as originally stated, loses its force and cannot be meaningfully raised against the theologian. To retain its force in a meaningful way, we must stick to the essentialist reading of ethics. For these reasons, if we can find a good response to the problem of evil that assumes the essentialist reading of ethics, then it would appear that finding the solution to the problem is very promising indeed.

Given our consideration, one could object that this claim seems to stipulate standards that God must meet in order to be God. More forcefully, one could contend that by defining the standards that God must meet in order to be God, I am already stipulating a God-independent standard that I expect God to meet in order for me to pledge my allegiance to him in worship. One could object that this very standard is the one that I take a lot of pain to avoid in my rejection of a God-independent standard of objective morality. In other words, the objection could quite conceivably contend that whereas I reject the standard up-front, on the one hand, in my attempt to underscore the importance of my thesis, on the other, I actually smuggle it back into my argument through the back door.

This objection is easy to meet in at least one crucial way. I am operating on the assumption that all human reasoning, including its ability to see that God must meet certain standards in order to be deemed worthy of worship, originates from God himself, irrespective of whether such information was issued by God through the processes triggered by the Big Bang or through some other form of divine creation. If human reasoning does indeed plausibly issue from God, then to be able to see, quite objectively, that God must meet certain standards in order to be worthy of our worship is itself an intuition that one arrives at through rational frameworks already set in place by God. In other words, one can see that God is the giver of just that standard that we, upon rational reflection, discover he must meet in order to be an object worthy of our worship. For this reason, the standard is not one objectively existing independently of God; rather, it is one issued by

God, which we intuitively grasp as true by some form of rational reflection. If this argument is correct, the objection loses its force.

A second objection that could be raised against this contention comes from process theology, a view contending that God need not be the most perfect being in order to be God. He need not have all the power in order to be worshiped. All we need is the assurance that he is the most powerful being. Its most famous proponent is philosopher Alfred North Whitehead. According to Lewis Ford, process theodicy, which is an offshoot of process theology, has argued that in order to solve the problem of evil, we need to revise our understanding of God's power. Admittedly, he is a very powerful being. However, he does not have all the power. He can meet real resistance from his creatures. The process theologian argues in this way because in his or her view, God does not exercise coercive power; rather, God exercises persuasive power. If he were thought to exercise coercive power, he would have to manipulate humans directly to do his bidding. This form of manipulation in no way gives humans the ability to exercise their free will. Rather, it determines them. In order for God to respect human freedom, he must go only as far as persuading human beings to act in a certain way. Process theology goes as far as admitting that even God cannot guarantee his own welfare.[10]

What can be said of this objection? First, it seems to solve the logical problem of evil. If God exists, perhaps one way to make sense of his existence along with the facts of pain is to deny that he has all the power. This impotence on God's part would then explain why so much pain exists. God is simply unable to eradicate the pain. However, this limitation on God's power comes at a heavy price, which leads to the second thing. That God is impotent in this way provides no guarantee for the realization of any possible victory over evil. Humans are left in some kind of existential limbo that offers no hope for relief from suffering. If God cannot even guarantee his own welfare, what reasons do we have for supposing that he will guarantee our welfare? Moreover, what reasons do we have for supposing that he is worthy of worship and adoration? On this reading, he comes across merely as a superhero that could be overpowered by a formidable enemy. This view must, therefore, be rejected, for it seems utterly hopeless.

We have seen that one reason to think my thesis is true is to consider that if God exists, he would be the sort of being worthy of worship by his creatures. Such a being must be thought of both as substantially and morally perfect. A second reason, closely related to the first, contends that if a substantially and morally perfect being worthy of our worship truly exists, he would no longer be worthy of our worship if he must bow to a law

10. Ford, "Divine Persuasion," 248–49.

external to himself, for at least one entity would exercise authority over him, in which case that entity would be higher in authority than him. If God is to be considered worthy of our worship, he must be the source or author of his own laws. Only this understanding makes sense when we speak of obeying God's laws, for they are quite properly his laws.

If the laws in question are not God's laws, then we would make no sense to speak of obedience or disobedience with regard to God. We would speak of breaking such a law without having to invoke the reality of God as its divine author. If such an objective God-independent law truly exists, the guardian or enforcer of such a law is not clear. In this kind of setup, one would merely need to know that the law exists, but one would not worry about the consequences, eternal or otherwise, of breaking the law for the simple reason that no one would stand behind the law in question in order to enforce it. Laws are innocuous if they have no enforcer.

Also, I contend that God would not bow to the aforementioned God-independent law and still be God. If we allow that God should bow to a law existing independently of him, we would imply that God is subservient to that law, thereby bowing to an authority external to him. An objective moralist maintaining that objective laws exist independently of God would have to show why God would still be the one he claims to be in spite of the fact that he has to be subservient to the law or morality in question.

Of course, one could argue that a good God will not only have to obey the law in question; he will also have to enforce it. If he fails either to bow to it or to enforce it, then he is no longer the good God that theists claim him to be. However, this consideration only serves to underscore the fact that he must bow to the law in question, which, in turn, seems to count against his nature as God. If such is the case, we are not guaranteed that justice will be served in cases of wrongdoing. On a more worrying scale for the theist, he is not guaranteed that he believes in a being for which a greater cannot be thought. One merely needs to posit the existence of that law as something greater than God.

I therefore contend here that objective value must be seen to exist to the extent that it issues from God's essentially good nature. Within this kind of framework and understanding, the problem of pain as well as the problem of evil must be raised. Outside this framework, the problem, whether of pain or of evil, seems no longer sensible, for we have no expectation that the atheistic attack should be based on a reading of ethics outside essentialism. Having set this framework in place, we now want to determine whether an entity of pain exists that is at the same time evil. This task is the subject of the next chapter.

5

Death and Evil

IN PREVIOUS CHAPTERS I have been contending that materialistic naturalists, of the sort J. L. Mackie alludes to, equivocate pain with evil and pleasure with good. More accurately, I have tried to expose the contradictions and oddities the naturalists in question encounter when we maintain that evil is always synonymous with pain and that good is always synonymous with pleasure. I have also taken trouble to argue that God must be seen to be the source of objective morality if the arguments from the materialistically inclined naturalists, based on the problem of evil, are to have any force. I have shown, albeit minimally, that even from the essentialist reading, the atheistic arguments remain innocuous. A more detailed critique will be offered in the last two chapters of this work.

In this chapter, I take a deeper look at an issue I highlighted somewhat briefly in the first chapter. The issue can be stated in the form of a question: Is there at least one instance of evil that is simultaneously an instance of pain? In other words, can we locate an example of pain, one which would command our assent that it is, in fact, painful, while at the same time unanimously see it as a prime example of evil? Put differently, can we reasonably suppose that an entity exists that is essentially evil as well as essentially painful? We find no controversy in saying that pleasure and good can and do occur simultaneously in some instances. What we find difficult to locate is an instance of pain that is also an instance of evil.

This question is perhaps a difficult one to answer for the following reason, which I have already discussed in earlier chapters: Unless we all agree as to what conditions must be fulfilled in order for something to count as evil, we will perhaps never arrive at the proper answer to this question. We must, therefore, settle on the ethical theory usually assumed by theologians and atheologians when dealing with the problem of evil. I suggest that the interlocutors in the debate usually base their arguments on the essentialist reading of ethics. This suggestion is based on my earlier contention that those who call the doctrines of Christianity to question do so on the supposition that certain important aspects of their doctrine of God fail to agree with their affirmations of the facts and reality of evil. I contended earlier that one would not meaningfully raise the problem of evil within Christianity unless one tries to show how the facts of evil fail to square with the claim that God exists.

Moreover, we would be imprudent to state the problem of evil without drawing attention to the fact that the believer's understanding of evil is based on his essentialist reading of ethics. This reading not only gives the interlocutors of the debate a common framework upon which to base their arguments but also allows them to work toward unanimity concerning what they would all believe are the sorts of entities that count as evil.

If we try to raise the problem on a utilitarian reading of ethics, Christians will rightly contend that they do not subscribe to the view that pleasure is the highest good. If we try to raise the problem on some form of deontological reading of ethics, Christians will definitely object to this kind of ethical understanding by drawing attention to the fact that they do not subscribe to the reading in question. In other words, Christians are bound to reject any form of objection raised against God via the problem of evil if the objector demands that Christians accept a reading of ethics different and far removed from the essentialist reading—or at least one that seems inconsistent with the sort of essentialism entailed by the Bible. For these reasons, I reiterate what I have been contending all along: In order for the problem of evil to have any teeth against belief in God, the objector must raise it in a way that tries to turn Christian doctrine on its own head based on its understanding on what counts as evil. This understanding of evil, I argue, is best explicated on essentialist terms.

Having settled on such a reading, we now proceed with the question I raised earlier in this chapter: does an instance of pain exist that is also an instance of evil on an essentialist reading of ethics? I noted earlier that finding such an instance is extremely difficult, even on other readings of ethics, including the Epicurean reading, a reading that many philosophical materialists uphold, especially with regard to death. Nevertheless, this chapter attempts to find one.

We may not succeed in finding a good example of pain that is also an example of evil by considering the instances of pain that humans commonly experience. However, we could have better promise if we look at the ultimate result that such pain could possibly bring. In other words, perhaps we might do better if we think that death might be just the example that is both painful and evil. Several *prima facie* reasons could be given for this possibility.

First, the one thing humans fear most seems to be the phenomenon of death. Does this fact perhaps point to the possibility that death is also an instance of evil? Consider that we do our best to avoid death if we can. Sooner or later, however, it catches up with us, through old age, failing health, or some fatal accident. Is it that death could be an entity properly considered both an instance of pain and an instance of evil?

The second reason, which I will later revisit at greater length, is that our pre-death experiences seem to point to the fact that, physically speaking, death is the highest and most excruciating form of pain anyone could endure. The physical, emotional, and psychological pain we seem to go through when a loved one dies is usually one reason we do our best to avoid it as much as we can. Moreover, the healing that follows the grieving period for those left behind never seems to come quickly enough. Many grieving individuals take time to recover from the emotional trauma that follows bereavement.

For this reason, one would want to suggest, quite understandably, that on the essentialist reading, death could be just the entity that is both essentially evil and essentially painful. However, we will see that even here, sustaining the claim that death is always an evil is difficult. I will proceed here by drawing attention to a possible essentialist argument that would defend the claim that death is both painful and evil. I will also show that even on such a reading, this claim is perhaps not a necessary truth, assuming we understand a necessary truth as a statement that cannot be false under any circumstance. In other words, we will see that the experience of death is not always also the experience of evil. To demonstrate this observation, we need to locate an example of death that is a counter-instance of this claim. If we find such an example, that is, one that would depict death as anything less than evil, we will have succeeded in showing that death is not necessarily an evil thing.

We have already noted how Epicurus contended that death is nothing to us. The answer to whether or not Epicurus was correct in this contention remains notoriously elusive within a materialistic framework of value. To be sure, the philosophical debate on this issue reveals an extremely rugged terrain, though quite rigorous, on both sides. The question philosophers find themselves trying to answer is whether or not death can be correctly viewed as an evil of some kind. Epicurus, of course, remained uncommitted to either side by maintaining that death is nothing to us—neither good nor evil. Some of the materialistic philosophers, committed to the belief that Epicurus was mistaken, proceeded to argue that death is an evil. Others found themselves in agreement with Epicurus.

Before proceeding, I note that many philosophers have offered their contribution to this debate over the years. However, a comprehensive survey of their views remains beyond the scope of this chapter, and certainly more than I would wish to pursue here. For this reason, I will offer, in what follows, only a brief survey of representative views on both sides of the debate as a way of demonstrating how, in a materialist reading of ethics, unanimity on whether or not death is an evil remains elusive, and to show that even among those agreeing that death is an evil, we still find sharp differences on exactly what aspect about death leads them to think it is, in fact, an evil. On a Christian essentialist reading of ethics, the story, of course is different, as we shall see. For now, let me begin with a few thinkers who found themselves at odds with the Epicurean conclusion, but who also found themselves at odds with each other in their interlocutions concerning what, exactly, about death makes it evil. I will then proceed to highlight the views of a thinker who tries to defend the Epicurean view.

In an article entitled "The Evil of Death and the Lucretian Symmetry," philosophers John Martin Fischer and Anthony Brueckner defend what they call "a deprivation account of death" against a potential vulnerability from a contrary argument offered by Lucretius, an ancient and medieval poet and thinker. They intend to defend the claim that death is really evil of a certain kind. In that argument, Lucretius noted how prenatal nonexistence plausibly functions as the mirror image of posthumous nonexistence. If so, then an individual's birth at time t_1 deprives him of the good he or she would have had if the individual had been born earlier, say at time t_{1-n}. For that reason, Lucretius could possibly argue, we remain justified to regret the fact that we were born at t_1 rather than at t_{1-n}.[1]

Fischer and Brueckner, however, note that although death need not be a bad thing, it can, quite plausibly, be a bad thing for its victim. According to them, a plausible explanation for the badness in question draws attention to the tendency of death to deprive its victim of a specific kind of good, namely, the individual's continued life. Hence, when an individual dies at a certain time, say at time t_2 rather than at a later time, say, t_{2+n}, then death is bad for that individual because it deprives that individual of the good he or she would have had.[2]

Still, both Fischer and Brueckner find this summary of their position quite vulnerable to Lucretian refutation. However, they still find what they call a *prima facie* problem of the deprivation account of the badness of death. They call it a "pro-bias toward future pleasure," (call it P_{btfp} for short).

---

1. Brueckner and Fischer, "Evil of Death," 784.
2. Ibid., 783–84.

By that expression, they seem, I think, to assume humans have a natural bias toward future pleasures yet to be experienced when compared to past pleasures never experienced—that is, past pleasures occurring at t_{1-n}. Stated differently, people hold asymmetric attitudes toward posthumous and prenatal nonexistence. They find P_{btfp} a deep-seated feature of human beings, one they believe is rationally defensible. However, Fischer and Brueckner do not build their response to Lucretius via the P_{btfp} model. They use a different approach on the assumption that the P_{btfp} model is rationally defensible.[3] For example, they argue that humans remain especially biased toward future pleasures, but remain quite indifferent to past pleasures. Death, though, deprives humans of future pleasures. It seems to deprive us of something we find arguably rational to care about.[4]

Feldman criticized this defense of the deprivation account. According to Feldman, Fischer and Brueckner offered an overly simplistic view of the deprivation account. They seemed to suggest that death deprives humans of something humans care about. Prenatal nonexistence, however, deprives humans of something to which humans remain indifferent. Fischer and Brueckner seem to agree. However, they still believe that the idea behind this simplistic version suggests a more nuanced way of employing the P_{btfp} model. More strongly, they contend that P_{btfp} can be defended rationally as follows: depriving an individual of something that individual finds rational to care about is, in fact, rational. However, prenatal nonexistence deprives humans of something for which they find irrational to care about.[5]

Brueckner and Fischer provide a more nuanced defense of this claim, which they call BF*, as follows: Suppose death is bad for an individual, call him or her X. Death is bad for X because the attitude of caring about the fact that X's death will deprive X of some pleasant experiences that X would, otherwise, have enjoyed, is a rational one, even if X may not know what those other experiences will be. However, prenatal nonexistence is not bad for X in this way, for at least one reason: even though prenatal nonexistence deprives X of pleasant experiences, caring about the fact that X's later birth implies X would be deprived of some pleasant experiences does not seem rational on X's part. According to Brueckner and Fischer, this defense of the deprivation account meets the objection Fred Feldman raises.[6]

For example, according to Brueckner and Fischer, a SIDS baby may not have the cognitive wherewithal to understand the future's relevant

3. Ibid., 784.
4. Ibid., 785.
5. Ibid., 786–87.
6. Ibid., 787.

aspects. Just the same, such a baby can be plausibly said to have an interest in good future and can, therefore, have a reason to care about such a future. Demanding that the baby, or for that matter, any individual, should have a conceptualization of what such a future might be seems unduly restrictive. Having a notion at a given time to care about something need not require that the individual in question should conceptualize that thing.[7]

Bueckner and Fischer believe that on their account, badness is not understood simply in terms of actual attitudes (for which Feldman accused them). Rather, the account is understood in terms of the rationality of certain attitudes. For this reason, they contend that having P_{btfp} is rational, and both claim that prenatal nonexistence is not a bad thing based on their observation that caring or having regrets about late birth—in contrast to early death—is not rational. An agent has a reason to care about anything in his or her interest. Being in possession of such a reason at a given time does not demand that the agent be in possession of the relevant conceptual apparatus at that time.[8]

According to Brueckner and Fischer, P_{btfp} might be thought to explain why an individual might be more concerned about being deprived of future pleasures than he or she might be about having been deprived of pleasures in the past. Since the individual cares about future pleasures, if death robs him of future pleasures, it will have robbed him of something about which he cares more. Prenatal nonexistence, however, deprives us of things we do not care about specifically because we remain indifferent about past pleasures.[9]

Materialist philosopher Fred Feldman, in his article "Brueckner and Fischer On the Evil of Death," does not find things this simple. If you consider the proposition that death deprives humans of something humans care about and that prenatal nonexistence deprives them of something to which they remain indifferent, *something*, in this context, denotes specific pleasant experiences we lose through death—experiences we care about. Fischer calls this claim BF *de re*, and it could be stated as follows: death is bad for a person X only if certain pleasant experiences exist such that X's death deprives X of those experiences, and X cares about those experiences. However, prenatal nonexistence is not so bad for X because even though some pleasant experiences do exist such that X's prenatal nonexistence deprives X of those experiences, X does not care about those experiences.[10]

---

7. Ibid.
8. Ibid., 788.
9. Feldman, "Brueckner and Fischer," 312–13.
10. Ibid., 313.

According to Feldman, BF *de re* does not seem to have a plausible demonstration of death's badness for X. Feldman finds this claim unacceptable because no pleasant experiences exist such that X cares *de re* about them and that death will deprive X of them. Consider, for example, the case of a loving family's healthy and smart infant. Suppose the infant will have a desirable life filled with pleasant experiences assuming all goes well. Since the infant is only six months old, he or she has no idea of those pleasant experiences and is certainly not anticipating them. Hence, the idea that those pleasant experiences are things the infant cares about *de re* is false specifically because the infant remains completely ignorant of them. Suppose, then, the infant dies of SIDS when he or she is six months old. That occurrence would be an incontrovertible example of a tragic death for the infant. Defenders of the deprivation approach would say this death is bad for the infant because it deprives the infant of his pleasant future experience, such as a birthday. However, the infant's death does not deprive the child of any future pleasure *that he cared about*, and hence, one cannot appeal to BF *de re* to explain why the infant's death is bad for the child—the infant is completely ignorant of those experiences.[11]

Feldman does not limit the illustration of his argument to infants alone. He tries to bolster his argument further by drawing attention to the example of a young woman about to complete her studies at college. Imagine the woman headed for an enjoyable career, a happy marriage and, quite possibly, a serene retirement later in life, provided, of course, she does not get killed in a bus accident at the age of twenty. According to Feldman, if she were to die at age twenty, her death would certainly be a huge misfortune to her. BF *de re* does not explain this misfortune.[12]

In short, even if we may all agree that X's death may be a misfortune for X, BF *de re* fails to locate or explain the misfortune. Feldman proposes a different kind of BF, namely, BF *de dicto*, which tries to locate the badness or evil of death as follows: death is bad for a person X only if X cares about the fact that if X dies, X will be deprived of some pleasant experience that X would, otherwise, have enjoyed. To be sure, X may not know what those experiences will be, but X cares about them nonetheless. Prenatal nonexistence, though, is not bad for X because although it deprives the person of pleasant experiences, X does not care about the fact that if X is born late, X will be deprived of some pleasant experience.[13]

11. Ibid.
12. Ibid., 313–14.
13. Ibid., 314.

Does BF *de dicto* fare any better than BF *de re*? According to Feldman, it apparently fails to address the SIDS objection, specifically because the infant lacks a concept of death and has no expectation of future pleasant experiences for him. Additionally, Feldman draws our attention to the example of an unduly pessimistic person who kills himself at age forty because he believes his future will bring only misery. In fact, pleasant experiences were in store for him such that he would have experienced an unexpected but desirable turn of events. In such an instance, the person's death would be a disaster for him, though he would not have realized it. However, BF *de dicto* does not locate the nature of this disaster.[14]

Owing to the fact that this formulation does not seem to work, Feldman suggests a third possibility, namely: death is bad for certain people because it deprives them of things *we* (rather than the victims of death) care about. This reformulation would then yield a different version of BF *de dicto*, which we could call BF *de dicto*$_2$, and could be formally stated as follows: death is bad for a person X if and only if other people care about the fact that if X dies, X will be deprived of some pleasant experiences X would have enjoyed. The problem with this reformulation is not difficult to see, according to Feldman. He finds no reason why *other people's* grave concerns about X's deprivations explain why X's death would be bad for X. Additionally, if other individuals mistakenly think that X's life seems headed for misery even though it seems poised to take a surprising turn for the better, then those individuals would not think that death will deprive X of any valuable thing. In this case, then, BF *de dicto*$_2$ suggests quite wrongly that early death would not be bad for X when, clearly, it is.[15] Notice how, in the debate between Brueckner and Fischer, on the one hand, and Feldman on the other, we find them disagreeing on how to locate the exact nature of death's evil even though both seem to agree that death is an evil.

Brueckner, Fischer, and Feldman are not the only philosophers defending the claim that death is a certain kind of evil. In an article entitled "The Evil of Death Revisited," philosopher Harry Silverstein offers a refutation of the Epicurean view of death (henceforth referred to as *EV*), refining the refutation from an earlier article published under the title "The Evil of Death." Silverstein believes one could, quite plausibly, dismiss *EV* quickly assuming one claims that something, call it Y, can be good or evil for an individual X, even if Y fails to make a difference, positive or negative, to X's experience. In other words, Y can be good or evil for X even if Y does not connect in any way, whether negative or positive, to X's feelings. If one

---

14. Ibid.
15. Ibid., 315.

makes this claim, then one rejects what Silverstein calls the "values connect with feelings view," or *VCF* for short. Moreover, one could reject *VCF* just as fast if one accepts the standard argument for the evil of death, as follows: the continued good life X experiences remains good for X, and if X continues living, then X remains a possible recipient of value. If one intelligibly regards X's life as good for X, then one must intelligibly regard the loss of X's life as bad for X. This argument, as it stands, refutes *EV*.[16]

Even after observing that these arguments seem plausible dismissals of *EV*, Silverstein seems to rethink this initial vantage point by postulating that neither the first nor the second dismissal of *EV* is ultimately successful specifically because even weak versions of *VCF* seem to rule out posthumous goods and evils. These versions include specific attempts to postulate merely possible, rather than actual, connections between an X-relative evil and X's suffering. As for the standard argument, consider the claim that the continued good life that X experiences remains good for X. For this claim to be relevant to *EV*, one must interpret it as making the claim that X's continued good life is better for X than X's death is good for X. From *EV*'s perspective, this claim remains implausible for the same reason that the simple claim that X's death is an evil for X remains implausible. Presumably, *EV* would hold that X's death is neither good nor evil for X.[17]

Thus, Silverstein finds no quick fix available to thinkers wishing to reject *EV*, noting how refuting *EV* entails formulating a serious argument. The argument, according to Silverstein, will include two key assumptions of the interpretation of *VCF*, as follows: First, the relevant connection between an X-relative evil, Y, and X's negative feelings is not that Y cannot cause those feelings. Rather, Y is or can be the object of those feelings. Second, future events and states can be objects of these very feelings in the required sense. This second claim requires the adoption of what Silverstein calls a four-dimensional framework. According to this framework, objects and events of different times are viewed as coexisting in a manner analogous to how we find objects and events from different places coexisting. Hence, the four-dimensional framework, *4DF* for short, allows or even requires us to see posthumous events and objects as coexisting in an eternal or timeless sense of the word.[18]

According to Silverstein, if we adopt this framework, one can plausibly claim that posthumous states of affairs exist, and that these states of affairs can, therefore, be objects of relevant and appropriate feelings in the same

---

16. Silverstein, "Evil of Death Revisited," 116.
17. Ibid., 117.
18. Ibid.

sense *VCF* requires. Stated differently, *X*'s death coexists with *X*, and for that reason, *X*'s death is a possible object of *X*'s suffering—it is an intelligible *X*-relative evil.[19] To be sure, this maneuver seems to be an attempt on Silverstein's part to defend what he calls a specific version of *VCF*, which he calls VCF_1 and VCF_2. The first version holds that the relevant connection between an *X*-relative evil, *Y*, and *X*'s negative experience is that *Y* is the object of *X*'s feelings. The second version is that future events can be objects of relevant negative experiences.[20] Silverstein's depiction of *VCF* portrays the materialistic philosophy I am trying to critique here, specifically because it seems to suggest values have a certain symbiotic, perhaps even synonymous, relationship with feelings—a view I find quite problematic.

Silverstein draws a distinction between the *de re* conception and the *de dicto* conception of *VCF* to illustrate the differences between how an object might connect, or for that matter, fail to connect, with feelings in certain cases. In his attempt to refute Rosenbaum's objection, he draws our attention to a certain assumption Rosenbaum accuses him of making: what remains important in saying whether posthumous events are bad for a person is that the event ought to be an object of feeling. According to Silverstein, Rosenbaum assumes that if something does not exist, it cannot be a cause of negative feelings because *Y* cannot be evil for *X* unless *Y* exists. For Rosenbaum, a causal relation is necessary.[21] Silverstein tries do refute this necessary condition claim, which I outline below.

Silverstein thinks if something does not exist, it cannot be the object of a person's feelings. He draws from an illustration Rosenbaum uses, which I will outline in greater detail when highlighting Rosenbaum's argument later in this chapter. For now, consider this brief version: Suppose *X* fears a Nazi invasion of Britain in 1945. Call that event *N*. Assuming that *N* did not occur, the claim "*X* fears *N*" turns out false. We would be wrong to claim that *N* is the object of *X*'s fear. This conception illustrates what Silverstein calls a *de re* conception. Slightly different from this conception is a *de dicto* conception. Silverstein and, possibly, Rosenbaum, would illustrate this conception as follows: Suppose *X* fears that *N* obtains. If *X* fears that *N* obtains, then it is true that *N* is the object of *X*'s fear. Silverstein employs the *de re* conception of *VCF* rather than the *de dicto* conception.[22]

How does the *de re* conception refute Rosenbaum's necessary condition claim? Silverstein appeals to the following example. Jim believes John's

19. Ibid.
20. Ibid., 122.
21. Ibid.
22. Ibid., 123.

wife Ann is having an affair with Phil, who happens to be John's friend, specifically because Jim overheard a conversation between Ann and Phil, and they happened to be discussing their affair. Jim, though, is mistaken because the conversation he heard was between Jan and Bill. Concluding that Jim would rather know about the affair between Ann and Phil instead of remaining in ignorance, Jim tells John that his wife Ann is having an affair with Phil. As things turn out, Ann actually is having an affair with Phil, and when Jim tells John this story, John gets totally distraught. Ann's affair with Phil turns out to be the object of John's misery. The affair, combined with Jim's mistake, cause John's misery. By itself, Ann's affair was not a causal antecedent of John's misery. Notice the connection Silverstein makes here: Ann's affair was not necessarily the cause of John's misery for it to have been an evil for John.[23]

How, exactly, does Silverstein's 4DF apply itself in this context? First, according to Silverstein, his 4DF does not imply that anything that exists always exists, which then falsely contends that on this view, dead people continue to exist. To avoid this conclusion as a possible source of confusion, Silverstein contrasts 4DF with what he calls the three-dimensional framework, 3DF for short. The latter abstracts from the "now" only, and is, therefore, spatially neutral. The former abstracts from the "here" and "now" and is both temporally and spatially neutral. Hence, suppose one says X exists in the 4DF sense. One leaves both the place and time of X's existence open. This claim can be designated as $X\ exists_4$. Suppose one says X exists in the 3DF sense. One leaves only the place of X's existence open, and this claim can be designated as $X\ exists_3$. Hence, to say that $X\ exists_4$ leaves the time and place of X's existence open, and it means that $X\ exists_4$ is true at every time if it is true at any time. Hence, $X\ exists_4$ is always true if it is ever true. It is also true everywhere if it is true anywhere. However, $X\ exists_3$ is only true everywhere if it is true anywhere. Thus, for both claims, anything that exists anywhere exists everywhere. On both readings of existence, they do not imply that X's existence extends throughout all space. Neither do they imply X's existence lacks spatial boundaries. More importantly, for $exists_4$, $X\ exists_4$ does not imply that X's existence extends throughout all temporal boundaries.[24]

Silverstein appeals to a time chart illustration to press his point. Imagine, for example, how time charts show the lives of English monarchs. A specific individual on the time chart, such as Henry VIII, either appears on the chart or does not. Of course, Henry VIII does appear on the chart. This appearance implies he always appears on that chart even long after his

23. Ibid., 124.
24. Ibid., 125–26.

death. It would be absurd, Silverstein would possibly argue, to claim Henry VIII goes on the chart when he is born and comes out when he dies. With respect to the meaning conveyed by exists$_4$, Silverstein finds this supposition rather strange.[25] This reading of existence would allow us to postulate that Henry VIII's death coexists with Henry VIII and, for that reason, his death was an evil for him. We can make analogous remarks about all deaths imaginable, presumably.

We consider one more defender of the evil of death view. In his article entitled "Fischer on Death and Unexperienced Evils," philosopher Ben Bradley contends that the Epicurean argument on death is a bad one. He refers to the argument that dead people experience no sensations—good or bad—and therefore being dead is neither good nor bad. Bradley calls this argument the experience argument, henceforth referred to as *E*. Bradley cites a specific aspect of John Fischer's argument as a counterexample to the Epicurean argument, namely, Fischer's contention that some things we find bad for us do not involve bad sensations at all.[26]

Consider Nagel's example: An individual, call him *A*, gets betrayed by another individual, call him *B*, and this betrayal happens behind *A*'s back. *A* never finds out about the betrayal and lives happily to his death. Consider also philosopher Robert Nozick's example of a person, call her *C*, secretly videotaped in her bedroom. People in Outer Mongolia watch the video. *C*, however, never finds out about the videotaping event. The event is bad for *C*, but *C* lacks any feelings about it. Finally, philosopher Jeff McMahan cites an example of another individual, call him *D*, whose daughter dies on a Himalayan adventure. The daughter's death happens minutes before *D*'s death. In all these cases, Fischer agrees that all individuals experience some kind of misfortune.[27]

Bradley cites a different kind of counterexample to *E*, as follows: John sends Ben concert tickets in the mail. Ben lacks any knowledge of the concert or the tickets, which he would have wanted and really enjoyed if he went to the concert. A certain individual, called Derek, steals the ticket from Ben's mailbox, and Ben still does not know about the theft. This theft, according to Bradley, is a misfortune to Ben, but Ben did not have any bad sensations resulting from the theft. The theft is bad for Ben because it deprives him of something good. For that reason, the theft is instrumentally bad for him. Nagel's, Nozick's, and McMahan's example involve bad events independent

---

25. Ibid., 126.
26. Bradley, "Fischer on Death," 507.
27. Ibid.

of what they bring about for their victims.[28] In other words, the events are intrinsically bad or, to use another expression, bad in themselves.

According to Bradley, the deprivation theorist would make the following claim about the badness of death as an objection to the argument; namely, death's badness for its victim consists in its preventing the victim from getting some intrinsic goods. Thus, the deprivation theorist would be targeting the second premise of the argument. Analogously to how illnesses and injuries prevent us from having the goods of life, death keeps us from having the goods of life. In contrast to illnesses and injuries, though, one is not suffering when one is dead.[29]

Nagel, Nozick, McMahan, and Fischer seem to target the third premise of the argument. They find some things bad for us, and these things are not bad sensations such as undiscovered betrayals, unknown misfortunes of loved ones, secret violations, and the like. They are not bad sensations nor do they cause any bad sensations to be bad. Stated differently, they remain intrinsically bad.[30] By intrinsic badness, Bradley notes how the thinkers in question attribute objectivity to value.

By making this claim, Bradley's keen mind locates a confusion highlighting the concern this work is attempting to address. After drawing the distinction between instrumental badness and intrinsic badness, he notes how thinkers subscribing exclusively (though, perhaps, unintentionally) to the former view reduce value to mere sensations, while thinkers subscribing to the latter view hold a more objective idea of value existing independently and without qualification.

Exactly how does the confusion arise? According to Bradley, that confusion can be located in the writings of Fischer. He claims to be defending the deprivation account that seems motivated to highlight the instrumental badness of death. However, his defense involves arguing for the intrinsic badness of events independent of whether those events deprive the victims of anything. According to Bradley, this state of affairs results in what he calls *a dialectical confusion*. Bradley, therefore, believes Fischer's example is not really a deprivation view, but a nameless one, apparently.[31]

Bradley proposes Fischer's view about death should be called the *more intrinsic badness view*. Bradley suggests the following description of this view: For any victim of death X, death is bad for X if and only if death causes something intrinsically bad for X. A few possible ways exist in which death

28. Ibid., 507–8.
29. Ibid.
30. Ibid.
31. Ibid.

could bring about intrinsic badness for X. For example, having X's desires frustrated is an intrinsic bad. Death frustrates many desires. For this reason, death brings about intrinsic evils. Bradley calls this argument *the desire fulfillment account of wellbeing*. Another example of the more intrinsic badness view is the *achievement-based account*, wherein the account views failure as intrinsically bad. On this account, if an individual X works hard on a project and X's death prevents X from completing the project, then X fails, and this is intrinsically bad for X.[32]

Therefore, according to Bradley, Fischer might seem to say that a premature death has the potential of adding some intrinsic badness to one's life story, possibly through frustrating a desire or preventing one from achieving a certain goal. Fischer appeals to unexperienced intrinsic evils rather than the more instrumental deprivationist reply to Epicurus. Consider the example of Ben's theft of the tickets. Following the deprivationist account, Derek's theft of the tickets is bad for me even though it causes me no bad sensations. Defenders of the experience requirement, Bradley says, would argue that Derek's theft of the tickets is bad for me only because it is possible for me to feel bad about the theft. Hence, Bradley thinks a modified experience requirement—one Fischer seems to endorse—is satisfied in the ticket-theft case. However, Bradley believes this modified experience requirement remains unsatisfied in the case of death. The modified experience requirement, then, runs as follows: something is bad for an individual X only if X can possibly feel bad about it.[33]

According to Bradley, this modified version of the experience requirement remains problematic, and this fact can be illustrated by the following counterexample. Suppose Ben never finds out about Derek's theft, but if Ben did, his upset feelings would have a minus 10 value. The modified version of the experience requirement fails to specify the extent of harm. In general, Bradley suggests, claiming that some feature makes an event harmful is wrong if we fail to specify the role that feature plays in determining the extent of the harm. Thus, the modified experience requirement merely requires the possibility of being the object of bad feelings in order for a given event to be harmful without playing a role in specifying the extent of the harm.[34]

Bradley proposes a third modification of the experience requirement; namely, unexperienced intrinsic goods or evils do not exist. Bradley finds this claim true. He believes the deprivationist objection to the Epicurean

32. Ibid., 509.
33. Ibid.
34. Ibid., 509–10.

argument remains compatible with this third version, thereby giving it a significant advantage over the Fischer/Nagel objection. For Bradley, the Epicurean need not rely on an experience to argue against the badness of death. Neither will he find deprivationist objections appealing. Rather, he will appeal to another difference between death and ordinary deprivations; namely, death is the end of one's existence. This fact explains why death cannot be bad for its victim, though having Derek steal Ben's concert tickets can be bad for Ben.[35]

In order to see this, Bradley proposes what he calls the timing argument, as follows: Death's badness for us implies its badness for us at some time. Death's badness for us at some time implies its badness for us before we die or after we die. Death is not bad for us before we die, neither is it bad for us after we die. Therefore, death is not bad for us. After listing several objections to this argument, Bradley gives us one possible objection he believes has some merit, as follows: death is bad for an individual X at times after X dies if and only if at some point in those times intrinsically good things would have been happening to X. In other words, X is worse off being dead than enjoying those intrinsic goods, thereby requiring us to say the dead have a zero-level of wellbeing. According to Bradley, an objection has been raised against this argument, namely, it requires attributing properties to nonexistent things. Bradley, however, finds the objection wrongheaded because in prudential evaluations we treat nonexistence as equivalent to existing with zero well-being.[36]

According to Bradley, Fisher rejects the fourth premise of the timing argument by noting how a betrayal can harm an individual posthumously, and death can do the same. Bradley follows the deprivation account in his objection by noting that death merely deprives one of intrinsic goodness. Nevertheless, the time of death's badness is the time that goodness would have obtained. From Bradley's perspective, one can suffer intrinsic evils such as betrayal even when one has ceased to exist. According to the deprivation view, death deprives its victims of good things, and for that reason makes a difference to how well things turn out for an individual. Fischer thinks that one's well-being level can rise and fall after one has died. According to the posthumous view, events can make a difference to how well things turn out for the dead person specifically because that person's well-being level can continue to rise and fall after the person's death depending on what happens.[37]

35. Ibid., 510.
36. Ibid., 510–11.
37. Ibid., 511.

Bradley finds a glaring drawback in Fischer's reply to the timing argument. According to Bradley, Fischer's reply seems to require one to say an individual can have a positive or negative well-being level even when the individual does not exist. A better way to develop Fischer's view is to suggest that death makes the victim's whole life worse than it would been otherwise by reducing its global value. This formulation seems to leave one unable to account for the full badness of death. This observation leaves Bradley to suggest that even if death is bad because of diminishing the value of the victim's life as a whole, it also seems bad in purely deprivational ways.[38]

Bradley then concludes his article by noting the following: to the extent that we desire to claim, and we should, that death's badness partly involves its purely deprivational, forward-looking, and episodic aspect, we will be forced to reply to the Epicurean concern that having a well-being level (even zero) after death remains impossible. For Bradley, we remain unable to avoid this worry when we appeal to unexperienced intrinsic evils.[39]

What do we make of these arguments? We can make a general assessment of all of them by drawing attention to Brueckner and Fischer's understanding of the deprivation approach as a way of locating the evil of death, though, as we have seen, not all of the thinkers already considered seem unanimous in their assessment of this argument's success in locating the evil of death. Briefly stated, the argument runs as follows: X's continued life is a good. For any state of affairs S, if S deprives X of X's continued life, then S is evil. Death is a specific state of affairs that deprives X of X's continued life. Therefore, death is evil. As stated, the argument seems successful. Almost all the thinkers hitherto considered, however, seem to believe the deprivation approach remains vulnerable to what philosophers in this debate have called the Lucretian symmetry argument, which contends that if one's posthumous existence is a deprivation of one's life, then one's prenatal existence is just as bad a deprivation of one's life. Brueckner and Fischer have tried to address this concern, as we have already seen.

We can locate a point of vulnerability of the symmetry argument adumbrated by Lucretius, wherein the thinker can see that one's prenatal nonexistence need not be seen as depriving the individual of his or her continued good life. Suppose I was born at time t_1 and that the circumstances in the world are such that if I had been born at an earlier time, say at t_{1-n}, I would have enjoyed a certain type of prolonged pleasure, call it P, a pleasure I am now incapable of enjoying. Regretting that I was born at t_1 rather than at t_{1-n} would perhaps seem rational. Suppose, however, instead

38. Ibid., 512.
39. Ibid.

of experiencing P at t_{1-n}, I really would have suffered some kind of prolonged evil, call it E. Regretting that I was born at t_1 rather than at t_{1-n} would in this instance seem rational rather than irrational. These two possible states of affairs imply that the goodness or badness of prenatal nonexistence does not rest on prenatal nonexistence itself. Rather, it seems to rest on unpredictable contingencies beyond our cognitive grasp. To be sure, we find a relevant difference between prenatal nonexistence and posthumous nonexistence. One is nonexistent, with respect to prenatal nonexistence, in a way radically different from one's nonexistence in posthumous nonexistence. As far as the former is concerned, the marks of one's nonexistence are absent. With respect to the latter, the marks of one's nonexistence seem present; namely, the individual's remains. With respect to the former, we find no loss of life. With respect to the latter, one experiences the loss of one's life. Therefore, we erroneously maintain that prenatal nonexistence deprives an individual of his or her continued life. To claim that it does sounds rather odd.

Having looked at four major objectors to the Epicurean view, we have at least one philosopher who seems to sympathize with Epicurus, and by extension, Lucretius. In his article, "How to Be Dead and Not Care," philosopher Stephen Rosenbaum offers a defense of what he calls a remedy for our attitudes toward death. Rosenbaum believes he needs to undertake this project because hitherto, the Epicurean account has not received a sound defense. Besides acknowledging that being alive is generally good, Rosenbaum additionally claims that when one dies, one ceases to exist in some important sense. Before proceeding with his defense, Rosenbaum makes some important distinctions between the meanings of the terms he intends to use, namely, dying, death, and being dead. Rosenbaum understands dying to be the process whereby one comes to be dead, thereby taking place near the end of an individual's lifetime. The process of dying may be either long or short, and it may be either comfortable or uncomfortable. Owing to the fact that dying takes place during one's lifetime, dying may be experienced. By contrast, Rosenbaum adds, death is the time at which a person becomes dead, and is different from dying.[40]

Rosenbaum then explains a third concept, which he calls "being dead." Being dead is the state of an individual after that individual has died. It is not part of a person's life. However, it is part of a person's history. Death, therefore, is located at the end of a person's dying process and at the beginning of a person's state of being dead. Rosenbaum then offers a reconstruction of Epicurus' argument as follows: A state of affairs S is bad for an individual X only if X can experience S at some time, call it t. Consequently, X's being

40. Rosenbaum, "How to Be Dead," 174.

dead is bad for X only if it is a state of affairs S that X can experience at t. X can experience a state of affairs S at t only if S begins before X's death. X's being dead is not a state of affairs S that begins before X's death. Therefore, X's being dead is not a state of affairs S that X can experience at t. Therefore, X's being dead is not bad for X.[41]

Before proceeding with his defense, Rosenbaum makes some qualifying remarks, including the observation that when Epicurus said "death is nothing to us," he is most plausibly interpreted as talking about being dead. Rosenbaum also observes that what people seem to find bad in this debate is not the moment of death itself, but the state of nonexistence, which he calls "being dead." The state of being dead is what people fear, and that fear is what Epicurus wishes to eliminate. Moreover, owing to the fact that a person's death may be a mere moment in time with little or no temporal duration, Rosenbaum is doubtful that an individual's death could be bad for the individual in question. Also, Epicurus' sympathetic proponents, such as Lucretius, take him to be concerned about being dead, and not death.[42]

Rosenbaum also makes additional remarks about experience, which seems fundamental to understanding the first premise of his argument, namely: A state of affairs S is bad for a person X only if X can experience S at some time t. To understand this premise, consider the state of affairs in which X cannot hear and never will hear. In such a situation, even the egregious performance of a Mozart symphony will not affect X at any time as far as X's hearing is concerned, assuming merely awful sound is what counts as bad performance detectable through normal hearing. Clearly, then, X cannot experience bad performance in an auditory way. The reason the performance is not bad for X is because X remains unable to experience it. X's deafness insulates X from the experience of hearing the performance which might otherwise be bad for X.[43]

Rosenbaum wants us to draw the following principle from this illustration: If a person X cannot experience a state of affairs S at some time, then S is not bad for the person. Dead persons cannot experience any states of affairs specifically because they are generally insentient. Therefore, no states of affairs are bad for a dead person. Therefore, according to Rosenbaum, a positive reason exists for believing the principle adumbrated earlier, namely: A state of affairs S is bad for a person X only if X can experience S at some time t. This principle is based on another assumption, namely, an individual X experiences a state of affairs S only if S can affect one in some way. On this

41. Ibid., 175.
42. Ibid., 176.
43. Ibid., 176–77.

reading of experience, X does not experience a situation merely by believing that S has obtained.[44]

Rosenbaum assumes that this sense of experience exists, namely, one entailing the process of awareness. He also notes, however, that a certain sense of experience exists of which the experiencer may be unaware. For example, one can undergo the experience of irradiation by low-level radioactivity and remain well unaware of it. Still, a clear requirement of experience is that the experiencer be causally affected in some way by the state of affairs in which the experience obtains. This requirement gives us a positive reason for believing the third premise of the restatement of the Epicurean argument above: X can experience a state of affairs S at t only if S begins before X's death. This understanding seems buttressed by the assumption that S causally affects X only if X exists after S begins to occur. After all, effects do occur only after their causes.[45]

Rosenbaum then draws our attention to an objection to the first premise, one raised by Thomas Nagel, as follows: quite possibly, what a person does not know may still be bad for the person. A person's friend may secretly betray that person without the person knowing it then or later, and such betrayal may involve vile and false rumors. Such a case counts as an example of evils a person might not consciously experience. Rosenbaum thinks, however, that such examples remain strictly and logically compatible with his first premise and do not refute it. According to Rosenbaum, the reason they seem innocuous to the first premise is this: that premise requires only that for a thing to be bad for a person, that person can experience it, perhaps unconsciously, at some time, and not that the person should experience it consciously. What the premise requires is that for S to be bad for a person, the person should *be able* to experience S at some time t, and not that the person *be aware* of the causal effects at t.[46]

According to Rosenbaum, Nagel denies the conclusion Rosenbaum gives by depicting death as a loss to its victim. Moreover, owing to the fact that losses are bad, Nagel concludes that a person's death is bad for the person. Rosenbaum, while admitting that calling a person's death a loss seems right, adds that the loss brought about by death is not like paradigmatic cases of losses, which humans characteristically view as bad for people. The loss of one's business to creditors provides a good example because in this case, one has the business, the creditors get it, and the previous owner no longer has it. In such a case, the loss really is something the victim is able

44. Ibid., 177.
45. Ibid., 177–78.
46. Ibid., 179.

to experience after it occurs, and this kind of situation seems consonant with the following principle: An individual X loses a good, call it G, only if a time t_1 exists at which X has G and at some later time t_{1+n}, X does not have G. If X ceases to exist when X dies, then being dead is not a loss of this paradigmatic sort in which losses are bad for a person because X remains unable to experience it. In other words, Rosenbaum argues that if being dead is indeed a loss, it remains insufficiently similar to paradigmatic cases of loss we deem bad for persons. Rosenbaum then asks for a special, rational demonstration to show why treating death as a loss would enable us to reject the first premise he proposes, neither of which Nagel and his cohorts offer. For this reason, to argue that death is a loss remains unconvincing.[47]

After critiquing Nagel's view, Rosenbaum turns to Silverstein. Rosenbaum finds Silverstein at odds with the third premise by proposing the following claim: An individual X experiences states of affairs S or events beginning after X's death specifically because such S obtains atemporally during a person's life. Rosenbaum, however, thinks Silverstein's hypothesis is unsupported and should, therefore, be rejected. Ronsebaum also finds Silverstein's second assumption quite unsupported; namely, his assumption that a person X having, at some time, an actual feeling about an event is necessary for the event to be bad for X.[48]

Rosenbaum draws attention to Silverstein's interpretation of Epicurus, namely, that bad is associated with sentience. Rosenbaum does not find this to be the only interpretation or the most obvious interpretation. Suppose we say that an individual X must experience an event consciously for the event to be bad for X. This statement does not entail that X must have certain feelings about the event, or about X's awareness of the event, or about anything.[49]

A third response Rosenbaum gives to Silverstein's objection is by way of illustration. To do this, Rosenbaum draws our attention to the following consideration: Britons in the early 1940s feared an invasion into their country by the Nazis. They even dreaded being governed by Hitler. Neither the invasion nor the governance of Hitler obtained as states of affairs. To be sure, they never will. Rosenbaum admits that these examples are states of affairs that had to exist for them to be objects of fear and dread. Just the same, Britons never experienced these events because they never occurred even if events which have never occurred or will never occur can, in a certain sense, be objects of our psychological attitudes. Hence, Rosenbaum thinks

---

47. Ibid., 179–80.
48. Ibid., 182.
49. Ibid.

Silverstein fails to distinguish between the *existence* of an event or state of affairs from the *occurrence* of an event or state of affairs. Some thinkers find no need to make such a distinction because, for them, existence and occurrence seem identical.[50]

Suppose, then, Silverstein identifies the classes of events. He would then seem forced to view that if events exist atemporally as he believes, they would also occur atemporally. The problem with this conclusion is that we would find no difference between past and future events if they occurred and existed atemporally and the set denoting this class of events would be empty, which seems absurd. To be sure, Rosenbaum argues, if one holds that all events exist atemporally but among them, some have occurred in the past and some are yet to occur in future, then with this distinction in place the third premise of the argument can easily be defended against Silverstein's attack. The premise reminds us, according to Rosenbaum, that X can experience S at t_1 only if S begins to occur before X's death. Understood in this way, objecting to this premise by stating that posthumous events or states of affairs exist timelessly during a person's life is no good. According to Rosenbaum, Silverstein would have to argue that X can experience S that does not begin to occur before X's death, and Rosenbaum does not see how S, understood in this way, could obtain for X. Therefore, Silverstein's proposal is ineffective against the third premise even if it might have independent merits.[51]

Before moving on to the Christian view, let me draw attention to Silverstein's comment on the kind of loss death brings. Recall his contention that the loss death brings about remains insufficiently similar to paradigmatic cases of loss we deem bad for persons. Apparently, Rosenbaum underestimates the loss death causes by finding it insufficiently similar to paradigmatic cases of loss. Death is more than merely a loss of paradigmatic cases of loss. Death is the loss of life, which is the very thing that remains capable of experiencing other forms of loss. To be sure, by drawing a contrast between the loss that death brings and other paradigmatic cases of loss, Rosenbaum underestimates the seriousness of this loss. Other kinds of loss entail dispossessions of some kind of material goods. With respect to dispossessions of one's belongings, one is no longer able to enjoy one's possessions. With respect to death, one becomes dispossessed of life, and life, I say, is a fundamental basis of owning anything.

I have provided a survey of the arguments on both sides of the debate on the evil of death offered by materialistic philosophers. I now turn to the view presented by Christian thinkers. I will merely provide the Christian

50. Ibid., 183.
51. Ibid.

view as an alternative to the materialistic philosophers' view, and demonstrate the advantage it has over materialistic philosophy. Notice how both sides of the debate assume, without argument, that once one dies, one ceases to exist. Apparently, assuming the Christian view of death is correct, as I believe it is, the central claim of materialistic philosophy becomes quite wrongheaded, as we shall see below.

A materialistic objector might press the point that the Epicurean view of death might be essentially correct because no one has so far demonstrated in any sufficient way that people have sensations after they die. In other words, given our scientific findings about death, we seem to know nothing or sense nothing or even feel nothing once we have breathed our last.

This objection might seem to have some force. Upon closer scrutiny, it fails for at least one reason: This view has been largely disconfirmed by near-death experiences. To be sure, near-death experiences sufficiently disconfirm the experience argument brought to our attention by Bradley. Perhaps accounts of near-death experiences are not consistent enough for us to draw any meaningful or reliable information about them. In other words, such accounts, though recorded, are inaccurate descriptions of what happens to an individual posthumously.

Just the same, even if such experiences remain inconsistent in some aspects, they still meet the minimal requirements of what an individual must live through in order to be regarded as having had a certain experience. Moreover, consider that even if accounts of near-death experiences are perhaps not consistent or uniform, amazingly, some resuscitated patients accurately recollect the medical room events following the announcements of their clinical deaths. Though I believe quite a strong argument for the reliability of near-death experiences can be made, the question of *reliability* of near-death experiences is not the aspect upon which I base my argument. I still hold that scattered instances of incoherence do not in any way undercut the possibility that some accounts of near-death experiences are reliable anymore than an incoherent account of our normal day-to-day experience undercuts the possibility that at least one account of our day-to-day experience is reliable.

What I want to underscore is the fact that the individual undergoing the near-death experience is, in fact, having *any* experience beyond death at all. In other words, even if incoherent, the fact that any person has had any experience at all is strong evidence that the dead do have sensations several indefinite minutes longer than the Epicurean view allows, for according to the Epicurean view, the atoms of the soul disperse once a person breathes his or her last. In other words, one loses sensation immediately upon dying. By contrast, emergency room reports seem to indicate that the Epicurean view of losing one's sensation upon death is perhaps not exactly correct. Even if sensation could be lost, quite possibly it is not lost immediately after one dies. In some sense, sensation is retained for a little while longer. According to the essentialist, however, it is retained for all eternity. For these rational, and perhaps scientific reasons, the Epicurean account of painlessness, or for that matter, lack of sensation, at death is inadequate.

These findings are important because they will go a long way in helping us to establish whether or not death is an evil. Given the Epicurean reading, death is neither good nor evil; it is simply nothing. Put differently, it is simply the absence of anything. However, if we can show that the Epicurean view is inadequate, the possibility of establishing the vileness of death should be done on another reading. As I suggested earlier, since the problem of evil is mostly a problem posed against Christian theology, we could possibly succeed (though I quite frankly think we will not) in establishing the evilness of death from this perspective.

From the Christian vantage point, as we shall see, Epicurus is wrong. The Apostle Paul, for example, refers to death as a sting. Both in Scripture and through common sense, the experience of dying is widely recognized as a dreadfully painful process. Not only is dying physically painful for the individual, it is emotionally painful as well, both for the dying and for the bereaved, for it involves the process of a physical separation between the dying individual and his or her loved ones. More so, it comes with such a finality that, from a human perspective, it cannot be revoked.

We would have great difficulty convincing a grieving individual that death is not painful. People grieve for long periods of time, finding their lives forever changed by the absence of their loved ones. Therefore, not just the dying person feels the pain of death; those left behind feel the pain as well. Moreover, the natural desire for survival evidenced by living things attests to our fear of death, presumably because we believe we could live without its dreadful advance. Death is therefore a painful thing. Attempts to convince us otherwise seem futile.

One might object that my take on the painfulness of death is undercut from the very source I intend to establish the cogency of the Christian world view of death through near-death experiences. Numerous accounts of near-death experiences, for example, do not seem to reflect the sort of painfulness with which I associate the experience of the dying process. Indeed, the objector might argue that if I adopt certain aspects of the near-death experience model as a reliable account of the occurrence of posthumous sensation, then I must admit that it undercuts my contention that death is painful. Hence, the objector might point to numerous accounts of disembodied selves floating painlessly through the air, approaching a tunnel-like alley at the end of which a bright shiny light appears, sometimes beautiful according to certain accounts and sometimes painful according to others. The fact that one can report an experience of beauty surely seems to suggest that death is not always as painful as I intend to portray it.

This objection does have some force. Notice, though, that it misses an important aspect of pain that every dying person seems to undergo. It is the dying process itself, occasioned by the labored breathing of the individual and indicated by numerous expressions of pain. In other words, shortly before the dying person breathes his or her last, considerable pain is experienced, or at least seems to be experienced, for every person that passes through the experience of death. I contend, therefore, that death is a painful experience, evidenced by the individuals going through that experience as well as by those left behind through the process of suffering. If we did not think death is painful, we would not do our best to keep it at bay. However, humans are not exactly innocent of trying to employ death-defying maneuvers in an attempt to stay alive. These attempts are best accounted for by the fact that humans believe death is dreadfully painful.

What about the other aspect of death, namely, that it is evil? To begin with, some theologians and Christian philosophers conclude, after considerable reflections on death, dying, and the problem of evil, that death is not altogether a bad thing. Without death, for example, the world would be overpopulated and we would not have enough resources to go around. Moreover, these philosophers continue to argue that death serves the purpose of minimizing the blow of pain, thereby ensuring that pain is not maximized any more than it needs to be. Philosophers such as Swinburne have made this contention.

Let me give a brief outline of Swinburne's argument. Swinburne lists several advantages of a world in which humans live a short, finite life, one culminating in a natural death. However, he contends that these advantages of death are lessened to the extent that humans believe that death is not the end. In Swinburne's view, death is only a bad thing to the extent to which it involves frustration of the desire to live. Just the same, the fact of death confers great advantages upon humans.[52] Hence, had Swinburne been a materialist, he would have agreed with the deprivation account of death proposed by Brueckner and his cohorts. As noted, however, Swinburne's belief in the afterlife leads him to conclude that death need not be a bad thing since the human soul survives after death.

What advantages, then, does Swinburne think death confers on the dead person? The first advantage, according to Swinburne, is his contention

---

52. Swinburne, *Providence and the Problem of Evil*, 212.

that death allows free-willed agents such as ourselves to do or to refrain from doing to each other the harm of taking away the other's existence. Put differently, it allows us to do to each other the sorts of harm that would eventually bring about death; but it also allows us to refrain from doing each other just this sort of harm. In that sense, death is advantageous.[53] Whether or not this view of death is some kind of advantage is open to question. However, Swinburne seems to think it is an advantage.

The second advantage of death, in Swinburne's view, is that it makes supreme sacrifice possible in the face of disaster. The argument here is that if we are immortal, then supreme generosity is impossible. Here, Swinburne seems to imply that it is a good thing for one to sacrifice one's life for the good of another. If such sacrifices were not possible, then heroic deeds that pay the ultimate sacrifice would be impossible.[54] An objector could, of course, argue that one need not lose one's life in order to perform heroic feats of the sort mentioned here. At any rate, Swinburne seems to have a point here.

The third advantage of death, according to Swinburne, is his observation that a world with natural death is one in which an agent's contribution has significance to it because that contribution is itself irreversible by the agent. It is good, argues Swinburne, that what people do should matter. Their actions do matter more if they have only a limited time in which to reverse them. Put differently, once a given individual has made a significant contribution to the society, the individual can undo the heroism behind that contribution by following an immoral course of action in the future. The longer one lives, the more likely it would be for such a state of affairs to obtain. The imminence of death helps to keep such immoral actions from occurring, or at least reduces the chances of their occurrence.[55]

Fourth, Swinburne argues that a world with birth but without natural death would be a world in which the young would never have a free hand. In other words, without death, the younger generation would always be inhibited by the experience and influence of the aged; for if the aged live forever, they would not only continue to possess old knowledge, but they would also acquire new knowledge. Presumably, therefore, Swinburne believes that death of the older generation allows the younger generation to be in possession of new knowledge—knowledge inaccessible to the now gone older generation.[56]

---

53. Ibid.
54. Ibid., 212–13.
55. Ibid., 213.
56. Ibid.

A fifth advantage of death, which Swinburne thinks is its greatest value, is the observation that it provides a limit to the suffering that agents can inflict on each other. In Swinburne's view, a God who did not put a limit to the amount of suffering that a creature can suffer would not be a good God. In Swinburne's view, limits are necessary to the intensity of suffering as well as to the period of suffering. Swinburne thinks that this limiting act is the role that natural death plays: it provides a limit to the period and intensity of suffering.[57] Hence, in light of Swinburne's argument, death is not necessarily a bad or an evil thing.

What do we make of these observations that seem to contradict, quite sharply, the materialists' arguments on the evil of death (following Brueckner, Silverstein, Fischer, Feldman, and Bradley) on the one hand and the value-neutrality of death on the other (following Rosenbaum)? We must admit that they *seem* to contradict those arguments. Indeed, from Scripture, in a sense death can be seen as a good thing. Psalm 116:15, for example, seems to suggest that death can be viewed as a good thing in some respects. It reads, "Precious in the sight of the Lord is the death of his saints." From Scripture's point of view, the death of a believer in God is not necessarily a bad thing.

We must also go back to the biblical reason why death afflicted human beings in the first place. Once we put that point in perspective, we will be able to see how death can be both a good thing in one light and a bad one when seen from a different light. Death seems to have come about as God's way of accommodating the infamous rebellion in Gen 3. In other words, it was a consequence that followed Adam and Eve's rebellious choice. To the extent that death came as a result of sin, it is indeed a bad thing. On the other hand, to the extent that God used it as a way of accommodating the sins of his rebellious free-willed creatures, it might be viewed as a good thing. We have no way of knowing what would have followed had God chosen not to punish Adam and Eve's rebellion with death. However, since non-eternal punishment seems to carry corrective goals with it, death might be seen in this sense as a good thing, at least for Adam and Eve.

I have already alluded to the view that death might not be bad after all. In light of these considerations, we must admit that given the evidence of Scripture and logical considerations presented by philosophers such as Swinburne, death is, after all, not necessarily an evil. In short, whereas we could plausibly admit that death is indeed painful, we would be hard-pressed to defend the claim that it is an evil thing. It cannot, therefore, be seen as an experience synonymous with evil.

57. Ibid.

These findings lead us to the following significant observation: death is not always evil. Put differently, an encounter with death is not necessarily an encounter with evil. Consider that almost all creatures regard death as the highest form of pain any sentient creature could experience. As painful as it might appear, the claim that it is always an evil is by no means a necessary truth. Indeed, as we have seen, even within Christian theology, some are willing to admit that death might be a good thing on some readings.

What are the possible implications of these findings? I think they are enormous for our purposes in this project. The enormity of these implications can be captured as follows. As already noted, death is arguably the highest form of pain sentient creatures could live through, including free-willed creatures such as ourselves. In order to show the possibility of locating an instance of pain that is also an instance of evil, death would arguably be the best candidate for just this sort of exercise.

Unfortunately, however, we have discovered that the highest form of earthly pain is not necessarily the highest form of evil. If this observation is correct, we have good reasons to believe that locating an instance of pain that is simultaneously an instance of evil is extremely difficult. More exactly, we will discover that the relationship between pain and evil is very likely not a synonymous one. The two terms are certainly not semantically equivalent, neither are they logically equivalent. This lack of semantic equivalence leads us to the suspicion that the problem of pain is perhaps quite different from the problem of evil. This suspicion will be the exercise to be pursued in chapter 8.

For now, we simply note that if the highest form of earthly pain can be shown to bear no exact resemblance to evil, then quite likely, instances of lower forms of pain may not necessarily be equivalent to evil either. In other words, if death can be shown to bear little resemblance to evil, then instances of less severe forms of pain may not bear this resemblance. If pain is synonymous with evil, then severe occurrence of pain should bear exact resemblance with evil; we should at least see that they have identical properties. However, we are hard-pressed to find occurrences that have both properties. We must therefore seek to reestablish the nature of the relationship between evil and pain.

Before we attempt this exercise, considering what theologians have termed the second death might be instructive. Whereas physical death is not necessarily an evil, could the second death, or eternal damnation in hell, be considered an instance of evil? The doctrine of hell implies a place of ultimate pain for those who willfully choose to go there through their rejection of God. Could we say with some theological, and perhaps even philosophical, plausibility that the experience of this second death is both evil and painful?

This contention seems to have some promise. For one, going by the teachings of Christian doctrine, hell is supposed to be a place in which God's full justice is meted out against those who willingly reject his offer of salvation. If, in fact, hell exists in the manner stipulated by Christian theology, it is a place where humans are separated from God. It would not be too much of a theological stretch to think that this form of separation from God is itself an instance of evil. It seems to be a place where dispositions that run contrary to God's will are fully actualized. In short, it is a place where God is absent. Put differently, the only place where God's absence would be truly and fully felt would be the place where ultimate pain meets with dispositions that run contrary to God's character. It would be the only place with no evidence for God's existence, owing to the full existence of evil and the full existence of pain.

Perhaps in this sense we can legitimately say that the experience in hell, that is, the second death, is both evil and painful. The doctrine of hell, in which God's absence will be fully felt by its inhabitants, leads me to formulate the following demand upon the naturalistic-cum-materialistic thinker if his or her argument against God's existence via the problem of evil is to be successful:

1. Arguments against God's existence via the problem of evil would be fully compelling if and only if rational creatures like ourselves inhabit a world W such that

    a. evil is fully present and all instances of good are completely absent in W, and

    b. pain is fully present and all instances of pleasure and happiness are completely absent in W.

World W in claim 1 is clearly not the world in which we live. In order for God to be seen not to exist, our earth must resemble W in all respects. An argument against God's existence via the problem of evil, I say, must meet the requirements and demands suggested by just this very world. Clearly, the sort of world in which we live does not in any way resemble W. It would be extremely difficult to show that it does, since this world, despite its share of pain, is not completely bereft of good. Pleasure and happiness are not lacking in it either. The only world that meets this condition is the sort of world depicted by the doctrine of hell. In other words, the doctrine of hell seems to satisfy the demands placed upon it by claim 1. If that is the case, the atheist living in W would be justified in showing that claim 1 does apply to him or her as well as to all inhabitants of W, but of course he or she will be absolutely correct because he or she will inhabit a place where God is no longer present. However, given the pain that inflicts inhabitants of such a world, the philosopher in question would doubtfully have time for such philosophical nuances.

I conclude, then, that perhaps the only place we can identify the kind of pain that is also an evil is where one has the experience of eternal damnation by rational creatures who willfully reject God's offer for salvation. I noted in chapter 2 that the existence of hell is a good thing not only because it is God's way of accommodating individuals who refuse to acknowledge him as Lord but also because it is a *carrying out* of God's divine justice for individuals who have unyieldingly given themselves to committing unjust acts. In this sense, the existence of hell is a good thing. However, the experience of hell is itself an evil that those who reject God have also asked for by their way of life here on earth. It is God's way of stating that if individuals consistently and unrepentantly choose to live as if God does not exist, then he will have no option but to respect their choice by letting them live in a place where God is, in fact, absent; and where God is absent, ultimate pain and ultimate evil meet in a way that leaves the deserving victim unable to distinguish one from the other. I now turn to the next chapter, which seeks to show that earthly pain cannot be used as evidence against God's existence.

6

God and Pain

WE HAVE SHOWN THAT pain and evil do not always imply each other, as the materialistic view seems, intentionally or unintentionally, to assume. When one talks of pain, logically speaking, one is not necessarily also talking of evil, and vice versa. We have also seen that good and pleasure do not always imply each other, either. This realization implies, then, that when we ask whether the existence of pain casts doubt on the existence of God, it is a substantially different question from when we seek to determine whether the existence of evil casts doubt on the existence of God. In this chapter, I want to explore the former question first.

I begin by asking if the existence of pain casts doubt on the existence of God. More pointedly, are we justified in believing that the existence of any instance of pain calls the existence of God to question? To use Plantinga's words, does the existence of pain provide a defeater for belief in God? I want to argue that it does not. If my contention in the previous chapters is hitherto correct, I want to argue that we do not seem to have any reasons for believing that because pain exists, we are thereby logically led to conclude that God does not exist. Nothing about the facts and reality of pain provides much evidence against God's existence. More accurately, we find no logical contradiction in holding that both the possibility that God exists and the facts of pain are conceptual pairs that contradict each other. Neither are we justified in sustaining the claim that the existence of pain and suffering is evidence against the existence of God. Or put differently, we would be erroneous to contend that the probability that God exists is low given the reality and facts of pain and suffering.

This finding is important for at least one major reason. As we have already seen, many materialistic philosophers who deliberate on religious questions repeatedly contend that the facts and reality of pain cast serious doubts on the existence of God. Once again, I allude here, as before, to the sort of philosophers who, according to J. L. Mackie, Christians try to refute. They contend that a loving, all-wise, all-powerful God of the sort postulated by Judeo-Christianity would not allow the occurrence of pain, especially what they call pointless pain. Hence, if God exists, he would not allow his creatures, and especially his children, to suffer numerous and repeated instances of pain—pointless or otherwise. I intend to deal with the notion of pointless pain in a different chapter. In this chapter, however, I want to examine the idea of pain in general to determine whether pain by itself is evidence against the existence of God.

Let me begin by making the following observation, which I will then defend. Philosophers who contend that pain and suffering supply us with evidence against the existence of God are in error, for they not only come dangerously close to equivocating evil with pain—a philosophical move that seems to me quite odd—but by this very equivocation they also fail to understand a fundamental aspect of the meaning of being a person with emotions and feelings. To have emotions is to have the capacity to experience and express feelings of joy and pain, and these are aspects that God must possess if God is to be understood as a person. Thus, the philosophers in question buttress their atheism under the erroneous presupposition that the God of theism would not allow his children to suffer instances of pain. We have already examined this error at length in previous chapters. What I want to underscore in this chapter is the claim that if, in fact, evil and pain are not synonymous terms, and we have seen that they are not, then the facts and reality of pain offer no evidence against God's existence.

Let me begin with a logical explication of this thesis. Theologians tell us that God is a person. We might, therefore, formulate initial observations as follows:

1. If God is a person, then God possesses the requisite elements of personhood.
2. God is a person.
3. Therefore, God possesses the requisite elements of personhood.

Of course, the implication is, if God does not possess the requisite elements of personhood, then God would not be considered a person. We can make this claim even stronger.

1. God is a person if and only if God possesses the requisite elements of personhood.
2. God is a person.

3. Therefore, God possesses the requisite elements of personhood.

We have changed the premise in the first argument to suggest that God being a person is a necessary and sufficient condition for his possessing the requisite elements of personhood. Let us examine the first premise of both arguments more closely. Are both premises correct? I think they are. That a certain being B is a person necessarily entails that B exemplifies the requisite elements of personhood. Affirming the personhood of B on the one hand, and denying that B is in possession of the requisite elements of personhood on the other, would be quite paradoxical. By way of an Aristotelian illustration, affirming, for example, that Socrates is human and denying that Socrates is a rational animal would be odd. If Socrates is human, then necessarily Socrates satisfies the conditions for which he would be called a rational animal. The first premises of both arguments appear to me quite beyond dispute.

The second premise, however, might seem contentious. In what ways are we to understand the claim that God is a person? The premise is stated on the assumption that God exists. More accurately, the premise suggests that if we assume that God, understood in the Judeo-Christian tradition, exists, then following the dictates of that tradition, God is indeed presented as a person—a being with intelligence, emotion, will, and a capacity to relate and communicate. Of course, this understanding of God is not in any way a proof for God's existence. The premise merely proceeds on the assumption that God indeed does exist, and that if he does exist, he satisfies the conditions for being a person. I will argue that God ought to be understood in this way—that is, as a person—if such an understanding is to be consistent with the Judeo-Christian understanding of God.

This understanding of God then leads us to consider the following question: what is the meaning when a being is in possession of requisite elements of personhood? As with our Socrates illustration, we would be correct in saying that the being in question is in possession of conditions that, if fully satisfied, would qualify that being to be a person. What, then, are these conditions? In all fairness, a being is in possession of personalistic attributes if, at the very least, the being in question thinks, expresses emotions, wills, and relates. Granted, these are perhaps not the only attributes; more items could be added to the list (e.g., life and self-consciousness are indeed important elements of personhood). However, the current list should suffice for our purposes.

These findings allow us to say the following: if God is a person, then God is a being who thinks, expresses emotions, wills, and relates. By suggesting that God is a thinking being, we infer that God is capable of rational reflection. Of course, if God is "that than which a greater cannot be thought," as Anselm postulated, then he is conceivably capable of the highest level of rational reflection. Determining the exact nature of God's thought processes is perhaps impossible; neither are we armed with the wherewithal to determine his thinking capacity. (Aristotle wrestled with this idea in his seminal work, which he labeled *Metaphysics*, though he was not exactly dealing with God as understood in the Christian sense.) However, God is indeed a thinking being.

Also, by contending that God has emotions, we maintain that God has feelings. He expresses feelings of joy; he also expresses feelings of disappointment, pain, and grief. With respect to the teachings of Christian theology, it is possible that our expressions of feelings of disappointments are analogues of God's expressions of the same. However, such expressions would seem to pale in comparison to God's way of expressing his feelings. We can still draw analogies between God's way of expressing his feelings and the human way of doing the same. Similarities could be legitimately drawn here.

Additionally, by suggesting that God wills, we infer that God has desires and motives. The Greek word *thelo* (to will) helps to articulate this aspect of willing. It reminds us that God has wishes that he desires to have met. The term may be somewhat misleading, for it seems to suggest that God has needs such that if those needs are not met he would, in some respects, be considered incomplete or imperfect. This supposition need not be the case, though. God is an eternally self-sufficient being, who really does not need anything from sources outside himself, but he nevertheless desires or wishes that his free-willed creatures have a relationship with him.

Finally, by suggesting that God relates, we imply that God is a communal being. In other words, he has the ability to establish an emotional connection with beings in possession of analogous attributes. Christian theism teaches that God lives in the community of the Trinity. Moreover, it also teaches that God loves his creatures because he is a relational being, and he wants his creatures to love him back in return. This desire on God's part does not mean, once again, that God needed someone to love and thereby created human beings to love him, such that if none loved him back, he would be in some sense unfulfilled. If this desire expressed some kind of lack on God's part, then Christian theism would be countenancing an imperfect God. Christian theism seems to suggest that God's love is already completed in the community of the Trinity. When he created us, his love was already complete and was perfectly experienced in the community of Father, Son, and the Holy Spirit. Hence, God is fundamentally a relational being.

The fact that God is relational points to one of the attributes essential to a person. They are what philosopher William Alston, in an unrelated context, calls personalistic predicates. In other words, they are predicates or attributes deemed essential for a personal agent to have. Alston has in mind the idea of an agent capable of executing purposes, plans, and actions, together with intentions, and the agent carries these intentions based on knowledge or belief. According to Alston, the agent in question acts in ways expressing attitudes and in ways guided by specific norms and standards. Such an agent, Alston would say, can communicate and form personal relations with agents possessing similar qualities. For Alston, we find the idea of God as a personal agent firmly rooted in Christianity, and communication between God and humans remains central to Judeo-Christianity.[1]

What do these findings suggest? To see their implications, we need to take each of them individually. Let's begin with the claim that God is a rational being. The contention here is that he is capable of rational reflection. He is a being that thinks, understands, imagines, remembers, premeditates, and so on. He is capable of using his divine mental capacities in a way consistent with what we would expect—or more accurately, in a way infinitely above what we would expect—of a rational being. If God is, in fact, a rational being, and he is the greatest possible being, his rational nature must imply that he has maximum knowledge—highest possible level of knowledge an omniscient being could have. He knows, understands, and remembers the creatures he has designed. He premeditates on what he brings about or causes to happen in their lives. He is fully aware of the situations and circumstances they find themselves coming up against. This fact means that God knows the pains of his children, and he knows them in a divinely intimate way. He knows their pain not merely by factual accumulation of data that allow him to infer that they are suffering; he also knows their pain by having cognitive and experiential access to their feeling. The existence of a rational entity like God implies the existence of a God who knows that something is the case, including our pain.

Let me now turn to the next thought, which I believe is even more instructing. The next thought suggests that God is a being who expresses emotions. Moreover, how he feels can in some way be communicated to rational creatures capable of grasping expressions of this sort. If God is capable of having emotions, or expressing emotions, he is capable of having feelings of joy and feelings of pain. In other words, God could have joy of infinite proportions. Also, God might have infinite proportions of painful feelings. If this conclusion is true, we can capture this understanding as follows:

1. If God is a being with emotions, then God is a being capable of joyous and painful feelings.
2. God is a being with emotions.

---

1. Alston, "Speaking Literally of God," 409–23.

3. Therefore, God is a being capable of joyous and painful feelings.

As with the first argument, we can strengthen this claim. We can contend, for example, that God's possession of emotions is a necessary and sufficient condition for God's capacity for joyous and painful feelings. Put differently, the argument could run like this:

1. God is a being capable of joyous and painful feelings if and only if God is a being with emotions.
2. God is a being with emotions.
3. Therefore, God is a being capable of joyous and painful feelings.

Assuming that God exists, is this argument correct? To establish its correctness, let us examine the first premise. We would seem correct to think that the ability to express joyous and painful feelings is itself based on being in possession of emotive faculties. In other words, having emotive faculties is a necessary and sufficient condition for expressing joyous and painful feelings. However, the premise seems to ignore the possibility of other types of feelings, some of which are neither joyous nor painful. Does God have such feelings? Are they logically possible with respect to God? I think so. We must, therefore, revise the first premise and have it include the full range of feelings possible for God to have. Hence, the argument could run as follows:

1. God is a being capable of having the full range of feelings from joy to pain if and only if God is a being with emotions.
2. God is a being with emotions.
3. Therefore, God is a being capable of having the full range of feelings from joy to pain.

This revised argument suggests that God has the full range of feelings allowed by the capacity of his emotive faculties. The full range thus includes feelings of joy, sadness, pain, sorrow, grief, and so forth. Indeed, a being with emotive faculties of the sort possessed by persons more or less like ourselves ought to exemplify feelings of this kind. Hence, our newly revised first premise is correct. If our newly revised first premise is correct, assuming that God exists, then so must be the second premise that follows it. Therefore, from a theistic perspective, the entire argument is not only valid; it also stands an excellent chance of being sound, for the theist who already admits that God is a person will at once see that he is a being with emotions. This admission, in turn, implies that he is capable of expressing the full range of feelings permitted by his emotive faculties, some of which include sadness and the like.

What this argument reveals, of course, is the contention I am trying to defend, namely, pain is not evidence against God's existence. In fact, pain is a part of who God is. Put differently, God experiences pain not merely at the natural level like the rest of us but also at the supernatural level. We can now begin to build a consistent set of statements using the two arguments hitherto presented as follows, and let's call it set A:

A = {God is a person; God has the requisite elements of personhood; God is a being with emotions; God is capable of joyous and painful feelings.}

If in fact we admit that God is a person, we must at the same time be willing to allow that he has the requisite elements or attributes of personhood. One such requisite element of personhood is the ability to express emotions. What then is the purpose of set A? It aims to show that if we list its members as premises of an argument, we will at once see the result of denying that God has the requisite elements or attributes of personhood. To deny that these requisite elements of personhood are attributes of God, if he exists, is to deny that God is a person, or at least to denude God's personality of the important element of emotions. We are then left with a being completely foreign to orthodox Christian theism.

Christian theology finds comfort in a God capable of having feelings. It finds comfort in a God capable of rejoicing when God's children rejoice, and it also finds comfort in a God capable of grieving with his children when they grieve. Moreover, if indeed God is (*qua* Anselm) that than which a greater cannot be conceived, we can reasonably think that his emotional capacity is infinitely higher than any we can imagine. He has the highest expressions of joy that only an infinite being like himself is capable of, and he has the deepest feelings of sorrow that only an infinite being can have. Hence, God is a being capable of feeling pain and does, in fact, feel pain.

Let us now examine the other aspects of God's personality to see what other facts could be revealed about God, if God is, in fact, a person. We noted that God wills. By willing, not only do we admit that he has desires; we also imply that he has specific motives to accomplish certain goals. Let us assume that God desires that his creatures love him. Suppose, for example, that he desires that human beings, whom he created in his image, should reciprocate the love he freely offers them. Drawing from Christian theology, we affirm that humans were created with free will. That means they can choose, out of their own volition and desire, to love God or not to love God. In other words, with respect to their free will, humans appear to have the power of contrary choice. They can choose to follow a certain course of action. However, they can refrain, out of their own volition, from following the course of action in question.

Suppose then, that a certain individual, infinitely loved by God, chooses not to reciprocate God's freely offered love. We can reasonably assume not only that God's desire will have been frustrated but also, and intimately connected to this point, that God's emotions will be wounded. Alvin Plantinga has argued, as noted in the first chapter, that God, having created humans with free will, would not preempt their freedom by determining them to do only what is right all the time. If he creates them with free will in order to preserve their freedom, he must allow them to act in a way consistent with their power of contrary choice. Hence, if they are created with the capacity for choosing God, they must also have the capacity for rejecting God. Freedom of the will would, therefore, be lost if God somehow forced his creatures to love him. Moreover, reason seems to indicate that this form of coercion would not in any way entail true love; for true love must come freely from a person's heart without coercion of any sort. This point allows us to add more elements to set A:

A = {God is a person; God is a being with emotions; God is capable of joyous and painful feelings; God has made creatures who are free to love or not love him; God is capable of loving his creatures.}

Let us now build another set, and call it B, whose elements describe human beings. The set would quite possibly look like this:

B = {God has created humans with free will; Humans are free to love or not to love God; Humans sometimes choose not to love God.}

Let us assume, for the sake of argument, that both sets A and B are correct depictions of the real world. We have no difficulty seeing the implications already discussed. If the claims in both sets are all true, then some members of both sets begin to yield interesting results about God and pain when those members form the premises of a single argument. If both sets are true, they will not only show that God's offer of love for his creatures will be rejected, but also that God will be grieved by just this very rejection. If he will, in fact, be grieved by this act of rejection, then we are looking at a God who suffers grief or, for that matter, pain.

God's desires, therefore, can be frustrated by those he has created to love him freely, even though he can, if he wishes, make them love him, and if God's desires can be frustrated in this way, we are led to believe that his feelings can be deeply hurt. We can then capture the argument in the following way:

1. If God is a being with a will, understood as an expression of God's desires, and God has created humans with free will, then God's desires can be frustrated by free-willed creatures.

2. God is a being with a will, understood as an expression of God's desires.

3. Moreover, God has created humans with free will.

4. Therefore, God's desires can be frustrated by free-willed creatures.

As with previous arguments, we proceed to evaluate this argument. Assuming that God is, in fact, a person, we at once see that he also must be a being with a will, understood as an expression of his desires. This teaching is not foreign to Christian theology either. What might appear somewhat suspect is the claim that God's desires can be frustrated by free-willed creatures. However, I do not see much difficulty in believing this postulate. Suppose God wants his creatures to love him freely, without attempting to coerce them to love him. If he has, in fact, created free-willed creatures, the possibility always exists that some of those free creatures will turn down his offer. If they do turn down his offer, God would logically grieve over this rejection. We see this happening repeatedly in the Old Testament. We read of Jesus' sorrow for Jerusalem in the New Testament. In these instances, God seems to grieve over the fact that his creatures turn down his offer of love.

Consider the following illustration. John deeply loves Mary. Mary is free to love John back, but she chooses not to. Perhaps she does not love John as much as John loves her. Perhaps she is interested in Peter, a classmate of John in their local high school. John's repeated attempts to express his love to Mary are met by indifference, and sometimes by sarcasm on Mary's part. John's emotions may well be deeply wounded by the fact of Mary's rejection.

Consider also, from Scripture, God's repeated attempts to love the children of Israel. He is often met with rejection by his children. The book of Hosea, for example, is dedicated to this very attempt. God asks Hosea to marry Gomer, a woman whom God himself describes as an adulterous wife. Possibly wondering what God intends, Hosea does indeed marry the prostitute. She then bears him three children. Each child is given a name that depicts what God is about to do to the inhabitants of Israel. The name of Hosea's first child is Jezreel, a name illustrating the fact that God is about to punish the house of Jehu for the massacre at Jezreel, and that he is about to put an end to the kingdom of Israel. The name of the second child is Lo-Ruhammah, suggesting that God will no longer show love to the house of Israel, specifically because they have sinned against him, or put differently, they have rejected him. However, God still relents, declaring that he will show love to the house of Judah. The name of the third child is Lo-Ammi, symbolizing the fact that the children of Israel are no longer God's people.

The strangest thing about the story is that Hosea's wife left Hosea for another man, thereby committing adultery, and God commands Hosea to go to his wife and show her his love a second time. God's command is very specific: "Love her as the Lord loves the Israelites, though they turn to other gods and love the sacred raisin cakes." In all fairness, the purpose of the story is to demonstrate God's willingness to love his children in spite of their sin. However, the rest of the book is a revelation not only of God's grief over the fact that his people have turned away from him but also of God's anger over this very same fact. He is deeply frustrated by the fact that his people keep turning away from him. From a biblical perspective, then, the consequent of the first premise is true, namely, that God's desires can be frustrated by free-willed creatures.

Some qualifications are needed here, however, for some might object that if God's desires can be frustrated by free-willed creatures, then we have no certainty that his will could finally be realized. This objection is powerful, and certainly does need to be answered. I think, however, the objection incorrectly assumes that this claim applies to every aspect of God's desire. It assumes, for example, that human beings can frustrate any of God's plans that he, as God, intends to accomplish. My contention is more focused on free will with respect to choosing or not choosing to love God. In principle, we can indeed choose to love God, and we can also choose to hate him. People make this choice frequently. God will not force us to love him if we do not want to love him. Of course, he can influence us to love him. He can, for example, endow us with gifts such as abundant life, health, food, clothing, and shelter. The person with enough wisdom to know that these gifts come from God will quite likely respond to God in a spirit of love and surrender.

However, this observation does not imply that God's attempt to get that individual to love him is coercion. Coercion is more of a forceful attempt to get an individual to perform or achieve a certain goal not meant for the individual but for the person doing the coercion. What God seems to do is to try to influence us through some form of divine persuasion to love him freely, and he does so precisely because he does not wish to preempt our free will.

Perhaps if we revisit the case of John and Mary, this point will become clearer. Suppose, after repeated but failed attempts to win Mary's love for himself John discovers a potion, which if Mary took, would make her love John at once, but once it wears off, she would resume her natural state of indifference toward John. Clearly, John will not believe that Mary truly loves him if she actually takes the potion and suddenly expresses feelings of affection for John. John knows that quite likely, in only a matter of time, Mary's indifference becomes a reality again. Love would not be coming from Mary's heart but from a deceptive form of affection quite meaningless in the long run.

God does not appear to be the sort of being to play similar love games with the free-willed creatures he has made. He wants their love for him to be free, without coercion and from their internal volition. With regard to other aspects of the universe, however, we would be correct to say that God can quite easily use coercion. If he wants to accomplish his decretive will, we might reasonably assume that God will use his coercive power for this very purpose. In the case of unconditional predictive prophecy, for example, we can reasonably expect that God will here direct events toward the fulfillment of his will. In this way, no free-willed creature can frustrate his will or desire.

Hence, I argue that free-willed creatures can frustrate God's desire to have them accept his offer of love. This inference seems to be quite in order. The teaching that humans have been created with free will, a teaching endorsed by most brands of Christian theology, can be used alongside the conclusion of the argument to underscore a truth I have been trying to adumbrate so far:

1. If free-willed creatures can frustrate God's desire by rejecting his offer of love, then God's feelings can be painfully wounded.
2. Free-willed creatures can indeed frustrate God's desire by rejecting his offer of love.
3. Therefore, God's feelings can be deeply wounded.

The teaching that God's desires can be frustrated by free-willed creatures entails the further teaching that his feelings can be deeply wounded. As already noted from the story of Hosea, the assumption that God's feelings are wounded is one that weaves throughout the book of Hosea. We find similar expressions of God's disappointment when we read the second book of Kings. These findings, in turn, underscore the important thesis that God is a being capable of feeling pain. Indeed, he is a being that suffers pain at a much higher level than we would know experientially. The findings also underscore the important point that if God is a person, as taught by Christian theology, he must be the sort of being capable of feeling our pain as well. He must be the sort of being capable of understanding the pain of his creatures. A being incapable of feeling the pains of his creatures is a being whose moral goodness is open to question—one that cannot be taken as divinely sympathetic to the needs of his creatures.

Conservative theologians remain widely in agreement in this regard. For example, Paul E. Little notes how God possesses all the element of personhood even though God is spirit. The elements are intellect, feelings, and will.[2] By feelings, Little refers to emotions rather than physical sensations we find in corporeal beings such as taste, touch, sight, sound, and smell. This fact does not deny that God lacks cognitive access to these physical sensations. To be sure, being omniscient, God knows what having these physical sensations entails.

Another Christian thinker accepting this understanding of God's personality is Bruce Milne. He argues, quite correctly, that the Spirit of God is a person, and he bases his argument on Eph 4:10. Milne notes how Paul's allusion to the possibility of grieving the Holy Spirit implies that God's Spirit is a person that can be grieved rather than a force that can be resisted.[3] Also, the Methodist theologian, Tyron Inbody observes how explaining God in theological terms allows us to say God is both unique and incomparable. Inbody then lists from Scripture a wide array of expressions he believes apply to God. He also notes that God has a wide array of intense feelings such as joy, delight, anger, grief, and regret.[4]

Similar remarks can be made about Jesus Christ. For example, Wayne Grundem's reading of certain passages of Scripture leads him to conclude, as others would quite likely conclude, that Jesus did possess a full range of emotions such as those possessed by humans. In John 11:35 he wept sorrowfully over Lazarus' death, in John 12:27 his soul was troubled at his imminent crucifixion, and in Matt 26:38 his soul was troubled at the Garden of Gethsemane.[5] All these theologians agree that as a personal agent, God possesses emotions and has often been depicted in Scripture expressing them in his interactions with human beings.

With regard to the Holy Spirit, for example, theologian Millard J. Erickson reminds us that the fact that the Spirit possesses certain personal characteristics is an indication of his personality. Erickson correctly notes these elements, some of which we have already seen, as will, intelligence, and emotions. These elements are traditionally regarded as the three fundamental elements of personhood. Evidence from Scripture includes Jesus' promise in John 14:26 that the Holy Spirit will teach his disciples all things, reminding them of everything he had taught them, and that he would do so precisely because he is the Counselor. Moreover, the will of the Spirit is

---

2. Little, *Know What You Believe*, 40.
3. Milne, *Know The Truth*, 222.
4. Inbody, *Faith of the Christian Church*, 89.
5. Grundem, *Systematic Theology*, 878.

evidenced by 1 Cor 12:11, which suggests that the Spirit decides or determines which spiritual gifts to endow upon believers. In Eph 4:30, Scripture affirms the possibility of grieving the Spirit of God. As with Milne, Erickson notes that while one can resist a mere force, one cannot grieve something that is impersonal.[6] Therefore, the teaching that God can suffer grief is fully affirmed in Scripture and explicated by theologians.

These postulations from Scripture imply the truth I set out to defend: Pain is as much a part of God's emotions as his emotions are an essential aspect of his personhood. We are then led to postulate the following argument to show that the facts of pain and the existence of God are not logically incompatible:

1. If the capacity to feel pain is an essential aspect of God's person, then God cannot be a person if God is incapable of feeling pain.
2. The capacity to feel pain is indeed an essential aspect of God's person.
3. Therefore, if God is a person, God must be capable of feeling pain.

We then arrive at the following conclusion about God, his person, and the facts of pain and suffering: if God is incapable of feeling pain, then God is not a person. To see this entailment, let us once again revisit some claims in previous arguments. They are now restated in the following list:

1. God is a person if and only if God is in possession of requisite elements of personhood.
2. God is a being capable of joyous and painful feelings if and only if God is a being with emotions.
3. If God is a being with a will, understood as an expression of God's desires, and God has created humans with free will, then God's desires can be frustrated by free-willed creatures.
4. If free-willed creatures can frustrate God's desire by rejecting his offer of love, then God's feelings can be wounded.
5. If the capacity to feel pain is an essential aspect of God's person, then God cannot be a person if God is incapable of feeling pain.
6. If God is a person, God must be capable of feeling pain.

Suppose we deny the consequent of claim 6 and instead hold that God is incapable of feeling pain. This denial will force us to claim that God is not a person. This claim, in turn, will force us to state that God is not in possession of requisite elements of personhood, which will then imply that

---

6. Erickson, *Christian Theology*, 878.

God has no emotions. But this statement will necessarily entail that God has no capacity for joyous or painful feelings, which will then imply that his desires cannot be frustrated by free-willed creatures. Moreover, it will force us to deny the antecedent of claim 3. In other words we will be forced to say the following about the antecedent: Either God does not have free will or he has not made creatures with free will. To claim, therefore, that God is a being incapable of feeling pain forces us to arrive at an understanding of God fundamentally different from that postulated by Christian theology. The following argument would, therefore, seem to me quite correct from a theistic perspective:

1. If God is capable of feeling pain, then pain is not evidence against God's existence but is a feeling that can be expressed through God's emotive faculties.
2. God is indeed capable of feeling pain.
3. Therefore, pain is not evidence against God's existence and pain is a feeling that can be expressed through God's emotive faculties.
4. Hence, by simplification of premise 3, pain is not evidence against God's existence.

Christian theology would seem to teach that given his omniscience, God would have to be the first person to understand our pain when we live through moments and periods of suffering. To be sure, Christians would be deeply disturbed to discover that God has no experiential knowledge of their pain. By experiential knowledge, I refer to the notion that God fully experiences the pain of his children more intimately than, say, a mother would feel the pain of her child. Christians want to be assured that God is aware of their pain. Christians want to know that God understands their pain at a much deeper level than Christians understand it as human beings. The full experience of his creatures' pain requires that God must be in the believers' suffering and must know most exactly how the believers feel. This knowledge on God's part is not possible unless God feels the believers' pain just as really and truly as the believers feel their own pain. This reason explains why, for example, the Son of God wept as he grieved with Lazarus' sisters over the death of Lazarus. Christian theology, therefore, affirms that God must be the sort of being capable of feeling the pain of his children.

Notice, however, that a God who feels no pain is precisely the sort of God the philosophical and materialistic naturalist wants the Christian to believe in. In other words, according to such materialist thinkers, if God exists, he must be the sort of being that disallows the facts of pain completely.

The following would, therefore, be the argument the materialistic naturalist could quite conceivably make:

1. If God exists, pain cannot exist.
2. Obviously, pain exists.
3. Therefore, God does not exist.

The second premise of this argument is clearly true. The first premise, however, is highly questionable for the believer. The believer would say, for example, that the antecedent of the premise—that is, God exists—is, in fact, true. The consequent of the premise, that is, that pain would not exist, is false. A true antecedent and a false consequent both yield a false conditional, as any standard text of logic will affirm.

The task for the believer is to show that the conditional, that is, the first premise, is false. In light of our stipulations concerning God's personhood, the falsehood of the first premise could be established as follows. The atheist wants the believer to affirm that God's existence must imply the nonexistence of pain whatsoever, whether among his creatures, or the sort of pain internal to God. However, this state of affairs would imply the existence of a God who would feel no pain. If God feels no pain, then his emotional constitution would be incomplete.

Let me pursue this state of affairs further as follows:

1. An emotional constitution of a personal entity P is complete if and only if P is capable of expressing both the full range of feelings permitted by P's emotive faculties, from the positive feelings of joy to the negative feelings of pain.
2. God is a person.
3. If God's emotional constitution is incomplete, then God's personalistic constitution would have to be incomplete as well.
4. Hence, if God is incapable of feeling pain, he would no longer be a complete person.

This finding is indeed surprising, for if God is no longer a complete person, he would no longer be a perfect person or, for that matter, a perfect God. In other words, the atheistic objector would be asking the Christian believer to settle for something less than the perfect, all-loving, all-powerful, all-knowing, and ever-present God of Christian theology. As many theologians note, a depersonalized God is no longer a rational agent; rather, a depersonalized God is the sort of being reduced to mere force, a view unacceptable to orthodox Christian theology. For this reason, Christians need not accept the terms of engagement stipulated by the materialistic thinkers such as those alluded to by J. L. Mackie; instead, they should believe boldly that God is a being capable of feeling human pain at a deeply divine level, and that God's capacity to feel pain is a most assuring fact for believers as an attempt to help them deal with the facts of their pain.

Quite possibly what I have presented here is really an exercise in logic that is not only epistemologically detached from reality, but woefully inadequate in providing us with reliable information about God, assuming he exists. What does the theologian, for example, have to say about God's capacity to feel pain? What does the Bible have to say about God's capacity to feel the same?

First, logic is precisely what it is because it is concerned with truth preservation. That is, if we begin with true statements as premises, we are likely to end up, by inference, with a true conclusion. If the statements presented about God's experience of pain are true, then by inference, we are likely to conclude that God's existence is not in any way undercut by the existence of pain. The argument presented so far in this chapter is based on specific presuppositions of Christian theology. The Christian theologian would like to think that his or her views about God are true. If God is presented as a person, then the findings at which we have arrived seem inescapable to me. We must, therefore, face the fact that God is a being who suffers. As noted above, we only need to see the excruciating experience of the Son of God to know that Deity, as understood in Christian theology, is not altogether unacquainted with grief and suffering. The Old Testament, as already noted, is filled with examples of a God frustrated by the sinfulness of his children. These appear to be biblical truths.

Second, the assumption of Christian theology is that God has created human beings as persons. If he has created them as persons, he has created them with the elements necessary for personalistic attributes, and some of these attributes include emotions. By creating them in this way, God was opening them up to the capacity for feeling pain and expressing those feelings. To be created in this way also constitutes the meaning of being created in God's image. Since God is a person, and he created us as persons, the fact that God, being a person, is capable of feeling pain also implies that we are capable of feeling pain as people. For this reason, we are able not only to feel pain but to express our feelings of pain.

Of course, one could still object with the following suggestion: Could God not create a world in which feelings of pain do not exist? For example, could God not create a world in which the elements of personalistic attributes preclude the possibility and the capacity for feeling pain? If such a world is a logical possibility, then God could and ought to have caused such a state of affairs to obtain. We would then live our lives without having to live through painful experiences. He could create, for example, a world in which people would be immune to death with no need for the experience of painful emotions such as grief. He could create a world in which we would be immune to the wounded feelings associated with broken relationships and ended friendships. Or he could create a world in which we would not feel the pain of putting our hands on a hot surface or cutting our flesh with sharp blades. God surely could create such a world.

Two responses need to be made about this objection. First, in a world of creatures with free will who must exercise their freedom to attain their own self-determined ends, God cannot guarantee that such a pain-free world would obtain if he must respect their freedom. A world in which people are free to act according to their self-determined interests is a world that will most likely be filled with pain. People will freely choose to hurt each other, or break associations, or let one another down. God would not create them free on the one hand and then determine them to do only that which is pain-free. He would have no point in creating them free if he must determine them to act only in ways that produce pain-free results.

Perhaps an example would help to clarify this view. Suppose God wants to create a square. If he creates a square, then, necessarily, the outcome will be a square and not a circle. To ask God to create a square that is necessarily a circle is to ask for a logical impossibility specifically because it is nonsensical. Similarly, to ask God to create a free-willed creature that he also determines to do what is right all the time is a logical fallacy. One is asking God to create free creatures who also happen to be determined. Put differently, one is asking God to create free creatures who are at the same time not free. Clearly this request entails a contradiction. A contradiction, however, is an imperfection in knowledge. Hence, by asking God to create a world in which free creatures are determined always to do only what is right, in the final analysis, is to ask of a perfect God to do an imperfect thing.

Closely tied to this observation is the second answer to the objection. Something is inherently problematic in asking for an exemption of pain in the life of creatures with personalistic attributes. Imagine for one moment that we were unable to feel pain and subsequently to produce corresponding expressions of such feelings. Admittedly, we would conclude that something is wrong. For example, suppose we could put our hands in fire and then end up not feeling the pain attending the act in which our hands come into contact with fire. Or suppose we could make deep cuts in our bodies with knives and then fail to feel the pain that should rightly follow such activities. In both cases, we will feel as if something is terribly wrong with our systems.

We will at once begin to sense the badness that comes with the absence of the ability to feel pain.

Another objection needs to be considered: Christian eschatological considerations affirm that God will eliminate all pain in the final apocalypse. Do we not have a promise somewhere that pain, grief, sorrow, and death will no longer be a thing of the future world in which we will live? If God can bring a state of ease from pain in the future, what keeps him from doing so now? Moreover, what reason did God not have for creating such a world from the beginning in the first place? If he had created such a world—which, given his omnipotence and omni-benevolence he should have—his creatures would then have been exempt from living through the experience of pain and suffering in the past and would be in a similar state in the present as well as in the future.

This objection is easily answered in at least two ways. First, I contend that pain, grief, and death are the sorts of things that were brought about by the disobedience of Adam and Eve. In light of the fact that they were beings created with free will, they could possibly have used their freedom to make wrong moral choices, which they did. Death, pain, and suffering resulted from this misuse of free will. Christian theology does teach that pain is the consequence of human rebellion. From a biblical perspective, therefore, rebellion against God and pain have a causal connection, with such rebellion being the cause of pain. God did not bring about the pain. However, by creating us as sentient creatures, he gave us the capacity to detect its occurrence.

Second, just because the New Heaven and the New Earth will indeed be free of pain is itself no indication that the capacity for feeling pain will thereby be eliminated. Whether or not this supposition is true seems to be something the Bible is silent about. However, it is reasonably possible that even after the Lord has wiped away all our tears, we will still have the capacity for pain, for our personalistic attributes will still be intact. What will be eliminated is the very thing that brought about the pain in the first place—sin. We will not have lost our attributes as persons once we are redeemed. If we do, it means we will have lost an important aspect of our personality. So what do we learn from Scripture with regard to this supposition? The lesson and assurance we get from Scripture is the elimination of pain rather than the elimination of the capacity to feel pain. This capacity is one that even God seems to possess in his eternal nature. In light of his immutability, we have no reason to believe that God will give up this capacity. More correctly, since sin is what brought about the pain we experience in the universe today, its elimination will also imply the elimination of pain. The capacity for pain will still be there, nonetheless, but the experience of pain will no longer be there.

A further objection could be stated as follows: Suppose we will retain every aspect of our personalistic attributes, including the capacity to feel pain and the capacity to make rational choices. In light of the eschatological considerations raised, we cannot even be assured that pain will be fully eliminated in the future world, for if God cannot create a world in which he will guarantee that his free-willed creatures will do good all the time, then the same observation seems to apply for the future world. God cannot guarantee that his redeemed free-willed creatures will do good all the time in heaven. Hence, we are not guaranteed that the consequences of sin, that is, pain, will be completely eliminated. We are not guaranteed that he will eliminate all sorrow, grief, pain, and death, which are the sorts of pain brought about by the acts of free-willed creatures.

This objection is perhaps the most forceful that one could raise against the view I have been adumbrating and defending in this chapter. What should we make of it? We need to take into consideration the entire context in which the salvation of human beings is brought about in order to answer this objection. Salvation of human beings is not the sort of thing that occurs only in a linear fashion in which humans are created with free will, sin follows, pain results, and then God saves them from sin and eliminates all sin thereafter. First of all, a relationship needs to be developed. It is a relationship of love between the person of God and the human person. Humans grow in their love and appreciation for God in a way that responds to the value they discover that God has placed on them, even to the extent of sacrificing his own life for them. A human person fully touched by the saving grace, mercy, love, and goodness of God will do his or her best to develop a relationship of true character reformation—one that seeks always to please God in light of what God has done. The human person that consistently rebels against God is one that chooses to have nothing to do with God. For this reason, if the rebellious person insists on wanting to have nothing to do with God, then God will have no option but to honor that wish, and the person will have to experience, in the final analysis, a life of eternal separation from God. It will be a life filled with pain—one that rebellious human beings have chosen for themselves.

By contrast, however, the person saved by God's grace, who now chooses to live a life of righteousness and holiness, one that seeks to please the Savior, will desire to be fully transformed by God's grace. Theology, once again, teaches that such a person will go through three important stages of salvation. Since the person willingly chooses to live a life of surrender to the Lordship of Christ, God will first ensure that the person is saved from the penalty of sin. Second, God will ensure that the person walks a life of surrender to God. In this case, God will ensure that the person experiences progressive salvation and sanctification from the power of sin—a view heavily endorsed by many theologians, especially by John Wesley. In the future, the person will experience eternal salvation from the presence of sin. When sin is eliminated, the pain brought about by its presence will also be eliminated. The assumption, therefore, is that the future world will be inhabited by people who love God too much to sin against him because the power and presence of sin that made this love possible will have been taken away. They will still have the capacity for pain. However, the cause of that pain will no longer be there. Hence, the objection loses its force.

The upshot of our consideration in this chapter is simply that the existence of pain and the capacity to feel it is no evidence against God's existence. Quite conceivably, God exists alongside the reality of pain. In fact, quite possibly God, having what I have hitherto called personalistic attributes, is capable of feeling pain and making known to us just this very possibility. This possibility seems to be what we learn from Christian theology. Moreover, this conclusion seems to be necessary from the point of view that sees God as a personal being capable of relating with us. Our conclusion in this chapter enables us to explore the exact nature of the relationship between pain and evil. If evil is not always synonymous with pain, what then is the nature of their relationship? If they do not always imply each other, can we say that one is a sufficient condition for the other? This question is explored in the next chapter.

7

Relation of Evil to Pain

WE HAVE BEEN OPERATING under the consideration that evil and pain are not identical entities. They do not imply each other logically, synonymously, or semantically in a way that we can say that evil is pain and pain is evil. In other words, we have discovered that their relationship is far from what materialistic philosophers commonly considers them to be. As noted, if we assume that they imply each other in these ways, we run the risk of making odd philosophical conclusions of the sort I have already suggested. The two terms refer to different entities and must, therefore, be seen in that light. This supposition leads us to ask the following question: If the relationship between evil and pain is neither that of logical identity, nor a synonymous one, what kind of a relationship is it? Are the two terms vastly different such that we cannot connect them in any meaningful way? Or can we say that we have at least one possible way of looking at the terms to determine how they are related to each other?

In this chapter I intend to argue that the relationship between pain and evil is not a synonymous one; rather, it is a cause-and-effect relationship. In other words, pain is the resultant effect of evil. Fundamentally, the kind of evil I have in mind here is the original act of rebellion of our ancestors, Adam and Eve. In other words, their rebellion made the actual experience of pain possible in this world. Whereas evil is not necessarily pain, and pain is not necessarily evil, the relationship that exists between the two, if any, can be captured by viewing evil both as the direct and, in some instances, the indirect cause of pain. We have already established, of course, that their relationship is not synonymous. At this stage we must establish the contention that they bear a cause-and-effect relationship to each other, with evil being the antecedent cause of pain. This consideration, however, seems to force us to ask several questions: Is the existence of evil a sufficient condition for the existence of pain such that if pain did not exist, then evil would not exist? Or could we correctly say that some instances of pain are not in themselves the resultant effects of evil? We could also ask: Is an occurrence of evil possible that does not, by its mere occurrence, bring about the occurrence of pain? These are important questions whose answers must be considered after defending the claim that pain is the resultant effect of an antecedent cause that might properly be deemed evil.

So far I have been proceeding on the assumption that a common definition for pain is available, and indeed this seems to be the case. More exactly, pain has its synonyms that philosophers of religion will not find contentious. Within Christian theology, for example, terms such as suffering, tragedy, and physical afflictions are all considered synonyms of pain. Emotional afflictions also seem to fall under this category. I proceed here on the assumption that this understanding of the definition of pain is not altogether controversial. When we talk about pain, we all seem to be in some kind of agreement as to what it entails. We agree, for example, that it involves some kind of physical or emotional discomfort, the sort of discomfort that sentient beings would rather not have.

However, as I have already argued, materialistic thinkers tend to conflate their understanding of pain with that of evil, resulting not only in a confusion of terms but also in a confusion of what the issues really are with regard to the problem of evil. I suspect they make this move on the understanding that even emotional suffering can be reduced to physical properties consistent with physicalism. For that reason, they would find emotional pain as physical, as the sorts of pain humans feel through the five senses, and that these painful sensations are what count as evil. Moreover, nothing else would count as evil. Only what causes pain does. I believe I have demonstrated, in a logical fashion, that this contention is erroneous. I stick to the contention that evil bears a somewhat different relationship to pain. I now turn to this contention.

I defined evil as an entity whose occurrence runs contrary to God's character. The notion of running contrary to God's character can be variously seen as an attempt to violate God's will, intentions, or purposes. Because God is considered absolutely good and holy, evil cannot be the sort of entity that we can locate in his being. If it is an entity at all, evil is the sort of entity that would be external to God. Moreover, evil has to be something that God allowed to occur, not causally from God's exercise of his coercive power, but permissively, that is, in the sense that God anticipated its occurrence when he made creatures with free will. He had to have anticipated its occurrence when he decided to make creatures with the capacity for contrary choice. God knew that creatures with free will are the sorts of things that would freely choose to love him or reject him. He must have anticipated that some of them would choose to reject him. This anticipation would seem a rational explanation for God to design creatures with the capacity to feel the resultant effects of evil choice, namely, the capacity to feel pain, the most obvious being the occurrence of death for the free-willed creature. Scripture affirms this anticipation, for God warned Adam and Eve that the day they would eat the forbidden fruit they would surely die. In other words, they would experience the most painful consequence of their sin.

If this anticipation is seen as a reasonable hypothesis, several observations can be made here. First, evil must be the sort of entity occurring externally to God. Put differently, evil cannot be seen as an entity occurring in God's being. For a holy God to countenance evil in himself would be contrary to his character. Second, evil must be fundamentally a moral phenomenon since it seems to arise from the exercise of free will. Let's consider the first observation more closely, and thereafter, the second one. If evil is that which runs contrary to God's character, or for that matter, God's will, then evil must be the sort of entity that occurs externally to God. We have already shown that evil is indeed that which runs contrary to God's character or will. If it runs contrary to God's character or will, it cannot be an entity internal to God. Therefore, it would seem to be the case that evil is the sort of entity external to God.

We must pause to ask ourselves whether this sort of argumentation is correct. The argument certainly seems valid. Is it sound, however? Let's begin with the conditional claim. If we subscribe to the essentialist reading of ethics, one I adumbrated in a previous chapter, then evil is indeed that which runs contrary to God's character, for the essentialist reading of ethics contends that we draw our idea and standard of good from God's essentially good nature. Hence, anything that runs contrary to God's nature or character is evil. If so, evil cannot be the sort of entity locatable in the being of God; otherwise, God would be seen as the sort of entity that contradicts himself or violates his own nature and will. However, God's perfect nature is such that he cannot violate or contradict himself. If he did, he would be less than perfect. In other words, if he contradicted himself, he cannot be trusted not only as a source of knowledge but also as the provider of the standard by which we can meaningfully conduct our lives. To retain his perfection, evil must be seen as a phenomenon existing or occurring outside of God's divine substance and nature.

God ought not to be seen as the cause of evil. Neither should he be seen as the one who brings about its occurrence. God's role basically involved designing creatures with free will who, in turn, chose evil from the exercise of their own free will. Having made creatures with free will, God allowed them to exercise their power of choice as a good thing. For God to design creatures with free will only to deny them the subsequent opportunity to exercise their freedom would be contrary to his good character. If he intended to create them with free will, he must also have intended to allow them to exercise their free will. However, allowing them to exercise their free will leaves room for the possibility that they will use their free will to choose wrong courses of action. Here then is where doing a good thing sometimes allows for the possibility of evil to occur without necessarily tracing the evil back to the doer of good as God seems exactly to have done. I believe Plantinga has sufficiently dealt with this form of argumentation in his free will defense.

An analogy, though possibly weak, might help to illustrate this truth further. When parents choose to have children, they do so in the hope their children will become responsible adults. Whereas parents are rightly considered the direct cause of their children's entry into the world, we seldom blame them for the wrong choices their children make, assuming, of course, the parents fulfill their duty of providing their children with the needed moral instruction. In other words, if after bringing their children into the world and doing their best to raise them as responsible citizens through proper moral instruction, the parents hardly get blamed for the wrong choices their children make once those children attain the age of moral accountability. On the contrary, the children are usually the ones to be blamed for their wrong choices.

Of course we can, with some degree of justification, blame parents whose children fail the moral test, if the parents failed to fulfill their duty of instructing their children. For example, parents who fail to instruct their children against committing crimes in any given situation are parents we would consider justifiably blameworthy.

From the ranks of Christian theology, a similar charge cannot be raised against God. God would be held morally blameworthy for the heinous acts that humans commit against their fellow humans if and only if God did not provide some frameworks for moral instruction. A version of the essentialist reading of ethics, of the sort endorsed by Lewis in *Mere Christianity*, seems to suggest that human beings are aware of a law that God has made available to rational creatures. The fact of the matter is that humans have flouted God's law in many significant ways.

Therefore, God should not be blamed for the wrongful moral choices of free creatures who fail to attain the correct moral maturity required of them. However, as previously noted, God anticipated a state of affairs to obtain, one in which some of his free-willed creatures would violate his rules. He, therefore, designed creatures with the ability to accommodate the resultant effects of evil, namely, the sensation of pain, the highest of which, of course, is death. This design was such that upon making choices that violate God's will, pain would ultimately follow.

I therefore say that evil is the antecedent cause, directly or indirectly, of pain. Assuming the events of Gen 3 are historical, we at once see how pain begins to be factored into the equation of evil. Pain in our earthly lives came about as the resultant effect of the evil choices made by our ancestors in the Garden. Pain may have existed before the creation of the world. For example, God may have been grieved or was pained by the rebellious angels in heaven who freely chose to rebel against him. Pursuing this possibility, however, is not the goal of this chapter at this time. Rather, I want to press the contention that evil seems to be the cause of pain. In addition, we also see that evil is not the sort of entity internal to God; it must occur in a manner external to him. In other words, God is not the originator of evil. It originates from free creatures who exercise their freedom, thereby freely choosing to make decisions that run contrary to God's will or character. Pain, however, is a phenomenon that can be properly understood to be felt by God.

The second observation I wish to make is that evil is fundamentally a moral problem. Many philosophers distinguish between moral evil and natural evil. They contend that moral evil is the sort of suffering brought about by free-willed agents. Natural evil, however, is the sort of suffering brought about by the processes of nature. An example of the former would include things such as rape, murder, adultery, and theft. An example of the latter would be things such as earthquakes, tornadoes, cancers (though some cancers are caused by human agents), and so forth. This distinction has been hitherto unchallenged within the ranks of philosophy of religion.

I want to argue, though, that this distinction is in fact a *category mistake*. If evil is seen or understood as that which runs contrary to God's will, character, or his essentially good nature, we must conclude that all occurrences of evil are moral, for they have as their intention the violation of God's will. I have already shown that evil is indeed that which runs contrary to God's will. Hence, all occurrences of evil are moral. Natural evil does not exist, unless by natural evil we refer to the sorts of evil brought about by free will, which we then understand as natural specifically because they issue from our natural composition as free-willed agents. Moreover, to assume that natural evil is the sort of suffering brought about by things such as earthquakes, tornadoes, cancers, and tsunamis is to equivocate pain with evil, a contention I think I have sufficiently demonstrated as erroneous. On the surface, of course, the aforementioned distinction between natural evil and moral evil may appear reasonable. A deeper look into the terms, however, reveals serious doubts about the accuracy of such appellations.

Having drawn attention to this consideration, I contend that if all we have is moral evil, then Alvin Plantinga's free will defense provides a satisfactory solution to the problem of evil. The importance of this consideration is underscored by the following fact: Swinburne thinks that Plantinga's free will defense might provide a perfect solution to moral evil, but it fails to provide one for natural evil. Besides committing the fallacy of equivocating evil with pain, Swinburne also makes the *category mistake* already considered. He thinks that moral evil and natural evil exist. Moreover, this dichotomy is one already assumed as correct by many philosophers of religion.

On the contrary, I contend that Plantinga's free will defense need not be required to provide a solution for natural evil, for my argument shows that natural evil does not exist. A summary of the argument could possibly run as follows:

1. If all occurrences of evil are moral, then the free will defense provides a satisfactory solution to the problem of evil.

2. All occurrences of evil are moral and not natural (assuming all my formulations are correct).

3. Therefore, the free will defense does indeed provide a satisfactory solution to the problem of evil.

The soundness of the argument involves showing that the antecedent of the conditional is true: all occurrences of evil are moral. Assuming that theism is true, the contention that all occurrences of evil are moral is a contention that can be proven consistent with the theistic worldview. Still, just because the antecedent of the conditional is true by itself does not render the entire conditional statement true. To be sure, the entire conditional would be false if we have a true antecedent and a false consequent. In order for the conditional to be true, we must first of all show that the consequent is also true. In other words, we must show that Plantinga's free will defense provides a satisfactory solution to the problem of evil. Showing that the defense succeeds in this endeavor, of course, would be a daunting task, for it would require us to apply the free will defense to all occurrences of evil. Perhaps an easier way would be to identify or locate an instance where the free will defense fails. Upon closer reflection, though, it appears that even here we are faced with a daunting task. Locating a situation in which Plantinga's free will defense against the logical problem of evil actually fails is extremely difficult. His defense is successful unless proven otherwise by possible forceful objections.

We must ask, then, what we mean by a satisfactory solution to the problem of evil. Obviously, we are not implying that the free will defense does in fact take away all instances of violation of God's will in the world. Neither are we suggesting that the free will defense is an antidote for pain such that the sufferer can in some way apply it in some therapeutic fashion to ease his or her pain. What I contend here is simply that the free will defense does solve the logical tension that seems to arise when we posit the existence of God while admitting the facts and reality of evil. Recall that Plantinga's intention was to respond to Mackie's charge that the postulates of Christian doctrine are positively irrational, and that one cannot contend, for example, that God is good and all powerful while maintaining that evil exists.

As already noted, Plantinga has successfully demonstrated how a good, all-powerful God exists at the same time that evil exists. He suggests that the creation of humans with free will enables us to see the logical outcome of such a contention. If God made creatures who are significantly free and does not preempt their freedom by determining them to do right actions all the time, then such creatures can, on occasion, make choices that violate God's will. The fact that significantly free creatures that God created acted in ways that violate God's will is in itself an explanation for the occurrence of evil in our world. This fact not only explains why evil exists in our world; it explains, I say, why all evil exists in our world today. I make this contention because moral evil is all the evil we have and contending that the world also has natural evil is erroneous. This contention, of course, is a much stronger claim than the one Plantinga makes when he postulates that logically, what we call natural evil is, quite possibly, the result of moral evil caused by nonhuman moral agents that are also significantly free—free perhaps in the sense that human beings are free.

Once again, one might object that this formulation ignores the obvious fact that natural evil exists. It seems to ignore, for example, the numerous occurrences of evil such as the earthquakes in Haiti, the tsunami in Indonesia, and Hurricane Katrina on the gulf coast. Hence, the objector would argue, rejection of the obvious distinction is wrongheaded.

This objection, as already noted, demonstrates an important confusion that normally exists by erroneously assuming that pain and evil are one and the same thing. As already noted, they are not. Also, pain seems to be the resultant effect of evil rather than a synonymous term for the same entity. My formulation does not deny that natural instances of pain and suffering do occur. I contend that they are just that—suffering. They are not what we would properly call evil.

In spite of this possibility, the objector could concede that my suggestion that evil be seen as a cause of pain seems to explain the occurrences of pain brought about by the act of free-willed agents. However, it does not explain, or at least fails to explain, the occurrences of pain brought about by natural causes. If pain is brought about by natural causes, then obviously no one can be blamed for it, and we are left with the sort of existential emptiness that characterizes the unbeliever who struggles with understanding the meaning of suffering. The theist, given my explanation, can at best blame nature for the suffering he or she is going through. The objector would argue that launching a protest against an entity that neither hears nor understands human predicament is pointless.

This objection is indeed forceful and, therefore, merits some attention. We can find no philosophical answer to the objection, unless, of course, we dabble in speculation. One such speculation could be seen as follows: The occurrences of natural disasters such as tsunamis, earthquakes, hurricanes, and tornadoes could all be traced back to God as their direct cause. Moreover, God could also be seen as the cause of natural occurrences of pain such as cancers and other examples of terminal illnesses. To what extent is this speculation correct?

The speculation fails for at least one reason: the potential for such events to produce deadly effects upon humanity leaves me to conclude that they were not in God's original plan for human beings. Death, for example, was not part of God's original plan for humans. Hence, the possibility that they could have occurred before the Fall must leave us wondering whether death could have occurred before sin came into the world. This contention that death could have occurred before sin does not appear feasible from a theological perspective. Death came about as a result of human sin, so we are told, and, therefore, not in spite of it. It would seem that a successful philosophical treatment of the cause of such events must factor in the reason for the reality and cause of death as one of its premises.

In this way, we open the door for another speculation that could quite conceivably run as follows: if God created free-willed creatures who later sinned against him, their sin somewhat affected their relationship with him. For that reason, some kind of epistemic distance emerged between God and his creatures—creatures that also include the nonphysical aspect of his creation. This distance, in some way, accounts for the fact that aspects of creation appear to have been left to themselves without God intervening to stop calamities from occurring. Of course, this suggestion is speculative at best and must not be accepted as a viable postulate. However, it does seem to have some promise. In fact, it seems to have an analogue in theology, which might as well be a theologically acceptable explanation.

Hence, to answer the objection in a satisfactory manner, perhaps we must draw from Christian doctrine. First, Christian theology does teach that the pain we experience in our world was brought about by the Fall of our first ancestors. Moreover, Christian doctrine also affirms that nature was affected by this very act of human rebellion. The act of rebellion broke the intimate relationship that existed between God and human beings. Thereafter, some kind of distance between creature and Creator came about. Moreover, the earth was cursed because of this very rebellion. This curse, resulting from human rebellion, possibly accounts for the anomalies in nature we see today. To be sure, death itself, considered the highest level of human pain, is a direct outcome of human rebellion. In the book of Genesis, God warns Adam and Eve that if they rebel against him by eating the forbidden fruit, they would die. Notice that this answer is somewhat parallel to the second philosophical speculation I postulated prior to formulating the answer. One gets the feeling that God is somewhat distant from his creatures. This feeling is consistent with Christian doctrine that contends that our sins have separated us from God (Isa 1:4–9).

From a biblical perspective as well as philosophical speculation, pain caused by natural processes might be traced to human sin. Whether or not this observation is true of all instances of pain is something we are yet to consider. For now, we would say the idea that pain is the direct result of evil has a very good chance of being accurate. This, then, completes the two observations I set out to consider in greater depth.

Let me now move on to the question I needed to examine earlier: Is the existence of evil a sufficient condition for the existence of pain such that if pain did not exist it would imply that evil did not exist? Put differently, are we justified in believing that all instances of evil are evidence in some way of the existence of pain? An argument affirming this state of affairs would run as follows:

1. If evil exists, then pain exists.
2. Evil exists.
3. Therefore, pain exists.

The argument presents the existence of evil as a sufficient condition for the existence of pain. Both premises would appear uncontroversial until we give them a closer look. Beginning with the second premise, what exactly do we mean by the claim evil exists? Since we adopted the essentialist reading of ethics at the beginning of this work, I advise evaluating the truth of premise 2 under this reading. However, the truth of premise 2 will be true under the essentialist reading only if God, upon whom the essentialist reading of ethics is based, does exist. I argued at length that in order for the debates surrounding the problem of evil to appear meaningful, they must be held under the presupposition that the essentialist reading of ethics is the correct one. Outside this reading, the debate would appear meaningless (see my contention in chapter 2). Hence, an evaluation of premise 2 ought to be carried out upon adopting the essentialist view, whether or not the evaluator believes that premise 2 is true. Under the essentialist reading of ethics, not only is premise 2 true, but premise 1 will also be seen to be true as well because the consequent of the conditional is hardly debatable.

However, the truth of premise 2 could be more firmly established on other grounds. If creatures with free will exist, then they are capable of making moral choices. If creatures with free will capable of making moral choices exist, then such creatures have in fact made both good and bad choices. Creatures with free will do exist. It is also true, as a result of this, that they are capable of making moral choices. Possibly, therefore, such creatures have in fact made both good and bad choices. The truth of this conclusion is confirmed by the facts of human behavior in our world. Free willed creatures have made choices widely regarded as immoral, evidenced by their participation in acts such as rapes, murders, and many instances in which the torturing of innocent children occur. Irrespective of the reading of ethics that we are willing to adopt, we seem to think, intuitively, that participating in acts of these sorts is wrong. However, if participating in this way constitutes making bad choices, then the acts themselves are evil. Hence, evil exists.

This result confirms the truth of our second premise. If it confirms the truth of the second premise, it also serves to underscore the truth of the first premise. Of course, following the truth-table method, the truth of the first premise is really dependent on the truth of the consequent alone. The truth of the consequent in this first premise seems indisputable. Hence, the truth of the premise itself is also indisputable. Thus, we conclude that the argument is both valid and sound, for it has both true premises and a conclusion that follows from the premises, which is itself true.

What might still be in doubt, however, is the causal connection existing, or the causal connection that I am supposing exists, between the antecedent of the premise and its consequent. As noted earlier, I argued that pain is the resultant effect of evil. Perhaps the reason this causal connection is evasive is because it is one that we would admit on *a posteriori* grounds rather than on *a priori* grounds, and must be established by experience. The latter connection is one that can be seen to follow through a mere inspection of the terms. If evil was a term synonymous with pain, then on *a priori* grounds this synonymy dictates that evil logically and semantically entails pain and suffering, and vice versa. We have seen that this hypothesis is false.

This result seems to bring about a hidden but possible truth about the argument. Evil does not appear to be a sufficient condition for pain, especially if the connection in question is one that must be confirmed by experience. To determine the nature of this insufficiency, one would have to cite an instance of evil that seems painless. Take, for example, the case of the student, Adam, cheating on an exam. This case seems to be an instance of evil. Pain would not always follow an individual who chooses to cheat in an exam. In fact, one might argue here that the cheater experiences the pleasure of being awarded a good grade. Or take the case of driving one's car ten miles per hour above the speed limit on some particular highway. Assuming that speeding is, in fact, an evil, not much pain is involved in committing this crime unless, of course, one gets a speeding ticket from the state trooper. Another example would be the case of two consenting adults committing adultery without feeling remorse for cheating on their spouses. Unless their spouses find them out, logically an individual can possibly commit this kind of evil without feeling pain from that experience. Therefore, we would have great difficulty proving that the existence of evil is a sufficient condition for pain. Then, the argument above, though valid, may after all be unsound, for it erroneously assumes that whenever evil exists, pain will also exist. We now see that evil can occur without the resultant occurrence of pain.

Of course, one could raise objections to these scenarios in the following ways. For example, with regard to the case of the exam cheater, one might argue that the student suffers pain of a psychological sort. Either the student is suffering from a sickness of the soul, about which Socrates talks in *The Republic*, or feels the pang of a disturbed conscience for earning a grade he knows he did not deserve. With regard to the sickness of the soul, Socrates argues that the human soul is in harmony if each of its three aspects is allowed to perform its proper function. For example, the first aspect, the aspect of reason, must be allowed to rule over the other two. The second, the spirited part, must perform its courageous duty of being an ally of reason. The third part, which he calls the appetitive part, must perform its duty of being subject to the rule of reason. A student who cheats on an exam basically allows the appetitive part of his soul to desire a grade he neither deserved nor earned. For this reason, his soul is in disarray. If his soul is in disarray, then his soul is in disharmony, and the student is a sick person. One concludes, following Socrates (and perhaps in agreement with Aristotle), that the student is psychologically disturbed, and therefore experiences pain of a certain sort.

However, more consistent with Christian doctrine, we might argue that the student is sinning, and all sin will be punished by God. For this reason, knowing that his sin will be punished, the student will never be at peace with himself unless he deals with the sin in question. His knowledge of this fact alone is sufficient to cause intellectual disturbance of a certain sort—the disturbance that comes with the knowledge that sin will be punished. Hence, even in the case of a student cheating on an exam, pain will not be elusive.

With regard to the example of driving well above the legal speed limit, one could take the Socratic as well as the Aristotelian approach. However, since we are dealing with the essentialist reading of ethics, the objector could argue as follows: Knowingly violating a rule that one knows one must obey is itself a sinful act. Sinful acts will be punished by God unless the sinner repents of them. The repentance itself is already based on the painful death of Christ. Hence, either way, even this act of driving above the speed limit is one that seems connected to some kind of pain—the pain itself being the death of Christ or some kind of divine punishment.

Finally, one could object to the adultery example by drawing attention to the fact that the adulterers are often plagued with guilt for their unfaithfulness. Moreover, as already noted, their spouses also suffer the consequences of their cheating. Equally painful is the fact that their relationship with their spouses is in danger of breaking. Experience shows that breakups are never easy. They are painful, whether one cheats or not. All these considerations indicate that finding an instance of evil that is not itself followed by painful consequences is extremely difficult.

An even more forceful objection against this argument is still possible. Worse, the objection might seem fatal. It is an objection against the contention that evil can occur without pain. It stems from Christian doctrine. Simply stated, the objection could take note of the following consideration. Apparently, the death of Christ is the resultant effect of all evil. But the death of Christ, presumably, was excruciatingly painful. If the death of Christ was the resultant effect of all evil, then it is not the case that an occurrence of evil exists that fails to bring about an instance of pain as its resultant effect, for every occurrence of evil can at least be seen to have a resultant effect of pain in the death of Christ. Therefore, no occurrence of evil exists that does not cause pain. Every occurrence of evil causes pain.

As noted, this objection might seem fatal to the claim that evil can occur without pain. However, a response to this objection could be formulated in the following way. The death of Christ is itself not a necessary result of the occurrence of evil. In other words, it is not an *a priori* truth that because evil exists, Christ was forced to die for the sins of humanity. Christ died of his own free will. He was not forced to die through the occurrence of evil. He could have chosen not to die if he wished, a fact that he himself makes clear to the soldiers who came to arrest him. Of course, Christian theology does teach that the death and resurrection of Christ were both necessary for our salvation from sin. However, this teaching is quite different from claiming, erroneously, that since evil occurred, Christ needed to die. Seen in this light, the previous objection loses its force.

Another objection to this formulation could still be raised from a slightly different angle. One could argue that the existence of hell is in itself an indication of the painful consequences of all evil acts. Hell exists for the purpose of punishing all forms of rebellion. More accurately, the pains of hell exist because evil exists. One could, for this reason, be tempted to argue that if an occurrence of evil is not atoned for by the painful death of Christ, it will face the consequence of eternal punishment in hell. Both alternatives are painful. The arguer would then conclude that no instance of evil fails to have a painful consequence.

This objection appears strong and we seem to have no way of answering it. Therefore, seemingly, whenever and wherever evil exists, pain will follow either immediately or later. The connection between evil and pain is both a causal and a necessary one, we might be led to conclude. Where we find one, we must necessarily find the other, sooner or later. This admission, however, does not imply that one is a synonym of the other.

If the relationship between evil and pain is some kind of a necessary causal connection, then the following argument would also appear correct:

1. If pain exists, then evil caused it.

2. Pain exists.

3. Therefore, evil caused it.

From a classical Christian vantage point, the truth of premise 2 seems indisputable, so I will not belabor it. However, what do we make of the first premise? Its truth is heavily dependent on the truth of the antecedent. If we are to go by the postulates of Christian theology, it does not seem farfetched to contend that evil brought about the facts and reality of pain in our world. This claim is made in Gen 3. Because we are adopting an essentialist reading of ethics, the claims of Christian theology must also be adopted. If we do, then premise 1 should be accepted as true. Hence, if both premises are true, and the conclusion follows, we conclude that the argument is both valid and sound. We must ask, though, whether this observation is correct. Can pain possibly occur without evil?

This state of affairs does not seem possible within the postulates of Christian theology. If pain is the resultant effect of evil, then necessarily, where pain exists, evil must somewhat be involved. In other words, when we see an instance of pain, somehow that instance is traceable to some occurrence of evil. Notice that this consideration is not in any way insinuating that pain and evil are synonymous; rather, it is contending that where one finds a certain cause, namely evil, one will also find its attendant effect, namely pain. One can maintain this truth without necessarily admitting that both terms are synonymous.

One can object to this formulation by supposing, for example, that some pains are caused by God. Does not Scripture, for example, remind us that God disciplines those he loves? In the Old Testament, for example, we read of a being who inflicts pain on his people. Also, the doctrine of hell depicts a God who directly brings about pain on his people. If we admit this state of affairs, we must at the same time admit that God does, in fact, cause pain. Pain is not exclusively the resultant effect of evil. Pain can also be caused by God.

This objection may *prima facie* appear forceful. However, it ignores an important fact. According to Christian theology, whenever God inflicts pain on his free-willed creatures, it is his way of responding to the evil his creatures freely choose. Thus, when God disciplines his children, he does so because his children are somewhat involved in sin, which they freely chose. He then necessarily inflicts pain on his children as a way of purging the sin in question from their lives. The idea that God inflicts pain on his free-willed creatures due to their sin is repeated in the Old Testament accounts of his dealings with them. The doctrine and reality of hell is also in place as a way of explaining God's way of dealing with the evil acts of free-willed creatures. Finally, we are well advised to go back to the doctrine of the Fall of human beings. The doctrine seems to reveal that pain is a consequence of sin—one that God seems to have built into the fabric of nature. It is a consequence that follows when his creatures freely choose to act in a manner contrary to his will. Hence, when pain comes about, sin must be blamed for it.

The fact of the matter is simply that we live in a fallen world. Its fallenness is caused or brought about by sin. Our ancestors' fall in the manner depicted in Scripture is a fact directly and causally responsible for the phenomenon of death, including all conditions that bring about the occurrence of death. Consequently, naturally occurring instances of pain and suffering are traceable to the fateful event in the Garden of Eden. Of course, it also means that instances of pain immediately caused by free-willed creatures are also indirectly attributable to the rebellion in the Garden. The Apostle Paul, for example, reminds us that through one man sin entered the whole world. The second formulation of the argument thus appears to have some promise. Pain, therefore, seems to be a resultant effect of the occurrence of evil. Our findings also imply that whenever evil exists, pain will always exist.

We must subscribe to the view that depicts the relationship between good and evil as a causal one for at least one reason. This view of the causal relationship between good and evil is consistent with the Christian doctrine of salvation, a doctrine that I outlined briefly in a previous chapter. Christian doctrine teaches that with regard to the future, we will be saved from the presence of sin or, for that matter, the presence of evil. In other words, evil will be removed from among us. If evil, the cause of pain, is no longer present with us, the pain that follows it will also no longer be present. The promise, therefore, that God shall wipe away all tears and do away with all pain is itself based on the promise that sin and evil will be eventually removed from among us.

We now come to an important question: why does a good and loving God allow evil to occur? In light of our findings, we reply with the following: a good and loving God allows evil to occur because he made creatures with the capacity to choose between good and evil, that is, with free will. If he denied them the ability to exercise their free choice, he would be violating his own intentions of creating them with free will. To preserve his goodness he must allow them to exercise their power of contrary choice freely without determining them to follow certain courses of actions that he would prefer them to follow.

We also consider the second big question: Why does a good and loving God allow his children to suffer? More penetratingly, why does God allow the occurrence of what appears to be pointless suffering? The second part of this question is perhaps more difficult to answer than the first question. Therefore, I will give it a fuller treatment in the final chapter. However, the first part of the question is easier to deal with, and I present an initial response as follows: In light of our findings, we once again reply that suffering is the causal result of human free choices. It is God's way of accommodating and dealing with the occurrence of evil brought about by the actions of free-willed creatures. God is not the cause of human suffering, however, but he has made us in such a way that when we sin against him, we must suffer the consequences of our sins. Without a doubt, every choice has its consequences, and bad choices will bring about painful consequences.

Still, one could press the following challenge: evil understandably comes about through the exercise of the choices of free-willed creatures. Also, God has structured the world in such a way that when evil occurs, pain follows as a consequence. What is not understandable is the fact that God is not doing enough to stop the instances of pain that follow from the occurrence of evil.

Several things need to be said about this concern. First, we are not exactly clear what counts as "doing enough to stop the instances of pain." What one person considers enough might not necessarily be enough for another. People handle different instances of pain differently. For example, a one mile run might be extremely painful for a person who fails to exercise. However, it might not be as painful for the physically fit. Hence, a person going through severe instances of suffering might think that God has done enough for him or her if, after a period of that kind of suffering, the person no longer experiences it. Similarly, a person might go through suffering that is relatively less severe and still believe that God has not done enough to eliminate the pain. Therefore, the worry that God seems to be doing less than he should to alleviate suffering is quite likely a misguided one.

Second, the occurrence of pain might just be of a sort needed for the character reformation of certain individuals. Lewis reminds us, for example, that character reformation is painful. That is, to become more and more like God, or for that matter, like Christ, sinful creatures will have to go through some instances of painful correction. Hence, for Lewis, in order to be even remotely close to God's goodness, sinful creatures such as ourselves will have to experience some kinds of pain. Hence, for God to stop the kind of pain in question, he would perhaps be acting counter to the goals of character reformation needed for those individuals.

Third, God could have, in fact, acted to prevent worse forms of suffering, of which we are completely unaware. We will never know, this side of heaven, how often God has prevented potentially disastrous plane crashes and catastrophic tsunamis. Of course, we are perhaps unable to prove, beyond the assurance of Scripture, that he has done so, but we cannot prove that he has not done so either. With regard to the proof that he has done so, Scripture does remind us that he holds everything together.

With regard to not being able to prove that God has not prevented the catastrophes in question, we would be wise to consider the following suggestion: Just because God does not appear to be doing something does not in itself imply that God is doing nothing. God might be working behind the scenes undetected by our cognitive faculties. For example, God might be doing behind the scenes precisely what he needs to do to alleviate suffering.

To see this possibility, consider the following illustration, which I used in my earlier book, *Heaven: God's Solution to Human Pain*. Imagine that both you and your friend decide to watch a highly publicized movie that has just been released. As the plot of the movie thickens, both of you decide you do not like how it is developing. Perhaps the bad guys in the movie are gaining an unfair advantage over the good guys. Your friend, therefore, decides to walk out of the movie theater, convinced that the bad guys will win. You, however, choose to stay and watch the movie until the end. As the plot unfolds, you discover much to your relief that the good guys finally win over the bad guys. You head home feeling satisfied that it was perhaps the best movie you have ever seen. You then relate the story to your friend who walked out of the movie quite prematurely. He then feels disappointed for missing out on the good part.

We are left to ask ourselves whether giving up on God by claiming that he is doing nothing to alleviate the evil is sort of like walking out of the movie before it is over. Put differently, are we reasonable to wonder, given the Christian vantage point, whether giving up on God simply because the plot of life is taking a turn we did not expect is a premature disposition? Life does have its twists and turns. Most of these take us by violent surprise. We are then jolted by the erroneous supposition that this unexpected turn of events is irreconcilable with the eschatological promise given to us in Scripture. Analogous to the movie illustration, I contend that this supposition is similar to giving up on life prematurely. We do not seem to be able to find enough justification for it. Given the essentialist view of heaven, we contend that God, as a wholly good being, can be trusted. If he can be trusted, his promises about the New Heaven and the New Earth are also trustworthy. Based on this element of trust, no turn of earthly events appear to counter the promise of enjoying both an evil-free and a pain-free eternal life in the New Heaven and the New Earth.

We are also assured that the existence of free will in the New Heaven and the New Earth does not pose a threat to the fulfillment of the promise of heaven. The threat, alluded to in an earlier chapter, can be stated in the following way: even if evil and pain are eventually removed from among us, the fact that humans will still have free will in the New Heaven and the New Earth gives us reason to suspect that new instances of evil could arise even in the afterlife. I already dealt with why I think this threat is nonexistent; hence, I see no need to repeat it fully here. Only a brief recapitulation is in order. First, humans will already be fully aware of the seriousness and ugliness of sin along with its horrific consequences. Moreover, they will also have been exposed to the majesty of God's love and beauty. They will, therefore, have developed a great love for God, one that would not have been possible with the occurrence and existence of sin. These considerations make believing that human beings will choose to rebel against God in the afterlife extremely difficult.

Also, another objection could be raised from historical considerations. If created beings in heaven did rebel against God, thereby bringing about their fall, nothing will keep redeemed saints from rebelling against God in the afterlife. What do we make of this objection? Is it a forceful one? I do not think so for the following reason: The angelic beings in question had no prior experiential knowledge of the implications of rebelling against God until, of course, after the fact. Human beings will indeed have this knowledge. Hopefully, the removal of sin, coupled with the sort of moral and character reformation that follows this removal, will be instructive enough to help redeemed saints avoid similar pitfalls. However, holiness in heaven will not be assured by merely learning from our past. It will be assured by countenancing the beauty of a holy God and being attracted to his being eternally. Christian doctrine seems to teach that sin is what keeps us from loving God as we should. Its removal will free us to love God more fully as we should.

This removal of sin does not mean that free will is an aspect of human beings that will be unnecessary eventually. It will be most necessary in heaven, for at that time, as free-willed creatures, we will make choices between alternatives that are all good. The meaningfulness of these choices will be underscored by the fact that we will know the meaning of having only good choices, having been exposed to the possibility of making bad choices and seeing their consequences. Put differently, the situation in the Garden of Eden will be restored, except for the possibility of eating the forbidden fruit.

8

The Problem

As already noted in an earlier chapter, if evil is not identical to pain and pain is not identical to evil, then the problem of evil, if indeed it is a problem, is quite different from the problem of pain. Stated in a different way, when we talk about the problem of evil, we cannot be talking about the problem of pain. Philosophers of religion, most notably Mike Peterson, have tried to classify different versions of the problem of evil as logical, probabilistic, gratuitous, and existential. Suppose we were to draw just these distinctions between evil and pain while maintaining these classifications. I would be curious to know what the problem really is.

I endeavor to pursue this exercise in this section. I want to show that since the problem of pain is distinct from the problem of evil, the various classifications in question should be taken as the logical problem of pain, the probabilistic problem of pain, the gratuitous problem of pain, and the existential problem of pain. We will discover that the problem of pain so understood fails to undercut belief in God's existence. Also, if we retain similar distinctions with regard to the problem of evil, our exercise will show that if the problem of evil is understood as a moral problem, it fails to render belief in God implausible or, for that matter, illogical. Let me begin with the first issue, the problem of pain.

The Problem of Pain

In the spirit of Mackie, what would the logical version of the problem of pain look like? I have already drawn attention to what it might look like in an earlier chapter. For the purpose of explication in this chapter, let me repeat it here. I believe that the problem looks like the following:

1. God is all powerful.
2. God is all good.
3. Pain exists.

Using Plantinga's method, let's call this triad set A. Presumably, Mackie would indeed have endorsed this form of argumentation since he used evil and pain interchangeably. However, as we have already noted, Mackie did not think the contradiction was readily apparent. To see the contradiction, he would have wanted us to add a fourth claim: good is opposed to evil in such a way that a good thing always eliminates evil as far as it can. Because Mackie uses evil synonymously with pain, we only need to reformulate his fourth statement in a way that yields the following set of statements:

1. God is all powerful.
2. God is all good.
3. Pain exists.
4. Good is opposed to pain in such a way that a good thing always eliminates pain as far as it can.

Let's call this set of statements set A^*. Mackie would have been quick to suggest that these claims would indeed make Christianity positively irrational. My suspicion that Mackie would likely make this move is plausible because Mackie fails to draw any meaningful distinctions between pain and evil. We would then need to ask ourselves whether Mackie would be correct in arguing in this manner.

Of course, Plantinga did show that the Mackiean triad has no inherent contradiction as originally formulated, despite the fact that Mackie believed there was one. What we want to pursue here is whether a contradiction can still be avoided if we revise our terms in a way that treats evil as a term whose etymological significance is different from pain. In other words, do the facts of pain logically contradict the existence of a good and all-powerful God? If so, what conditions need to be satisfied for such a contradiction to obtain? In other words, how would we show that such a contradiction exists?

We could follow Plantinga's rigor in showing that there appears to be no contradiction in maintaining all three claims. Thus, we could argue, as Plantinga did, that the triad is not formally contradictory; neither do we see any evidence of implicit or explicit contradictions. What do we mean by these terms? Let's begin with a formally contradictory set of statements. A set of statements is formally contradictory, Plantinga argues, if upon the application of the laws of logic to that set we derive an explicit contradiction. For example, consider the following set of statements:

1. If pain exists, God does not exist.
2. Pain exists.
3. God exists.

Let us call this set B. If we apply the laws of logic to statements 1 and 2 of set B, we will arrive at a fourth claim, which will then yield set B* as follows:

1. If pain exists, God does not exist.
2. Pain exists.
3. God exists.
4. God does not exist (after conditional elimination on 1 and 2).

We then arrive at an explicit contradiction between claims 3 and 4. Of course, no theologian affirms the sorts of claims we find in set B*. Following Plantinga's critique of the Mackiean triad, we note in our reformulation that this contradiction is not the kind that Mackie believes the theologian is making. In other words, Mackie is not charging the theologian's doctrine for affirming formal contradictions.

Perhaps then Mackie thinks the theologian is making explicitly contradictory claims. For example, suppose we have a set of statements as follows:

1. God exists.
2. Pain exits.
3. God does not exist.

Let's call this set C. When we combine the set of statements in this set, the resultant conjunct will yield a necessary falsehood. Therefore, we ask ourselves whether the necessary falsehood plaguing this set is the sort of necessary falsehood we would find plaguing set A. Upon a close examination, we discover that the combination of the members of set A fail to yield a necessary falsehood because at least one possible instance exists where if all the members of the set are true statements, the resultant conjunction cannot be false. In order for set A to be necessarily false, the result of the conjunction of all its members must yield a falsehood in all its instances. However, set A does not appear to be plagued with this falsehood, even when we do not know the truth-value of its members. Set A is, therefore, not logically contradictory.

The theist will be the first to admit, however, that set A does not purport to prove that God in fact exists. What the theist would be justified in maintaining is the contention that he or she does not live with a logical contradiction by maintaining the triad represented by set *A*. In other words, the theist believes that all the statements in that set are, in fact, true. Moreover, he or she suggests that the truth of claim 2 in set *A* is somewhat entailed by the truth of claim 1. The theist would argue, for example, that if God exists and God created free-willed creatures who somewhat reflect his being as a person, then he or she can logically imagine the occurrence of pain in the world. If one affirms the antecedent of this claim while denying its consequent, then one believes or upholds a falsehood. As already argued in a previous chapter, if one believes in the existence of a personal God who made free-willed creatures, then one must believe in the possibility of the occurrence of pain inflicted by those creatures. If the possibility becomes actual, one should not at all be surprised. The conclusion we arrive at here, then, is simply that set *A* is not logically contradictory. It would perhaps be more accurate to think of set *A* as a contingent (in the logical sense) set of statements.

Nevertheless, we might argue that while set *A* is not a forceful repudiation of Christian doctrine, set *A** is. Raised in the Mackiean spirit, this argument fares no better than the previous argument about set *A*. In light of our findings in previous chapters and as already noted here, clearly if God is a personal being with emotions, he is capable of experiencing pain. If so, we can find no logical contradiction in thinking that the reality of pain undercuts positive claims about God's existence. In other words, the existence of pain does not eliminate the fact and reality of God.

However, some theologians would go as far as suggesting that set *A* is a necessary set of statements if God is a person, for his personhood entails the capacity to feel and experience pain, whether pain occurs or not. This claim does have the potential to generate some heated debate. For our purposes, however, it is enough to think that set *A* is a contingent set of statements. If it is, we are not in any way sustaining a contradiction by thinking that set *A* consists of members whose statements are true. In short, the logical problem of pain fails to undercut belief in God.

We now move to the probabilistic problem of pain. To help formulate the probabilistic problem of pain, we might need to revisit the probabilistic problem of evil. Following Peterson,[1] we note several versions of the probabilistic problem of evil. The first one could be stated as follows:

1. God's omniscience and omnipotence imply that he is capable of creating any logically possible world.
2. God's omni-benevolence implies that he would choose to create the best world his omnipotence would allow.

---

1. Peterson et al., *God and Evil*, 47–48.

3. God's omniscience, omnipotence, and omni-benevolence imply that he would have created the best of all possible worlds.

4. This world is not likely the best of all possible worlds.

5. Therefore, an omnipotent, omniscient, and omni-benevolent God does not likely exist.[2]

Peterson notes how J. W. Cornman and Keith Lehrer presented a version of this argument. Plantinga contends that both Cornman and Lehrer suffered from Leibniz's lapse. More accurately, Leibniz's lapse seems to presuppose that there is such a thing as "a best of all possible worlds." The problem with this presupposition is that whenever one mentions what one thinks is the best possible world (*BPW*), one is left with the possibility of envisioning a better world than *BPW*. To see this possibility, consider the analogy of numbers. For any number one designates, one can always find another number that is greater. Similarly, for any *BPW* one envisions, one has the possibility of envisioning a better one.[3]

Plantinga considers that perhaps the argument could be strengthened by substituting *BPW* with a more palatable consideration: of all the logically possible worlds within God's power to create, he should have created one with a better balance of good and evil. Consider also that God can control the amount of natural evil in the world. This control is possible for God even if he will not override the freedom of his significantly free agents.

In his response to this argument, Plantinga contends that it fails for at least one reason: Plantinga argues for the possibility that all the evil in this world is broadly moral evil. For this reason, of all the possible worlds within God's power to make, none of them will contain a better balance of broad moral good with respect to broad moral evil. Because, quite possibly, the so-called natural evil is broadly moral evil, of all the worlds within God's power to create, none may be better than the other with respect to moral good versus moral evil. Plantinga's conclusion here, then, is that the existence of the great amount and variety of evil fails to render God's existence improbable.

Another contention, which Peterson calls the personalist interpretation of the problem of evil, is as follows: the probability that God exists is very low given the facts, reality, and amounts of evil. Two major objections were raised against this contention. First, the accuracy of the discipline arising from the theory of probability is far from settled. It is replete with margins of error that, at best, force us to make approximations regarding the facts of the case. In light of these, probability theory is perhaps not reliable in helping us arrive at

2. Ibid., 48–49.
3. Ibid., 49.

meaningful conclusions about the existence of God with regard to the reality of evil. Second, the probability theorist usually assigns figures based on his personal bias. When the probability theorist argues that the existence of God is very low with respect to the facts and reality of evil, his personal bias allows him to arrive at the *very low* judgment. Put differently, an atheist will presumably assign a low figure to indicate the improbability of God with respect to the facts of evil. A theist, quite understandably, will assign a higher figure. Thus, we are no longer dealing with objectivity here, but with personal biases, opinions, and feelings about God's existence.[4]

In all versions of the probabilistic problem of evil, none draws any distinction between evil and pain. Assuming that we drew such a distinction, is the probabilistic objection strengthened or weakened? In my opinion, the latter is more obvious. Let's begin with the first one. Are we correct in contending, for example, that the existence of pain makes this world worse than the *BPW*? Of course we are not. We have already seen the possibility of envisioning instances of pain, some of them extreme by our standards, that could also be considered instances of good. The mere occurrence of pain does not, by its occurrence, militate against the possibility of the good. The *BPW*, if there be such, could have instances of pain. In a world with free creatures, such a possibility is not difficult to imagine, even in cases with an overbalance between good and evil in favor of the good. Hence, even with the strengthened version of the probabilistic argument, not much is achieved.

Let me turn to the personalist interpretation of the problem of evil. Notice here that even without having to worry about the distinction between evil and pain, the personalist interpretation of the problem of evil seems to fail before it takes off the ground. To underscore its nonstarter status, let's reframe the argument in light of our findings so far. Suppose we contend, analogously to the probability theorist, but with an important modification, the following: the probability that God exists is very low with respect to the facts and reality of pain. Would this inference in any way undercut, or at least render, God's existence improbable?

First, it does not seem to do so because of the two responses to the objections already raised. These two would seem quite useful here. However, the argument has a third problem, now that the distinction between evil and pain has already been made. If pain is a feeling that is not foreign to the character of God, it cannot be used as evidence against God's existence, much less, as reason to demonstrate the improbability of God. The capacity to feel pain and express it meaningfully seems to be something quite normal for a personal being like God. When his children turn away from

---

4. Ibid., 53.

him, rejecting his offer of love, as a person he is bound to feel pain in much the same way that he delights in his children when they freely choose to love him. Moreover, just this very capacity to feel pain is what might be considered evidence for human personality, which, if rigorously pursued, could give reasons for us to doubt the claim that our personality arose from impersonal sources and lean more toward the suggestion that our personality must have arisen from a personal source. Hence, the probabilistic problem of pain seems impotent as an objection against God's existence.

Next, we turn to the problem of gratuitous pain. In order to formulate the problem adequately, we need to see how the problem of gratuitous evil is presented. Peterson seems to contend, in his outline of the problem, that it has been presented in three different ways. The first version contends that God does not have any morally sufficient reason to permit the occurrence of evil. The conclusion of this contention would, therefore, be that God's existence is undercut and disconfirmed by the facts and reality of evil. This objection was answered by the consideration that to attain certain goals, the existence or occurrence of evil is necessary. Theists who provide this response take note of the fact that even atheists do subscribe to this view. Possibly, then, at least some reasons could exist for the occurrence of some instances of evil, reasons which God could have. Hardship, for example, is connected to the development of character.

Notice that this response assumes, as does the objection, that evil and pain are synonymous. Perhaps, for our purposes, we need to rename gratuitous evil as gratuitous pain. The argument would then read as follows: God does not have any morally sufficient reason to permit the occurrence of pain. We should now be clear what the response to this objection might be. If pain is the resultant consequence of sin, then we conclude that sin is indeed a morally sufficient reason for the occurrence of pain. Moreover, since God is a being that experiences pain, arising from the sinful rebellion of his creatures, his existence is not undercut by the occurrence of pain. To be sure, his existence seems to be affirmed by the facts and reality of pain.

The second version of the argument against God's existence from gratuitous evil contends that extensive amounts of extremely intense kinds of evil seem to exist in perplexing distributions, some of them very severe, in patterns that simply defy comprehension. The fact that they appear in a way beyond human imagination seems to call into question the existence of a wholly good God. The theistic response focuses on the contention that the evils occur in large amounts. It draws attention to the fact that the objection assumes that God would allow only certain amounts of evil. However, it also observes that we would be hard-pressed to establish and quantify just how much evil would be too much for God to permit. The response continues by claiming that God could permit the occurrence of many instances of evil—evil of the sort that could perhaps strike us as extreme amounts, as long as those amounts serve God's good purposes.

Notice, once again, that this version conflates evil with pain. If we apply our findings to this contention, an adequate response could be formulated thus: the frequency of the instances of pain occurs in direct proportion to the frequencies with which acts running contrary to God's will do occur. If this case is true, God should not be blamed for the frequencies of those acts; human beings as well as nonhuman free-willed agents are the ones to blame. Because intense kinds of pain can logically exist in perplexing distribution, the antecedent sinful causes of the occurrences of those pains, which are equally logically possible both from human and nonhuman free-willed agents, did happen in perplexing distributions. Hence, such pains ought not to be blamed on God but on humans or those free-willed agents.

The third version of the argument is also called the evidential argument from gratuitous evil, or pointless suffering. The contention is simply that if God does exist, then gratuitous evil ought not to exist. Clearly, gratuitous evil exists, which of course leads the contender to conclude that God does not exist. Peterson notes several points about gratuitous evil, some of them being that it is the sort of evil that God could have prevented without losing some greater good, or that God could have prevented without having to allow the occurrence of some greater evil. The idea is that gratuitous evil is not a prerequisite to attaining a greater good.

A response to this objection, one worth considering, comes from Stephen Wykstra. In his view, he notes that the atheistic contention is simply that some evils seem pointless; hence, they are indeed pointless. However, Wykstra notes, this inference is a mistake on the part of the atheologian, for the atheologian seems to contend that pointless suffering fails to serve any purpose of a divine being. The problem with this contention is that the atheist thinks he knows what this divine purpose ought to be. Wykstra draws attention to the possibility that God would certainly know purposes and goals beyond our cognitive reach. Humans should not expect to know all the goods for which God permits evil.

Notice, once again, that even here, evil and pain are terms used synonymously. I defer my response to this issue and promise to deal with it in greater detail in chapter 9. However, let me make a quick observation here. If all instances of pain are the resultant effects of some antecedent sinful choices from free-willed creatures, then what we call pointless suffering is perhaps not pointless after all. If our considerations in previous chapters are correct, those instances of what we call pointless suffering can be traced back to the acts of some free-willed agent, human or nonhuman, misusing his or her power of contrary choice. Therefore, the pointlessness of a given instance of pain possibly arises from the fact that the sufferer is hard-placed to explain the antecedent cause of pain, which in reality is there.

On an instructive note, these findings demonstrate that the problem of evil is quite different from the problem of pain. Moreover, it shows that if we state the problem of evil as the problem of pain, we immediately see that we are dealing with a weaker objection. Perhaps the reason we find the issues in this debate problematic is because we fail to draw distinctions between these two terms. Upon realizing that evil and pain are somewhat different entities, the forcefulness of the major objections seem to be less impactful. Let us now turn to the problem of evil, evil understood as that which runs contrary to God's character and God's will.

Problem of Evil

If the problem of evil is not the problem of pain, what then should it be? How should it be understood? I will follow the format of the first section in this chapter to see exactly how best to construe the problem. First, we need to revisit our definition of evil. For our purposes here, let me define evil as that which violates God's will. Following the Mackiean triad again, it is fair to say that the logical problem of evil could be stated as follows:

1. God is all good.
2. God is all powerful.
3. Instances of violations of God's will exist.

Let us call this set D. To see the innocuousness of the claim that D is irrational, we do not need to run through Plantinga's explication of formal, explicit, and implicit contradictions. All we need is to show that set D is not a logically contradictory set. As initially stated, a logically contradictory set is such that the conjunction of all its members yields a necessary falsehood. If the conjunction of the members of D yields a necessary falsehood, we will conclude that D is logically contradictory. Presumably, when we engage in this exercise, we discover at least one instance in which the conjunction of the members of D is true. Hence, D is not necessarily false. If it is not necessarily false, we conclude that it is not logically contradictory.

Recall Mackie's contention, however, that the contradiction to which he alluded was not readily apparent. To see the contradiction, he contended that we needed to add another claim, which would then yield the following set, which I will call D^*:

1. God is all good.
2. God is all powerful.
3. Instances of violations of God's will exist.
4. Good is opposed to violations of God's will in such a way that a good thing always eliminates violations of God's will as far as it can.

What do we make of this argument? If D turned out contingent rather than logically contradictory, then perhaps the addition of claim 4 would render D^* logically contradictory if the existence of evil is logically incompatible with the existence of God. Depending on how we symbolize each claim from 1 through 4, we discover that the conjunction of those claims fails to yield a logically contradictory set of statements. At least one instance exists in which the set of statements could all be true.

However, if all of them could be true, then claim 4 could also be true. If claim 4 is possibly true, then perhaps we confirm Mackie's worry. I think, however, that even if claim 4 is true, it is perhaps not a necessary truth. Possibly, God can allow instances of violations of his will without such violations undercutting belief in his existence. Indeed, this possibility is one of the key postulates of the free will defense.

Let us take a closer look. If God is good and God is all powerful, then God will want to eliminate all instances of violations of God's will, and he will want to do this as far as his omnipotence will allow. Can we find a logical contradiction in this claim? Assuming that evil is understood as violations of God's will, I believe Plantinga's free will defense has sufficiently shown no contradiction here. If God has created beings with free will, that is, beings capable of moral good as well as moral evil, he would be preempting rather than preserving their freedom by determining them to do good all the time. In order to preserve their freedom, he will need to allow them to exercise their capacity for moral choice to the fullest extent possible. In light of this brief consideration, we conclude that no contradiction abides in holding that an all-good and all-powerful being exists alongside creatures capable of violating his will. The free will defense seems to be an acceptable solution to the logical problem of evil or, more accurately, the logical problem of violations of God's will. The solution seems to suggest, quite successfully, that no logical problem attends instances of violations of God's will.

We now move to the probabilistic problem of evil, herein understood as the probabilistic problem of violations of God's will. Recall the argument by Cornman and Lehrer, arguments that could be restated, for our purposes, as follows: God's omniscience and omnipotence implies that he could have created any logically possible world. His omni-benevolence implies that he would choose to design or create the best world he could. His omniscience, omnipotence, and omni-benevolence is a sufficient condition for his creation of the best of all possible worlds. However, the actual world in which we find ourselves is unlikely to be the best of all possible worlds. Hence, God, understood as omnipotent, omniscient, and omni-benevolent, does not likely exist.

The assumption from this contention is simply that the existence of evil, understood as instances of violations of God's will, counts against the contention that this world is the best of all possible worlds. In light of the success of Plantinga's free will defense, we find no reason to suppose that the probabilistic argument succeeds. To be sure, allowing that God created free-willed creatures who often violate his will would be consistent with God's existence. Because of the possibility of choosing to love him or reject him, the notion of free will makes sense.

Plantinga has already exposed the flaw attending the contention that this world is the best one possible. I will, therefore, not restate the argument here because it applies to Lehrer and Cornman's objection irrespective of whether we look at evil as pain or evil as violations of God's will. Consequently, I will look at a different approach somewhat briefly considered in other chapters in this work.

Cornman's and Lehrer's objections believe that this world would be a better world with less evil in it than we already have. The task we are left with is to try to think of ways in which this world could be better. This exercise is difficult, but it is worth a try. Presumably, this world would be better if free creatures always did what was right. This observation seems fundamentally correct. However, if God has left creatures to exercise their freedom, he cannot guarantee, as Plantinga has already argued, that they will freely and always choose to do what is right, at least not in our pre-eschatological life. Their freedom to choose what is right is up to them, not up to God. Moreover, in light of the fact that we all come into this world morally immature and cognitively incapable of apprehending the full nature and beauty of God, I doubt that such a state of affairs could obtain, that is, a state of affairs in which moral creatures freely choose to do what is right.

Perhaps one way to guarantee that the creatures should always freely choose what is right is to argue, contra-Plantinga, that an omnipotent God is capable of creating worlds in which creatures freely choose to do his will always. However, such a state of affairs is impossible to obtain without God preempting the freedom of his creatures. As I have already argued, God's act of designing a creature already predetermined to love him would make the exercise of loving him, on the part of that creature, quite meaningless. A creature already predetermined to love God is no more meaningful than a robot already predetermined to "love" its designer at the flip of a switch.

Think of the situation in this manner: If a brilliant scientist, bereft of spousal love, were to design a robot who in every sense of the word resembled a human being, except that it could not freely love its master unless a certain button is pressed to activate the love, one surely could not admit that the robotic love is meaningful. It would be more meaningful if the love in question came from the robot's free exercise of its will, which of course it does not have. Similarly, those demanding that God ought to design free creatures that he can at the same time determine to love him always are demanding that God ought to design humans with such robotic features, which seems to me a less desirable world. Put differently, a world in which God determines his creatures to always do what is right is, after all, a less desirable state of affairs than one in which God allows creatures to exercise their powers of contrary choice.

In light of these considerations, perhaps we would be wise to revisit an objection considered in an earlier chapter, namely, if God cannot guarantee that his free-willed creatures will always do what is right, we have no reason to suppose that the eschatological promise of eternal righteousness envisioned in the apocalypse would actually obtain. If true, we have no hope of eliminating instances of violations of God's will. However, Christian apocalyptic literature such as the book of Revelation and the book of Daniel seem to indicate that such righteousness will obtain. If true, then clearly God must be the kind of being who will guarantee that his free-willed creatures will always do what is right.

What should we make of this objection? True, Scripture gives the promise of a world in which a state of eternal righteousness will consistently obtain without the possibility of being undermined by evil. Can we possibly uphold such a promise without necessarily contending or at least believing that God cannot guarantee that his free-willed creatures will always do what is right? Does maintaining such vantage points result in a logical contradiction of sorts?

As I have already noted, I do not think we have a contradiction here. Perhaps making the following consideration, espoused by Christian theology, could diffuse the apparent tension. A state of eternal righteousness of the sort promised by Scripture is based on the supposition that God's children will either have experienced some kind of moral transformation or have a cognitive awareness of the seriousness of the consequences of sin, or both. Moreover, they will experience the beauty of God's holiness in that eternal state of redemption. According to Christian theology, it is the sort of beauty never before seen by the eyes of mortal flesh. God's children will realize the moral transformation in question after a lifetime of walking with God. The assumption is that having experienced the joys and spiritual satisfaction that follows from walking in a daily relationship and communion with God, the child of God will freely want to relate with God more and more.

Also, the child of God will develop a cognitive awareness of God's hatred for sin by actually witnessing God's personal dealing with those who reject his free offer of love. They will see the magnitude of God's hatred for sin in a way that will make them realize that though they are free with regard to the choices they make, they are not free with regard to the consequences that follow the choices in question. In other words, God's free-willed creatures are free to make their own moral choices concerning their relationship with God. However, they must also be willing to live with the consequences of those choices.

More importantly, however, they will countenance the beauty of God in its fullest splendor. Since I have dealt with this aspect of God's beauty more fully in my book *Heaven: God's Solution to Human Pain*, let me offer a brief summary of my contention in that book. I contend that the beauty of God's holiness will be maximally attractive to the extent that the redeemed saint will freely choose to embrace it. Violating God's beauty will, therefore, not be an option for the saint, for he or she will freely choose to preserve this beauty with utmost care.

An illustration will help to explain this contention: Assume your most cherished companion sends you a gift that, in your opinion, is extremely precious. Because you cherish your relationship with that cherished companion, you will want to preserve the gift with the utmost care. You will not mishandle it, neither will you subject it to harsh treatments of the sort that could destroy it. Because of your love for your cherished companion, you freely choose to preserve the precious gift bestowed on you. Similarly, because of their love for God's beauty, which they will see in its fullest extent at the end of time, God's children will freely choose to preserve that beauty rather than violate it.

This realization implies the following: In light of the fact that God's redeemed children will experience moral transformation, and in light of the fact that they will be fully aware of the seriousness of sin as well as of its consequences, we reasonably suppose that the promise of an eternal state of sin-free righteousness will be fulfilled. Christian theology, therefore, teaches that God's children will not be determined to do right all the time; rather, it teaches that in light of their experiences of redemption by God from sin as well as of moral transformation through the sanctifying work of the Holy Spirit, we have every good reason to believe that redeemed saints will freely choose to live lives of absolute holiness before their holy God. Moreover, coupled with the fact that God's beauty will be right before their eyes, and that sin's ugliness will appear exactly for what it is, we hold that the promise of eternal righteousness will be fulfilled and sustained eternally among God's children. If this consideration is even remotely a logical possibility, it serves to show the possibility of envisioning a state of affairs to be actualized in the apocalyptic world in which righteousness will be upheld without God having to preempt the freedom of his children by determining them to do right all the time.

This demonstration, of course, results in another objection; namely, if this state of affairs could obtain in a later state of existence, why does God not bring it about in our current state of existence? If God will bring about a world of eternal righteousness in the future, without having to determine his creatures to do what is right always, what keeps him from bringing about such a world in the present state of things? Why has he not put frameworks in place to allow the bringing about of such a world? What do we make of this objection?

This objection, I believe, is easily answered once we consider the factors adumbrated previously. First, we bear in mind what the theologians tell us: Christians in this life are still very much in the process of moral transformation. If so, perhaps we are premature in expecting them to uphold a state of eternal righteousness consistently without violating God's will at some stage in their earthly lives. Stated differently, whereas this state of affairs seems at least initially possible in a logical sense, on an equal basis it cannot be guaranteed to obtain consistently.

Second, the enormity of sin and its abhorrence in the sight of God is something of which Christians are at least theoretically aware. The practical consequences of sin and how it bears on the individual person is yet to be fully realized. Nevertheless, Christians hope that these consequences will be fully realized on the Day of Judgment. Without the believer's experiential awareness of the eternal consequences of sin and its ugliness (either through an understanding of the implications of Christ's death on the cross or through witnessing, directly or indirectly, the punishment of unrepentant sinners), we always have the possibility of the Christian violating God's will at some point in his or her life.

Third, believers are aware of the beauty of God, but only in a practical sense. They are not in a state in which the absolute beauty of God is fully captured by their cognitive faculties. Put differently, they are cognitively ignorant of the glory that attends the sort of divine being about which theologians talk. Thus, things less beautiful, and often sinful, attract them from the beauty of God. As noted, they can only be fully committed to God in the moral sense upon countenancing God's absolute glory and majesty.

We are then led to see that spiritual immaturity in this life, a lack of full awareness of the consequences and ugliness of sin and an epistemic ignorance of the beauty of God sets the believer in a situation in which a consistent Christian life is not fully guaranteed. These three factors, and perhaps a few more not mentioned here, would be the sort of factors that explain why a state of affairs in which believers always and freely choose the good fails to obtain.

Another objection that could be raised against this view is the question of those who die without attaining the requisite spiritual maturity that would somehow enable them always to choose the good. If indeed such individuals die without attaining full spiritual maturity, then we are not guaranteed that such individuals will always choose the good in heaven. Would this objection be an argument against my contention? I have no scriptural answer to this objection. What I can offer at best is a logical possibility that, if true, should render the objection innocuous. However, I do not imply that the response is, in fact, true. Rather, my contention is that the response that follows below is at least logical, and if it is logical, it dulls the force of the objection.

My contention is that this objection is not a forceful one for at least one reason: Even if the requisite spiritual maturity has not been attained on the part of the individual, two factors are still at play. First, the individual in question will at least have at his disposal the history of God's dealing with those who rebelled against him. That is, they will have access to the consequences of sin by merely referring to the history of God's dealing with embracers of sin. Second, they will be cognitively aware of the beauty of God and the ugliness of sin and its consequences. Having both at their disposal, they will not only be able to make comparisons that will enable them to see the rationale behind choosing a life of eternal devotion to God, but they will also be able to find the motivation to choose that very life. Moreover, they will want to choose just that life on the supposition that they will find the beauty of God maximally attractive.

These considerations, therefore, bring us back to where we started. Whereas we can envision a better world in which free-willed creatures always do what is right, certain factors must be taken into consideration before such a world obtains. The question of moral maturity, the seriousness of violating God's will, the ugliness of sin, and the joy of beholding God's beauty must all be set in their proper context. Perhaps no such thing as the best of all possible worlds exists. Lewis suggests that this world is perhaps the only possible one that God could have created.

As Peterson has shown, and as we have already seen in the previous section, the probabilistic argument adumbrated could still be strengthened. Having defined evil as a violation of God's will, the probabilistic argument could be strengthened by admitting, first of all, that God could create an infinite number of logically possible worlds. Among these worlds, one could argue that a good God ought to have created a world bearing a more acceptable ratio between good and instances of violations of God's will. The argument could also press the consideration that God has the power to control the amounts of natural evil without having to override the freedom of moral creatures.

The argument fails for several reasons. First, if we can build a case for the claim that evil is best seen as violations of God's will, which I believe I have done successfully, we have no such thing as natural evil. All instances of evil are moral evil. Plantinga leaves room for the possibility that all evil in this world is broadly moral evil, without necessarily affirming this statement as fact. I, however, make the stronger claim that this statement is in fact the case given that Christian theism is true. If all evil is moral evil such that their occurrences are brought about by the actions of free-willed creatures, the frequency with which instances of violations of God's will occur in this world is more or less what we expect to see. Indeed, that frequency is what we *do* see.

Second, the argument fails to show how the instances of violations of God's will count against the existence of God. We seem to have no reason to believe that sinning individuals—that is, individuals who violate God's will—render God's existence impossible or unlikely. If God has created beings with the capacity to choose him or reject him freely, we should not be surprised that some do choose to reject him when others choose to love him. Indeed, precisely because free will exists do we make an inference to God as the best explanation for the occurrence of free will. Thus, the strengthened probabilistic argument is innocuous as an objection to the existence of God.

The personalist interpretation of the problem of evil fares no better under this reading. I refer here to the reading that views evil as violations of God's will. It runs as follows: the probability of God's existence is very low, with respect to the amount of evil in this world. Under our reading or understanding of evil, we restructure the argument as follows: the probability of God's existence is very low, with respect to the number of violations of God's will in this world. We are not exactly clear what the phrase *very low* denotes. If we were to go by the logic of probability, the phrase could, at most, suggest a likelihood, with respect to God's existence, that is below 50 percent. We are now left to determine whether any objective basis influences our assignment of this figure.

Upon closer examination, we must at once ask the following question: what about the instances of violations of God's will count against the likelihood that God exists? With regard to the frequency with which instances of violations of God's will occur, nothing within that logical framework allows us to arrive at the conclusion that the probability of the existence of God is below 50 percent. Arriving at some sort of objective quantification that will enable the probability theorist to arrive at a definite figure that quantifies the unlikelihood of God's existence is extremely difficult.

The atheistic probability theorist may hinge his or her argument on the consideration that a good God ought to reduce the frequency with which instances of violations of his will occur. This kind of thing, the atheist would argue, is something any person would do if that person's rules are violated. The person in question will step in to bring to an end the number of times his or her laws and rules are flouted. We see this picture played over and over again in our systems of justice. Laws are put in place, for example, to ensure order, with police officers and judges called upon to enforce those laws. However, with God the situation seems different because God does not seem to be stepping in to stop his free-willed creatures from violating his rules. He does not seem to step in, for example, to stop rapists or pedophiles from committing the sorts of crimes attributed to them. If he truly exists, we should have decisive indications that he is doing something to stop the frequent injustices as well as instances in which his will is being violated. However, he does not. For this reason, we are led to suspect that he does not exist.

This sort of argument would perhaps lead the atheologian to present the personalist interpretation of the problem of evil. We are then left to wonder whether this presentation of the problem of evil is correct. Several things need to be said about this argument. First, if God should step in to curb every instance of evil in the manner demanded by the atheist, quite likely not one of his free-willed creatures would be spared from his punitive wrath because, as the theologians remind us, we are all guilty of violating his will. The objection is often raised under the erroneous assumption that the objector is perhaps more righteous than the rapist. The fact of the matter is, we are all guilty before God—a fact powerfully illustrated by Lewis' *Mere Christianity* and by the powerful doctrines of Scripture. Hence, to insist that God should step in every time his free-willed creatures violate his will is a demand that, if met, would not spare anyone, including the objector.

If my argument above is correct, it should lead to the next consideration, namely, the fact that God chooses to remain apparently passive in cases where his will is violated is in itself an act of mercy on his part. By such passivity, we can fairly say that God is giving his rebellious, free-willed creatures a chance to take advantage of the opportunities for moral reformation that he places before those very creatures. Needless to say, this apparent passivity on God's part will have to imply at some point that violators of his will, such as rapists and psychopaths, could go unpunished, much to the dismay of their victims, who will rightfully demand that their molesters be apprehended and justly punished. Sometimes they do get punished, and sometimes they do not. However, the fact that God is seemingly passive still gives them time to repent even under such circumstances.

This consideration leads us to the third response to the objection. God's apparent passivity in the manner stipulated is no reason to suggest that he is indifferent to those who violate his will. Drawing once again from the dictates of Christian theology, we read of a promise from Scripture that every course of action that has been followed in violation of God's will and intentions will be judged and punished, unless of course the person has expressed remorse and repentance over those actions and has decided to follow a path of spiritual reformation that yields in total devotion to the Lordship of Jesus Christ. Hence, just because God is seemingly doing nothing about the sins of his free-willed creatures in the present is no indication that he is doing nothing at all, neither is it an indication that he will not do anything at all. In light of the fact that he is giving violators of his will the opportunity to repent of their deeds, and in light of the fact that he will eventually punish all acts of rebellion against his will, we have reason to believe that on the assumption that theism is true, God is doing something about the evils in this world—evil understood as violations of God's will. In light of these considerations, the concern of the personalist interpretation of the problem of evil is innocuous.

I believe that this third response to the objection I cited also answers, to some considerable extent, the concern I alluded to in the third chapter, namely, that if pain is not synonymous with evil and pleasure is not synonymous with good, then the problem of evil is perhaps located by raising the complaint that God appears passive and unconcerned about his children's suffering. In other words, he does not seem to be doing anything to stop the instances of pain that his children are undergoing. This contention would imply that God is morally at fault in maintaining this passive state. Notice that this objection applies to both cases with which we are dealing, that is, it applies to both pain and evil irrespective of whether we are discussing the problem of pain or the problem of evil.

However, my consideration appears to answer this objection sufficiently. In spite of the fact that God may seem to be as passive as initially thought, he is not passive with regard to his children's suffering. The frameworks he has set in place to deal with the pains and evils in this world are such that he must give his children time to experience the requisite character and moral reformation before he finally steps in to bring an end to those instances in which his will is violated.

The final version of the problem of evil to which I would like to draw the reader's attention is an obscure version, raised by Dostoyevsky's book, *The Brothers Karamazov*. Once again, I did draw attention, in the third chapter, to this version of the problem. The version could be stated as follows: If you were God and could foresee that the world you are about to create will be the sort of world in which at least one innocent child will be violently molested by some rapist, would you create such a world? The challenge, of course, appeals to the humane aspect of our personality. When this question was raised in the dialogue between Alyosha and Ivan Karamazov, it was supposed to be a rhetorical question, one whose answer was supposed to be entirely obvious. Of course, Alyosha expected Ivan to answer in the negative. How could your humaneness allow anyone to put in place frameworks that would bring about the torture of innocent children? A good God would not allow this kind of situation to happen.

This objection is indeed very difficult to answer. It definitely merits a whole chapter, which is the subject of the next chapter. It is the question of innocent suffering. However, several things need to be said about this objection. First, it seems to contend that God is morally at fault in allowing such a state of affairs to obtain in a world that he has designed. Second, it seems to contend that God has absolutely no reason to create a world in which innocent children suffer. I believe Hasker has provided a sufficient response to the atheologian vexed by this perplexing occurrence. In addition to Hasker's contention, I would like to offer some thoughts worth considering when the atheist raises this objection. What are some of the most promising ways to answer this very difficult objection?

First, we will see that we are not exactly justified in believing or even contending that God has absolutely no reasons for bringing about a world in which innocent children suffer. Second, I will contend that the atheist has no justification required to raise this question at all, and that his question self-destructs before it takes off the ground. Third, I will show that an individual already willing to accept the claim that God exists can only properly raise this question. In other words, only under theistic presuppositions does the raising of such a question actually makes sense. If these considerations have any merit at all, we could suggest that the objection has been sufficiently met.

However, I am quick to point out the following warning: The fact that this objection can be met does very little to comfort an individual undergoing periods of excruciating pain. The person in question needs some kind of psychological healing, or as Plantinga describes it, some pastoral care. A philosophical attempt at answering the sufferer's questions will quite likely be taken by the victim as somewhat offensive. Moreover, we often (though not always) fail to think logically under instances of intense physical pain. However, an answer can still be given in a manner that should strike the honest seeker of truth as intellectually satisfying. Arriving at this answer is what I try to accomplish in the next chapter.

In the meantime, the upshot of this consideration is merely that if we distinguish the problem of evil from the problem of pain, clearly both of them need different responses. Moreover, the distinctions allow us to present more focused responses to both cases in a way that deals with the enormity that thinkers usually find in them. Finally, we discover that when separated in this way, both pain and evil can receive a separate treatment in a manner that should sound intellectually satisfying to the believer. The problem of pain, in its different aspects, fails to cast doubt on belief in the existence of God. Similarly, the problem of evil, even when considered in its different versions, fails to cast doubt on belief in God's existence. Of course, this conclusion sounds somewhat premature in light of the fact that we have not quite responded to the last objection. We now have the opportunity to consider the question of pointless suffering in the next chapter, to which I now turn.

9

The Why Question

In a highly, though perhaps unintentionally, provocative article entitled "The Evidential Argument from Evil," William Rowe draws our attention to the fact and reality of intense human suffering, with a view to showing that the existence of specific instances of pointless suffering leaves us to conclude that God does not exist. Rowe notes that instances of intense human and animal suffering occur daily and plentifully, and these are clear cases of evil. He admits, however, that the existence of these instances of suffering would be justified if their occurrences bring about instances of greater good, which would otherwise not occur.[1] Rowe contends that instances of intense suffering exist, sufferings of the sort that God could have prevented without losing some greater good thereby, or allowing the occurrence of equally intense or worse instances of suffering. Hence, since God would prevent intense suffering of this sort unless doing so would result in losing some greater good or permitting worse occurrence of evil, Rowe concludes that God does not exist.[2]

A good example of pointless suffering could be illustrated as follows. Suppose lightning strikes a dead tree, which then results in a forest fire. A fawn gets trapped in the fire, is horribly burned, and lies in terrible agony for several days before death relieves it of its agony. According to Rowe, the fawn's suffering seems pointless. For one, it does not appear to bring about any instance of a greater good. Neither does its suffering prevent an equally intense or worse instance of intense suffering. Even theists, Rowe observes, would claim that God could have prevented this kind of suffering.[3]

Even if we cannot prove (Rowe does not think we can) that the first premise of this argument is true—that instances of intense suffering exist,

---

1. Rowe, "Evidential Argument from Evil," 325.
2. Ibid.
3. Ibid.

which God could have prevented without losing some greater good in the process or allowing the occurrence of equally intense (or more intense) instances of suffering—at least we have rational grounds for believing that the premise itself is true because in light of our experience or knowledge we rationally believe that a certain claim is true. Hence, we reasonably believe that the premise in question is true. For example, all instances of intense suffering are unlikely related to a greater good or to the prevention of an equally intense, or worse, form of suffering.[4]

A very forceful critique of Rowe comes once again from Plantinga. A summary of his argument against Rowe's challenge would be in order here. According to Plantinga,[5] Rowe seems to argue as follows:

1. We know of no good of the sort that warrants God, a perfect being, in allowing evils such as the rape and murder of a five-year-old girl (call this E1) or the painful death of a fawn in a forest fire (call this E2).
2. Therefore, no good exists that justifies God in permitting E1 and E2.
3. Therefore, God does not exist (call this not-G).
4. Only an actual good could warrant God in allowing E1 and E2.
5. However, we know of no actual *good* sufficient to justify a perfect being in permitting E1 and E2.

According to Plantinga, the main problem with the argument lies in the inference from 1 to 2. He offers a counterexample to reveal what he believes (rightly, I think) are flawed assumptions behind Rowe's line of argument. Although I cited this counterexample in chapter 3, it is worth repeating here. Suppose I fail to see a St. Bernard inside my tent while looking for it there. I could reasonably conclude, in this case, that no St. Bernard is inside the tent, for a St. Bernard has difficulty avoiding detection inside a small tent, assuming that my cognitive faculties are functioning properly. Suppose, however, I look inside my tent and fail to see *noseeums*. Concluding that *noseeums* have not inhabited my tent would, perhaps, be erroneous; for even if they were inside my tent, I would be unable to see them, owing to their smallness.[6]

Plantinga then asks us to consider whether God's reasons, if any, for permitting E_1 and E_2 are more like St. Bernards or more like *noseeums*. Suppose God has a reason for permitting evils such as E_1 and E_2, and assume we try to determine what the reason in question might be. We are not likely,

---

4. Ibid.
5. Plantinga, *Warranted Christian Belief,* 465–69.
6. Ibid., 466.

Plantinga thinks, to come up with the right answer. Even if God has such reasons, we are perhaps not justified in believing that we should be the first to know of them. Moreover, in light of our considerable cognitive and, for that matter, epistemic limitations, we ought not to be surprised that his reasons for some of his actions completely escape us. Hence, suppose no good we know of justifies God in allowing E_1 and E_2. This fact alone does not guarantee that such good, with respect to what we do know, does not exist, or that God has no reason for permitting E_1 and E_2.[7]

Plantinga considers other arguments against the existence of God in light of the facts of evil. Since Plantinga has dealt with those arguments at length and quite adeptly, I have no reason to regurgitate his rebuttals here. The reason I draw attention to Rowe's argument is specifically because his argument zeroes in on the thorny issue of pointless suffering. Plantinga thinks there might just be a reason for what we are led to think is an instance of pointless suffering even if we are hard-placed to find that reason.

On the contrary, Swinburne believes he can find a possible reason. In his attempt to respond to this challenge, he appeals to possible lessons that humans tend to learn from instances of tragedy, which would otherwise be deemed pointless. He asks us, for example, to imagine a state of affairs in which a loved one gets killed in a horrific automobile accident. Swinburne would argue that taken in isolation, the accident would, from our perspective, appear pointless. In the overall scheme of things pertinent to the accident's immediate context, though, the event itself has the potential of inspiring some kind of resolution among concerned citizens and activists. They would aim, for example, to champion the enactment of bills that would forestall possible occurrences of future accidents. In such a case, relatives of past accident victims would see that the death of their loved one was not in vain. The case in question spurs the authorities concerned to make the immediate context of their world a safer place to live in. That is, without the kind of tragedy that befalls them, those concerned would possibly ignore calls to follow beneficial courses of action. In the absence of tragic instances of this kind, no one would be aware of the need for preventative measures.[8]

In Swinburne's view, something similar to this consideration can reasonably apply to Rowe's example of the fawn caught in a forest fire. Suppose relatives of the accident victim find it a blessing that their tragedy opened up the possibility for someone else to benefit from the corrective measures designed to forestall the possible occurrence of future tragedies. We can see with equal plausibility how the death of the fawn in question provides

---

7. Ibid., 466–67.

8. Swinburne, *Providence and the Problem of Evil*, 103.

empirical knowledge for other sentient creatures in similar situations. Those creatures will discover, from that experience, the importance of not only staying away from the fire by migrating to safer grounds, but also of preventing their young ones from burning. By making this contention, Swinburne would thus argue that the kind of intense suffering that might appear pointless to us does in fact have a point. Logically, therefore, the fawn's death was not in vain. Some lesson was learned by its occurrence.[9]

Plantinga and Swinburne are essentially correct when they contend that even in cases of suffering that might seem horrendous to us, reasons for those instances of suffering are possibly available. However, as we will see, Marilyn Adams will contend that in many cases those available reasons will still be inaccessible to us. Of course, the fact that those reasons are available does very little to ease the suffering of the victim. As we shall see later, the suffering victim needs more than mere reasons; the victim desires some kind of relief and healing, and this no longer falls in the realm of philosophy. Merely noting, at this point, that reasons are available for what might appear to be instances of horrendous suffering seems enough for our purposes.

Coming back to Rowe, I wish to redirect the reader's attention to the now familiar theme of this book. Rowe seems to make the materialistic mistake, in my view, of equivocating evil with pain. Plantinga's response does not draw this distinction either, for obvious reasons. He is responding to Rowe on Rowe's own terms. To be sure, he does not draw this distinction when he responds to other materialists, besides Rowe, who try to cast doubt on the existence of God using the facts of evil as evidence.

Moreover, Rowe seems to make one more mistake. He thinks that pointless evil exists. He believes, for example, that the death of a fawn in a forest fire is quite likely a good case of pointless suffering, sufficient to cast doubt on the existence of God. In light of this contention by Rowe, we must pause to ask what might very well be considered an existential question: Is the atheist even rationally justified in trying to determine why pointless suffering exists?

More specifically, when dealing with the reality and facts of pain, are we intellectually justified to ask the *why* question (also referred to as Q_w in this chapter) on the presupposition that atheism is true? By Q_w, I refer to the sort of question that looks for reasons or explanations for the occurrence of a specific instance of suffering. For example, we might be compelled to ask why innocent children died pointlessly during the Holocaust or why some innocent child died of cancer at some specific point in time or why,

---

9. Ibid.

following Rowe, a fawn died in a forest fire. Humans seem naturally inclined to ask such questions.

Asking a question of this sort on a theistic reading of the universe seems to make existential sense. In other words, in order for the question to be meaningful at all, the questioner must ask it within a framework that presupposes the existence of God. What is not clear from materialistic naturalists is whether Q_w could be legitimately posed on a naturalistic reading of the universe. By a theistic reading of the universe, I refer to a worldview that sees the universe as the product or work of a divine supernatural being, properly called God. By a naturalistic-cum-atheistic reading, I refer to just the opposite, namely, one that not only denies that God created this universe but also denies that such a being exists.

Thus, on a theistic reading, for example, one might seek explanations—supposedly from the Bible, theology, or more accurately, from God—for a certain occurrence of what one takes to be some form or version of pointless suffering. Under such circumstances, the sufferer feels entitled to know the reasons for his or her pain, and even if the answer may not eventually be forthcoming, at least the sufferer knows and feels, or thinks he knows and feels, that someone, namely God, does have the answer.

This sense of entitlement implies that the sufferer assumes a being exists, a being that he thinks could be blamed, or one against whom an honest protest could be launched for allowing a given instance of pointless suffering to occur. The protest is honest because the sufferer feels some kind of entitlement to an answer for why he or she is suffering. It is not a protest that registers disbelief in God, neither is it one that complains against God. Rather, it is a protest that simply wonders why God permits or even inflicts the kind of suffering now faced by the believer in him; it is a protest that seeks an explanation for the suffering in question.

In such an instance, at least the sufferer experiences a degree of existential satisfaction in assigning blame to an entity that, in the sufferer's opinion, ought not to have allowed the instance of pointless suffering. The sufferer then feels justified in waiting for an explanation for why he or she suffers. In fact, the sufferer must feel the need for an explanation for the obvious reason that pain and suffering are indeed obstacles to Christian belief. However, as Plantinga notes, the fact that there are serious obstacles to Christian belief does not in any way imply that they undercut Christian belief at all. One can still find obstacles to Christian belief without necessarily holding that the belief in question is false.

For example, in the Old Testament we find countless examples of pain and suffering that fit this very picture. Job is a case in point. His pain and suffering did present some obstacles to the extent that he could not square them with his beliefs about God or what he thought he knew about God's manner of interactions with human beings. Still, he did not doubt the existence of God. In the New Testament we read of Jesus' famous question, "My God, my God, why have you forsaken me?"[10] Many others have found themselves angry with God in the grip of their own pain or the pain of people close to them.[11]

Plantinga argues that in such cases one can become resentful, mistrusting, antagonistic, and hostile. However, even in these biblical cases, we do not find them thinking that they have established evidence that would undercut belief in God. Hence, Jesus and Job, or even the psalmist, are not tempted to abandon their belief in God. To be sure, they face a problem of a different order. The problem is a pastoral one rather than a philosophical one, of whether, in their opinion, God can be trusted with their lives.[12]

Of course, wondering whether Jesus doubted his Father's purposes as he hung on that cross would be odd. What we can say with certainty is that Jesus did not like his experience on that cross—the experience of having to bear the sins of the world and having to see his own Father turn his back on him. As noted in chapter 1, this repugnance for his experience is evidenced by his agony in the Garden of Gethsemane.

With Job, the Psalmist, Jeremiah, and Habakkuk, though, the question of trust comes into play quite reasonably. Could God, whose existence was not an issue to them, be trusted in the midst of the suffering they witnessed either in their own lives or in the lives of those to whom they ministered? That was the question with which they wrestled. Nevertheless, for all of them, including Jesus, we can safely say that they loathed the instances of pain and suffering in which they found themselves, and they felt the need for some remedial action on God's part.

Suppose, therefore, that we experience an instance of pain or suffering. Perhaps a close friend or significant family member dies of some dreadfully painful disease. According to Plantinga, we might find ourselves reasoning as follows: God is doubtlessly in possession of those great attributes theologians tell us about. Moreover, we do not doubt that God has excellent reasons for allowing a brother or sister or father or mother to die of this dreadful disease. In fact, Pantinga continues, we cannot come up with better reasons, for his reasons are easily and utterly beyond us. However, what he has permitted is appalling, and we find it unreservedly loathsome. In fact, we wish we could meet him face to face so that we could tell him exactly

---

10. Matt 27:46
11. Plantinga, *Warranted Christian Belief*, 482.
12. Ibid., 482–83.

how we feel. According to Plantinga, a problem of this kind is not really an evidential problem. In other words, it would not be the kind that would lead us to call God's existence into question.[13]

Let me now underscore a point I made earlier. The sufferer feels the need to know why he or she suffers as she does. In a sense, the sufferer needs to know who is to blame for his or her pain. Moreover, when blame is assigned, the sufferer hopes that the recipient of the blame is capable of understanding the seriousness of the pain in question. Merely assigning the blame to the blind forces of nature does no good. The blind forces of nature do not understand the seriousness of the pain experienced by the victim in question; or, simply put, the blind forces of nature have no understanding of any kind.

When we assign blame in this way to the so-called blind forces of nature, we do so because we feel short-changed by something. We do so because we feel something is wrong. In spite of these feelings, the materialistic atheist has nothing to appeal to for an answer even though he or she somehow senses an inner urge to launch just such an appeal. This inner urge is unavoidable because it is part of human nature that desires to be satisfied.

Logically speaking, the atheist should not raise this question in light of his atheistic vantage point. In other words, for the atheist, his or her belief that *that* blind force of nature is insentient gives no justification to posit Q_w, for Q_w is posited on the assumption that the one who permits or brings about one's suffering understands the gravity of one's pain. The atheist would thus be intellectually content with leaving the question unanswered.

Existentially speaking, however, the atheist finds him- or herself naturally wired to ask this very question. The question arises irrespective of whether one is a believer in God or not. What we are forced to wrestle with as human beings is whether our answers to Q_w are big enough to fill that void created by the urge. If we present the blind forces of nature as an answer to Q_w we discover that it fails, in a very existential way, to quench the feeling of being short-changed.

Logically speaking, then, the atheist might have a well-articulated answer. Existentially speaking, however, he or she feels the void created by urges left unmet. Herein lies the struggle the sophisticated unbeliever lives through when faced with a specific instance of pointless suffering. I dare say that herein lies the source of the bigger question on the meaning of life. Alas, no answer would of course be forthcoming for the naturalist.

Even if Charles Darwin, for example, made it possible for Richard Dawkins to be an intellectually fulfilled atheist, it is possible that an existential void remains in both of them, for not even the theory of natural

---

13. Ibid., 483.

selection can fill that void. It would be pointless to question natural selection for bringing about certain painful states of affairs, since natural selection, whatever it is, bears no answer to existential struggles of this sort.

On the contrary, to posit God both as the answer to and the filler of the void created by this inner urge is an existentially formidable view because in many ways the seeker gets some hope that the suffering he or she countenances will find a satisfactory explanation from a being that has access to reasons for what, otherwise, seems pointless.

For the theistic sufferer, then, God's nonexistence would signify the absence of meaning in suffering, which is admittedly very tragic, for in such a case, he or she would have no existential satisfaction in knowing that an answer to Q_w is available. The theist would have no one toward whom to launch a protest. However, if God does exist, the theist thinks he or she knows that his or her protest against the occurrence of pain, at the very least, has been understood by God. Moreover, he or she draws comfort from the hope, crystallized by faith, that God will make things right in the long run. Q_w, then, seems to make sense given the acceptance of such a worldview. More accurately, on a theistic reading of the universe, Q_w seems to command intellectual legitimacy.

However, suppose one adopts an atheistic reading of the universe. We might legitimately wonder whether the atheist is justified in posing Q_w in the manner I've adumbrated. In other words, does posing Q_w with respect to suffering have any intellectual legitimacy in a worldview that rules out any possibility that God exists? Although tempting for the atheist to ask the question, I shall argue that he or she is not justified to do so, and here's why.

Q_w is the sort of question one asks precisely because the questioner, as previously noted, feels entitled to an answer. If the answerer is nonexistent, or is supposed not to exist, as the atheist would have us believe, posing Q_w is pointless. For an individual p to ask another individual q for reasons why q allows a certain event to occur when p believes that q does not exist seems quite absurd. In other words, since the naturalistic atheist already adopts a worldview that rules out the existence of the very being he or she is willing to blame for the occurrence of a specific instance of what he thinks is pointless suffering, he or she is not entitled to an answer to Q_w because, given the atheistic worldview, the being capable of holding the answer to Q_w is the very being the atheist believes does not exist. One cannot expect a nonexistent being to provide answers for any question, let alone Q_w. Perhaps the atheist's demand for an answer to Q_w from the very being whose existence he denies is self-defeating. I therefore establish the following:

1. If a certain subject S believes that some cause C does not exist, then S is not intellectually justified to blame C for bringing about a certain event E.

2. A certain subject S does indeed believe that some cause C does not exist.

3. Hence, S is not intellectually justified to blame C for bringing about a certain event E.

This argument is indeed valid. The premises give us reasons to believe the conclusion. What we might question is its soundness. In other words, even if the premises do seem to guarantee the conclusion, are we entitled to believe that the premises themselves are true? Do we have reasons, for example, to believe that the antecedent of the first premise entails its consequent? That this belief is well-justified is, I think, intuitive. This point can be quite easily established.

To see this point, let me begin with an illustration. Imagine you are a professor taking your regular roll call with the goal of updating your class attendance. On the first day of class you announce you will be updating your students' attendance records on a daily basis. Most professors under such circumstances normally place check marks against names of students already in attendance. In this way, if you are some such professor, you are able to take note of students already present as well as those not in attendance.

Let us now assume you decide to use a different method of attendance-taking. Instead of calling out names, you formulate a requirement of an awkward sort. On your first day of class, you require, for example, that all the *absent* students register their absence by speaking out in class. Hence, you announce: "Would all the absent students please speak up so I can record your absence?" Or perhaps you say, "Would all the missing students please write the word 'absent' against your name?" While the question sounds grammatically correct, it is awkward. Of course the absent students would not know of such a requirement at the time of its stipulation. Moreover, the students already in attendance would rightly point out the absurdity of the question, or at the very least refuse to take you seriously. More worrisome is the possibility that they might question your sanity. They would rather not sit in a class conducted by professors with odd requirements or even attend a school that hires them.

For the sake of argument, then, let us adopt the naturalistic worldview, a worldview that rules out the possibility of the existence of God by contending that material physical nature is all that exists. Let us then assume that under this worldview, the atheist is confronted by an instance of suffering he believes is pointless. Perhaps, following Rowe's example, he sees a fawn perishing in a forest fire, and nothing in the vicinity gives any indication that the fawn's death has some purpose to it. Or perhaps the atheist knows of an instance where a cat pounces on an innocent rat, digs its claws into the poor rodent's back repeatedly, solely for its amusement.[14] The atheist then begins to wonder, if God exists, why would he allow the occurrence of pointless suffering of this sort. He then, validly (but unsoundly, as I will show), argues that God would not allow the occurrence of pointless suffering in this way. Hence, he concludes, God does not exist.

Having tried to rule out God's existence via logic, he is still faced with Q_w. He finds himself wondering why such instances of suffering happen. He does know the *how* part of it. He can explain, for example, that with regard to the fawn perishing in a forest fire, the fire itself was caused by a thunderstorm that ignited one of the dried up trees, and because the trees had flammable leaves, they quickly burst into flames that not only consumed them, but everything else housed by the twigs and branches. What he fails to explain, though, is the *why* part of it. He, therefore, believes he must pose Q_w. However, he has ruled out the very existence of the one who could not only provide the basis for asking the question but also provide the answer for the question itself. Hence, once he begins to pose Q_w, in a manner similar to the professor demanding that his absent students speak up to register their absence, the unbelieving thinker makes an interesting but absurd demand. The only person who could answer Q_w has already been ruled out from his worldview. We are now ready to make a more pointed argument as follows:

1. If a subject S believes that God does not exist, then S is not intellectually justified to blame God for allowing what he thinks are instances of pointless suffering, call them P, to occur.

2. A certain subject S believes that God does not exist.

3. Hence, the atheist is not intellectually justified to blame God for allowing P to occur.

As with the first argument, this argument seems to me both valid and sound. To ask the *why* question when the one to provide the solution is absent seems to border on the absurdity as previously illustrated. Seeking answers to questions of this kind when the source of the answer is deemed absent or his existence is ruled out is absurd.

This argument might be pushed a little further. The naturalistic atheist has already ruled that the instance of suffering in question is itself pointless.

---

14. For similar examples, see Puccetti, "Loving God," 231.

In other words, it is the kind of suffering he or she would consider as serving no major goal or overall purpose. It is perhaps a random instance of suffering, or perhaps it is an instance of suffering brought about by what Richard Dawkins would call the blind forces of nature.[15] The atheist is, in fact, more than willing to admit that such instances of suffering and pain abound. As we have seen, precisely because of such instances of suffering, they are willing to rule out the existence of God, for they believe that such kinds of pain could not be permitted by a good, loving, and all-powerful God. Therefore, in their view, the pointlessness of some kinds of suffering makes God's existence implausible.

If indeed such instances of suffering are pointless, I would contend that posing Q_w would be extremely odd, if not downright irrational, with regard to pointless suffering. In other words, admitting on the one hand that a given instance of suffering is pointless, while on the other, feeling compelled to pose Q_w with regard to the existence of the supposed instance of pointless suffering would be extremely anomalous. More accurately, the person would be asking the question, "Since pointless suffering exists, what is the point of its existence?" On any reading of the universe, whether atheistic or theistic, the question is meaningless. If the suffering is pointless, asking for its point makes no sense. More accurately, the question is self-defeating, irrespective of how grammatically correct it might present itself. One might as well be asking for the shape of a shapeless entity, or for the dimensions of a dimensionless entity, or, more distressingly, for the materiality of an immaterial object. Logically construed, such a statement might run as follows:

1. A subject S seeks the point of some pointless entity.
2. S therefore assumes that an entity E exists that has a point P, and also does not have P, where P of the first conjunct is identical to P of the second conjunct.
3. To seek the point of pointless suffering is to believe that pointless suffering should both have and not have the property P simultaneously.

Hence, if the subject in question contends in a manner captured by claim 1, claims 2 and 3 should be seen to follow. If all these instances sound absurd, an atheist positing Q_w with regard to an instance of pointless suffering presupposes an absurdity of sorts because Q_w seeks to find the point of a given instance of suffering. If so, by asking just this very question with regard to pointless suffering, the atheist is not being intellectually honest with himself or herself, and of course with his or her hearers as well. To

---

15. Dawkins, *Blind Watchmaker*, 5.

admit that the instance of suffering is pointless is to admit that Q_w cannot be legitimately asked of that instance of suffering. All the aforesaid should be sufficient to show that posing Q_w with respect to pointless suffering on an atheistic reading is a self-defeating disposition.

Let me now raise the following consideration. Q_w points to an issue that belongs to the bigger question concerned with the meaning of life. Many theistic philosophers hold that the meaning of life turns out to be a legitimate question only when we are willing to admit a theistic worldview.[16] Outside this worldview, the intellectual rights for such a question begin to fall apart. Hence, theists would contend that without the existence of God, we would never know whether or not life has meaning. In other words, the question would not even be legitimately raised. To question the meaningfulness of all of life from a God-denying perspective is to run the risk of adopting a self-defeating vantage point, for one is casting doubts on the meaningfulness of the universe, of which that question is a part. Second, one must presuppose that the question, which is itself a part of life, is meaningful before one begins to cast doubts on life's meaningfulness. Hence, to try to show that all of life is meaningless by questioning the meaningfulness of life, one already presupposes that the question one asks is already meaningful. If the question is itself meaningful, then all of life cannot be meaningless.

As Lewis reminds us, if life did not have any meaning, we would never know that it did not have any meaning.[17] To avoid this self-stultification, we must tread on grounds considered intellectually safe. Theism suggests that every event that occurs in the universe must occur under God's jurisdiction. Put differently, no event occurs without God's notice. Whereas some events do occur without God causing them, they nonetheless fail to surprise God, given his omniscience. Theism therefore holds that God can and does order the occurrence of all events to the fulfillment of his purposes, whether or not those purposes are cognitively accessible to us.

An atheist would conceivably object to this argument by admitting that he or she does not, in any way, seek the point of pointless suffering and would therefore claim, for example, that given the atheistic worldview, he or she does not see the intellectual justification for posing Q_w with respect to pointless suffering. On the contrary, the believer in God really raises Q_w and tries to look for answers to satisfy Q_w. However, an atheist feels perfectly satisfied subscribing to a worldview that, having admitted pointless suffering exists, sees no need for raising Q_w. Just the same, if God exists as claimed

---

16. Philosophers such as Michael Martin believe (erroneously, I suppose) that one can find meaning in our universe even if God does not exist.

17. Lewis, *Mere Christianity*, 46.

by the theists, then the onus is on the theists themselves to explain why God allows the occurrence of what seems to be pointless suffering. In light of this picture, let me revisit an argument by the atheist, which I adumbrated earlier. The atheist could be seen to argue as follows:

1. If God exists, he would not allow instances of pointless suffering to occur.
2. Clearly, however, instances of pointless suffering do occur.
3. Hence, God does not exist.

Whereas this argument may seem valid, the theist need not buy it. The theist could admit that premise 1 is in fact correct. However, he or she could respond to the objection by contending, as already noted, that the naturalistic-cum-materialistic atheist mistakenly believes that pointless suffering exists. The theist, for example, could attack the second premise, which contends that God allows instances of pointless suffering to occur. In light of the theistic contention or worldview, the theist has no reason to concede that pointless suffering occurs. A given instance of suffering appearing pointless from our perspective in no way proves without question that the suffering is objectively pointless. From the dictates of Scripture, the theist believes that God orders all events, those caused by him as well as those caused by his free-willed creatures, to the fulfillment and completion of his purposes. The theist, therefore, need not buy into the atheistic worldview contending that some instances of suffering are pointless. From the theistic perspective, then, the second premise is false. Hence, the entire argument is unsound.

Marilyn Adams takes us deeper into this view. According to Adams, arguing that Christianity is false because God's existence is incompatible with a world like ours is not helpful, especially when the atheist erroneously views God as a pleasure-maximizer. Christians never believed that God was a pleasure-maximizer in the first place. Similarly, in her view, showing that God could coexist with some kinds of evil, such as those, for example, caused by the misuse of free will, is not enough. A full account must show the compatibility of divine perfection with evils in our world. Adams believes this demonstration is necessary because the internal coherence of Christianity is at stake. Hence, a successful argument for its consistency must draw from premises internal to Christianity, premises obviously acceptable to its adherents.[18]

---

18. See Marilyn Adams' view in "Horrendous Evils and the Goodness of God," 334–37.

Adams contends that standard strategies for dealing or solving the problem of evil are powerless in the face of horrendous evils. For one, God cannot be said to be good or loving to individuals within whose lives horrendous evils remain undefeated. Adams uses the phrase "horrendous evils" almost synonymously with pointless evil, for she describes it as the suffering that gives a person *prima facie* reason to doubt whether that person's life could be a great good to that person on the whole.

Adams then asks us to suppose, for the sake of argument, that horrendous evils occur in what Leibniz called the best of all possible worlds. This understanding would not be helpful to a truck driver who accidentally runs over his beloved child. The truck driver has no consolation in knowing that the accident in question was indeed the price that God had to pay in order to create a world with the best balance of moral good over moral evil. Neither would this thought prevent an infant born in a cannibalistic culture from wishing that it had never been born.[19]

What, then, are motivating reasons for one to believe in God in light of the facts of pain and suffering? According to Adams, we are still able to think of reasons to believe in a God who fails to give us a life that is a good to us—one who permits us to suffer horrendous evils. Such motivating reasons come in several varieties. First, we have reasons that we can readily understand when we are informed about them. For example, we can understand why a mother would permit her child to undergo painful heart surgery. We understand this example because the surgery is the only humanly possible way to save the life of the child. Adams is not clear whether the child is also thought to understand this reason. My impression is that the child may or may not understand, depending on its age.

Second, we would be able to grasp reasons cognitively, emotionally, and spiritually if only our memories were larger and our attention span wider. For example, I can memorize the street plans of a small town. This capacity is not beyond the realm of possibilities. However, I may not memorize the road networks of the whole country, for such is a task requiring relatively larger memory and wider attention span. According to Adams, some of God's reasons for permitting some instances of pain may be such that our understanding of them would require more sophisticated cognitive abilities on our part in order to grasp them.[20]

Third, a much higher level of reasons exist than the previous two. We find ourselves too immature—cognitively, spiritually, and emotionally—to understand. For example, consider a two-year-old's inability to understand

19. Ibid., 336.
20. Ibid., 337.

its mother's reasons for allowing it to undergo heart surgery. Adams is in agreement with Plantinga when she notes that our ignorance of God's reasons for allowing horrendous evils are more of the third type than of the first two types. The assumption here is that God does indeed have reasons for allowing horrendous evils to happen, but those reasons are simply inaccessible to us. We would not understand them even if we tried.

In addition to the question of motivating reasons, Adams leads us to consider the notion of assurance. Take the example of the two-year-old again. In spite of undergoing excruciating heart surgery, the two-year-old is still reassured, in some vivid way, of its mother's love. She draws this love, indeed experiences it, from the direct care and presence of its mother throughout its painful experience. The story of Job suggests something similar with respect to what the atheist would consider painful suffering. God does not exactly give Job his reasons for allowing Job to suffer. However, he does imply that Job would not understand those reasons even if they were made available to him. Notice also that just like the two-year-old is assured of its mother's presence and love, Job receives instructions on the nature and extent of God's power. At this point, Job sees God's goodness face to face. In other words, he experiences God's love and power in the midst of his suffering.

Plantinga seems to focus on this very issue as well. He contends that a person whose cognitive faculties and processes are functioning properly, that is, in the manner in which those faculties were meant to function, would have an intimate knowledge of God that is also vivid, detailed, and explicit. The person would have an intense awareness of God's presence, glory, goodness, power, perfection, wonderful attractiveness, and sweetness. The person would be as convinced of God's existence in much the same way that he or she is convinced of his or her own existence. Hence, confronted with pain and suffering, the person might ask why God permits it. But finding no answer, the person will not doubt God's existence; rather, he or she will conclude that God has a reason that is beyond his or her ken.[21]

From a Christian viewpoint, both Adams and Plantinga seem quite right in this regard, unless, of course, contrary evidence within Christianity can be adduced to challenge their view. The problem for suffering Christians is not whether or not God exists. That question is already settled for them. What Christians try to deal with is the attempt to understand why God would allow them to suffer in the manner so experienced. Christians understand that reasons could be made available in the immediate future. But Christians also understand that even if such reasons are made available, they may not be cognitively mature enough to grasp them. At this level, they

---

21. Plantinga, *Warranted Christian Belief*, 485.

choose to maintain their trust in God even in the absence of such reasons, for they are already buttressed in their assurance of God's love for them from other quarters. Moreover, they believe that in the final analysis, when they will attain a level of spiritual maturity to understand the reasons, God himself will take the initiative to present the reasons to them.

Adams' reasoning here seems quite plausible. Moreover, together with Plantinga and Swinburne, she gives a powerful voice to respond to unbelievers who call God's existence to question via this avenue. I also believe all three give significant reassurance to believers who struggle with the same issue. Recall Anselm's contention that God has reasons for his existence within himself. In other words, he is a necessary being and does not derive this necessary quality from sources external to himself. His necessity is such that the reasons for his existence are internal to him. Given this understanding, everything that God brings about, or causes to exist, are all dependent on him. God would not be acting in a manner consistent with his character, therefore, if he were to cause pointless events or allow them to happen. Hence, to be consistent with his character, all events that God brings about or allows to happen are not in vain. For this reason, the theist would not admit that some supposed instance of pointless suffering is in fact just that. Given the aforesaid, and in light of Scripture's promise that all things work for good to them that love God,[22] no event, painful or otherwise, is pointless from God's perspective.

Some raise the objection that one can contend that life has meaning without necessarily tracing that meaning back to God. In other words, we need not posit the existence of God to know that life is meaningful. As evidence for the truth of this claim, atheists point to just this universe to prove that it is completely natural without any supernatural entities (e.g., God, angels, demons, and souls) inhabiting it, but it is nonetheless meaningful. In other words, it has a purpose, which if we see it as fulfilling would leave us to conclude that it is a meaningful world.

Two things need to be said of this claim. First, this view seems to run contrary to the dictates of modern science, which refuses to attribute any overarching purpose to the universe. Thus the atheist, mostly influenced by the scientific worldview, contradicts himself in this regard. Championed by Charles Darwin in the 1800s and overwhelmingly adopted by biologists today, scientists take pains to argue that meaning or purpose so understood does not exist, broadly speaking, as an overarching purpose toward which the world is moving. Admitting the existence or possibility of a purpose is to come dangerously close to postulating the existence of the supernatural, which they think is a problematic way of conducting their scientific enterprise.

---

22. See Rom 8:28.

The denial of the meaningfulness of life, which came as a consequence of the rejection of the purposefulness of life, was in itself a rejection of Aristotle's first and fourth cause. Aristotle's fourth cause, for example, also heavily adopted by Thomas Aquinas, gave both philosophers the background for the formulation and legitimatization of the design argument. However, as today's naturalistic biologists will vigorously contend, the world is not designed, even though it appears designed. It is a world that came about by chance through the blind forces of nature. Hence, if an honest atheist subscribes to this naturalistic framework, the atheist cannot in any way consistently believe that the universe has an overall objective meaning or purpose to it and at the same time maintain the scientific-cum-biological presupposition that the universe is an undesigned product of the blind forces of nature.

A second observation that I believe needs to be made can be stated in the following way: The atheist, following the naturalistic frameworks of biology, will admit that the universe has no overarching meaning and purpose. However, the atheist might still maintain that *we* can assign meaning to the universe. In this way the universe can be seen to be meaningful. Hence, for example, we can find meaning and purpose in doing what we enjoy doing. We can find meaning and purpose in fulfilling our parental or family duties. We can find meaning and purpose in pursuing certain careers. This vantage point would then supply us with the meaning we seek.

This way of finding meaning appears very relativistic. The difficulties with this form of relativism become apparent when we make the following considerations. What might be meaningful for a given individual might not necessarily be meaningful for another individual, in the long run. Having no objective overarching meaning to life but only the relativistic meaning that we could assign to it implies that what we accepted as our common longings, which we think all human beings have, are no longer common, but vastly different. Thus, to use my favorite apologist's line, perhaps some would find great meaning and satisfaction in loving their neighbor, while others would find equal gratification in eating them! If the universe becomes meaningful for us only when we assign meaning to it, then nothing prevents this kind of scenario from unfolding. To be sure, the society would be unlivable if we promulgate this view as a law.

Of course, one might say that we could all agree about what we could take to be meaningful and then pursue it as a goal. In this way, the populations of the earth would all have one purpose to pursue—one for which they perhaps need to live and one that appears objective for all. This state of affairs sounds logically possible. However, we are not guaranteed that human beings are capable of arriving at such a consensus. Given the ideological conflicts we witness in our world today, very little, or nothing, seems capable of securing this state of affairs for us. We are not in agreement, for example, as to the kind of political system we think we could all adopt as a world. In areas where we seem to be in agreement, conflicts still emerge. Moreover, even if we are to arrive at just this sort of consensus, we have no guarantee that future generations will not repeal it. I dare say, in addition, that the mere possibility of conflict, even when a consensus is within reach, is in itself an indication of a deeper longing that is not only not being met with respect to the atheistic worldview but is also being denied of our very humanity. It is being denied because we are prescribing an inadequate solution for a deep inner longing.

All these considerations lead us to conclude, then, that without a theocentric worldview, the question of meaning cannot be legitimately asked. If the question of meaning cannot be legitimately asked, any particular instance of Q_w with regard to the issue of the so-called pointless suffering is itself a misguided one if asked from the perspective of a God-denying view. Only within a theocentric framework can the question be meaningfully asked because the theistic believer lives with the expectation that an answer is forthcoming.

Having made these observations, let me bring this book to a close. We discovered, in earlier chapters, that the Bible seems to show that pain in our world came about as a direct consequence of sin, whether we are dealing with individual sins or sin as a category. We have also discovered, in chapters two and three, the logical fallacy involved in naturalistic-cum-materialistic explications of the problem of evil wherein evil and pain seem to be deemed either synonymous or nearly synonymous. These pairs do not necessarily imply each other in a reciprocal way.

I have also argued that in order for us to have fair terms of engagement, we need to adopt an essentialist reading of ethics that would enable us to locate the exact meaning of evil and good. I contended that only from an essentialist reading of ethics would there be any meaningful debate between the interlocutors. We then considered whether, on this earth, a certain sense of evil and pain might converge in a way that would allow us to see them as synonymous. I concluded that finding such an instance would be extremely difficult. Turning our attention to pain, I showed that the existence and facts of pain in no way count as evidence against the existence of God, for the simple reason that God himself is a being that suffers, perhaps in ways more intense than his creation.

In light of all these findings, I thought it necessary to locate the exact relationship between evil and pain. I concluded in the seventh chapter that the relationship is that of causal entailment, such that pain turns out to be the resultant effect of evil. Scripture seems to teach this very conclusion. Moreover, I concluded that if pain is the causal effect of evil, then the problem of evil is quite different in scope from the problem of pain. Thus, if the problem of evil is redefined in a way that captures evil as that which runs contrary to God's character, it turns out that the existence of free will, which God created, is a logical explanation for the existence of evil, and if pain is seen as an experience that even God lives through, then the existence of pain cannot be evidence against the existence of God. In this last chapter, I considered the notion of pointless suffering. As troubling as the occurrence of pointless suffering might be, I have shown in this final chapter that it does not exactly count as evidence against the existence of God.

The upshot of this entire consideration is something that has been largely ignored by materialistic thinkers. Once we remove the doctrine of the human fall (irrespective of how one wishes to understand it) from the equation, the problem of evil and pain will always present severe intellectual difficulties for Christian believers. Once the doctrine of natural selection was accepted by Christian believers in a way that did away with the events analogous to those described in Genesis 3, Christian philosophers of religion have often groped in intellectual darkness for possible answers to the challenge.

However, thinkers such as Lewis, Polkinghorne, and Collins have shown that maintaining scientific integrity in our understanding of Scripture, in a way that honors both science and religion, is still possible. Trying to demonstrate this symbiosis is beyond the scope of this project. Instead, my purpose here was to show that pain and evil are terms or entities that do not imply each other in a manner that would lead us to think that they are synonymous. The fact of the matter is that they are different. Moreover, when we show that they are different, the intellectual difficulties arising from believing in the facts of pain, evil, and the existence of God seem to dissipate. As long as we still live in this fallen world, pain and evil will still be a reality. The believer hopes for a day when both will be eliminated. Indeed, this elimination is the hope provided by eschatological considerations of the Christian tradition, and that hope is big enough to fill the existential void raised by instances of intense pain that seem pointless to us.

Bibliography

Adams, Marilyn McCord. "Horrendous Evils and the Goodness of God." In *Philosophy of Religion: Selected Readings*, edited by Michael L. Peterson et al., 333–42. 4th ed. New York: Oxford University Press, 2009.

Adams, Robert M. "Must God Create the Best?" In *The Problem of Evil: Selected Readings*, edited by Michael L. Peterson, 275–88. Notre Dame: University of Notre Dame Press, 1992.

Alston, William. "Speaking Literally of God." In *Philosophy of Religion: Selected Readings*, edited by Michael L. Peterson et al., 409–23. 4th ed. New York: Oxford University Press, 2009.

Aquinas, Thomas. "Summa Theologica." In *The Problem of Evil: Selected Readings*, edited by Michael L. Peterson, 31–38. Notre Dame: University of Notre Dame Press, 1992.

Aristotle. "Nichomachean Ethics." In *The Basic Works of Aristotle*, edited by Richard McKeon, 935–1126. New York: Modern Library, 2001.

———. "Physics." In *The Basic Works of Aristotle*, edited by Richard McKeon, 218–397. New York: Modern Library, 2001.

Armstrong, D. M. "The Nature of Mind." In *Fifty Readings in Philosophy*, edited by Donald C. Abel, 209–19. 3rd ed. New York: McGraw-Hill, 2008.

Arnobius, of Sicca. "The Seven Books of Arnobius against the Heathen." In vol. 6 of *The Ante-Nicene Fathers: Translations of the Writings of the Fathers Down to AD 325*, edited by Alexander Roberts and James Donaldson, 413–539. Grand Rapids: Eerdmans, 1994.

Augustine, Saint, Bishop of Hippo. *Concerning the City of God against the Pagans*. London: Penguin, 1972.

Bentham, Jeremy. *Introduction to the Principles of Morals and Legislation*. New York: Hafner, 1965.

Bradley, Ben. "Fischer on Death and Unexperienced Evils." *Philosophical Studies* 158 (2012) 507–13.

Brandt, Richard B. "Hedonism." In vol. 3 of *The Encyclopedia of Philosophy*, edited by Paul Edwards, 432–34. New York: Macmillan, 1967.

Brueckner, Anthony, and John Martin Fischer. "The Evil of Death and the Lucretian Symmetry." *Philosophical Studies* 163 (2013) 783–89.

Bryce, Hamilton. "Introduction to Arnobius." In vol. 6 of *The Ante-Nicene Fathers: Translations of the Writings of the Fathers Down to AD 325*, edited by Alexander Roberts and James Donaldson, 405–11. Grand Rapids: Eerdmans, 1994.

Burley, Mikel. "Harry Silverstein's Four-Dimensionalism and the Purported Evil of Death." *International Journal of Philosophical Studies* 16 (2008) 559–68.

Cahn, Steven M., ed. *Classics of Western Philosophy*. 5th ed. Indianapolis: Hackett, 1999.

Campbell, Keith. "Materialism." In vol. 5 of *The Encyclopedia of Philosophy*, edited by Paul Edwards, 179–88. New York: Macmillan, 1967.

Chisholm, Roderick. "Which Physical Thing Am I?" In *Metaphysics: The Big Questions*, edited by Peter Van Inwagen and Dean W. Zimmerman, 291–95. Malden, MA: Blackwell, 1998.

Cicero. *On Moral Ends*. Edited by Julia Annas. Cambridge: Cambridge University Press, 2001.

Clement, of Alexandria, Saint. "The Stromata, or Miscelannies." In vol. 2 of *The Ante-Nicene Fathers: Translations of the Writings of the Fathers Down to AD 325*, edited by Alexander Roberts and James Donaldson, 299–568. Grand Rapids: Eerdmans, 1994.

Collins, Francis S. *The Language of God: A Scientist Presents Evidence for Belief*. New York: Free Press, 2006.

Craig, William Lane. *Reasonable Faith: Christian Truth and Apologetics*. 3rd ed. Wheaton, IL: Crossway, 2008.

Darwin, Charles. *Origin of Species*. 3rd ed. New York: Oxford University Press, 1996.

Dawkins, Richard. *The Blind Watchmaker: Why the Evidence for Evolution Reveals a Universe Without Design*. New York: Norton, 1987.

Dembski, William A. *The End of Christianity: Finding a Good God in an Evil World*. Nashville: B & H Academic, 2009.

Descartes, René. "Meditations on First Philosophy in Which the Existence of God and the Distinction Between the Soul and Body Are Demonstrated." In *Classics of Western Philosophy*, edited by Stephen M. Cahn, 343–77. Indianapolis: Hackett, 1999.

Dostoyevsky, Fyodor. "Rebellion." In *The Problem of Evil: Selected Readings*, edited by Michael L. Peterson, 57–66. Notre Dame: University of Notre Dame Press, 1992.

Epicurus. "Letter to Herodotus." In *Epicurus: The Extant Remains*, translated by Cyril Bailey, 173–274. Oxford: Clarendon, 1926.

———. "Letter to Menoeceus." In *Classics of Moral and Political Theory*, edited by Michael L. Morgan, 359–61. Indianapolis: Hackett, 2001.

———. "Principal Doctrines." In *Classics of Moral and Political Theory*, edited by Michael L. Morgan, 362–64. Indianapolis: Hackett, 2001.

Erickson, Millard J. *Christian Theology*. 2nd ed. Grand Rapids: Baker, 1998.

Feldman, Fred. "Brueckner and Fischer On the Evil of Death." *Philosophical Studies* 162 (2013) 309–17

———. "Some Puzzles About the Evil of Death." In *Life, Death, and Meaning: Key Philosophical Readings on the Big Questions*, edited by David Benatar, 220–40. New York: Rowman and Littlefield, 2004.

Flew, Anthony, R. M. Hare, and Basil Mitchell. "The Falsification Debate on Religious Belief." In *Classics of Philosophy*. Vol. 3, *The Twentieth Century*, edited by Louis P. Pojman, 347–50. New York: Oxford University Press, 2001.

Ford, Lewis. "Divine Persuasion and the Triumph of Good." In *The Problem of Evil: Selected Readings*, edited by Michael L. Peterson, 247–66. Notre Dame: University of Notre Dame Press, 1992.

Grundem, Wayne. *Systematic Theology: An Introduction to Biblical Doctrine*. Grand Rapids: Zondervan, 1994.

Harris, Sam. *The Moral Landscape: How Science Can Determine Human Values*. New York: Simon and Schuster, 2011.

Hasker, William. "On Regretting the Evils of This World." In *The Problem of Evil: Selected Readings*, edited by Michael L. Peterson, 153–68. Notre Dame: University of Notre Dame Press, 1992.

Hick, John. "The Problem of Evil." In *Fifty Readings in Philosophy*, edited by Donald C. Abel, 89–99. New York: McGraw-Hill, 2004.

Hobbes, Thomas. "Social Contract Ethics." In *Great Traditions in Ethics*, edited by Theodore C. Denise et al., 91–104. 11th ed. Belmont, CA: Thomson-Wadsworth, 2005.

———. *Leviathan: Or the Matter, Form, and Power of a Common-Wealth Ecclesiastical and Civil*. London: n.p., 1651.

Hume, David. *Dialogues Concerning Natural Religion*. New York: Hafner, 1962.

———. *An Enquiry Concerning the Principles of Morals*. Lasalle, IL: Open Court, 1938.

———. *A Treatise of Human Nature*. Edited by L. A. Selby-Bigge. London: Clarendon, 1896.

Inbody, Tyron. *The Faith of the Christian Church: An Introduction to Theology*. Grand Rapids: Eerdmans, 2005.

Irenaeus, Saint, Bishop of Lyon. "Against Heresies." In vol. 1 of *The Ante-Nicene Fathers: Translations of the Writings of the Fathers Down to AD 325*, edited by Alexander Roberts and James Donaldson, 309–567. Grand Rapids: Eerdmans, 1978.

Kant, Immanuel. "A Grounding for the Metaphysics of Morals." In *Classics of Western Philosophy*, edited by Stephen M. Cahn, 827–66. Indianapolis: Hackett, 1999.

Kaufman, Frederik. "Pre-Vital and Post-Mortem Non-Existence." In *Life, Death, and Meaning: Key Philosophical Readings on the Big Questions*, edited by David Benatar, 241–64. New York: Rowman and Littlefield, 2004.

Kim, Jaegwon. *Philosophy of Mind*. 3rd ed. Boulder, CO: Westview, 2011.

Leibniz, Gottfried. "Discourse on Metaphysics." In *Classics of Western Philosophy*, edited by Stephen M. Cahn, 463–83. Indianapolis: Hackett, 1999.

———. "Theodicy: The Abridgement of the Argument Reduced to Syllogistic Form." In *Philosophy of Religion: Selected Readings*, edited by Michael L. Peterson et al., 282–87. 4th ed. New York: Oxford University Press, 2009.

Lewis, C. S. *Mere Christianity*. New York: Simon and Schuster, 1996.

———. *The Problem of Pain*. New York: HarperCollins, 1996.

Little, Paul E. *Know What You Believe*. Downers Grove, IL: InterVarsity, 2008.

Long, A. A., and D. N. Sedley, eds. *The Hellenistic Philosophers: Translations of the Principal Sources, with Philosophical Commentary*. Vol. 1. Cambridge: Cambridge University, Press, 2002.

Luper, Steven. "Annihilation." In *Life, Death, and Meaning: Key Philosophical Readings on the Big Questions*, edited by David Benatar, 199–220. New York: Rowman and Littlefield, 2004.

Mackie, J. L. "Evil and Omnipotence." In *God and Evil: Readings on the Theological Problem of Evil*, edited by Nelson Pike, 46–60. Englewood Cliffs, NJ: Prentice-Hall, 1964.

———. *The Miracle of Theism*. Oxford: Clarendon, 1982.

Martin, Michael. *Atheism, Morality, and Meaning*. New York: Prometheus, 2002.

Mill, John Stuart. *Utilitarianism*. London: Longmans, 1897.

Milne, Bruce. *Know The Truth: A Handbook of Christian Belief*. Downers Grove, IL: InterVarsity, 1998.

Nagel, Thomas. *Mind and Cosmos: Why the Materialist Neo-Darwinian Conception of Nature is Almost Certainly False*. New York: Oxford University Press, 2012.

Okello, Joseph B. Onyango. *Heaven: God's Solution to Human Pain*. Bloomington, IN: Westbow, 2010

Olson, Eric T. "The Epicurean View of Death." *Journal of Ethics* 17 (2013) 65–78.

Origen. "Against Celsus." In vol. 4 of *The Ante-Nicene Fathers: Translations of the Writings of the Fathers Down to AD 325*, edited by Alexander Roberts and James Donaldson, 395–669. Grand Rapids: Eerdmans, 1978.

Peterson, Michael L. *God and Evil: An Introduction to the Issues*. Boulder, CO: Westview, 1998.

———, ed. *The Problem of Evil: Selected Readings*. Notre Dame: University of Notre Dame Press, 1992.

Peterson, Michael L., et al. *Philosophy of Religion: Selected Readings*. 4th ed. New York: Oxford University Press, 2009.

Pike, Nelson, ed. "Hume on Evil." In *God and Evil: Readings on the Theological Problem of Evil*, 85–102. Englewood Cliffs, NJ: Prentice-Hall, 1964

Plantinga, Alvin. *God, Freedom, and Evil*. Grand Rapids: Eerdmans, 1974.

———. *Warranted Christian Belief*. New York: Oxford University Press, 2000.

Plato. "Gorgias." In vol. 1 of *The Great Dialogues of Plato*, translated by Benjamin Jowett, 505–87. New York: Random House, 1937.

———. "Republic." In vol. 1 of *The Great Dialogues of Plato*, translated by Benjamin Jowett, 591–879. New York: Random House, 1937.

Pojman, Louis P. *Ethics: Discovering Right and Wrong*. 5th ed. Belmont, CA: Thomson-Wadsworth, 2006.

Puccetti, Roland. "The Loving God: Some Observations on Hick's Theodicy." In *The Problem of Evil: Selected Readings*, edited by Michael L. Peterson, 231–46. Notre Dame: University of Notre Dame Press, 1992.

Quinn, Philip L. "God, Moral Perfection, and Possible Worlds." In *The Problem of Evil: Selected Readings*, edited by Michael L. Peterson, 289–302. Notre Dame: University of Notre Dame Press, 1992.

Rosenbaum, Stephen. "How to Be Dead and Not Care: A Defense of Epicurus." In *Life, Death, and Meaning: Key Philosophical Readings on the Big Questions*, edited by David Benatar, 173–88. New York: Rowman and Littlefield, 2004.

Rowe, William. "The Evidential Argument from Evil." In *Philosophy of Religion: Selected Readings*, edited by Michael L. Peterson et al., 324–32. 4th ed. New York: Oxford University Press, 2009.

Russell, Bertrand. *A History of Western Philosophy, and its Connection with Political and Social Circumstances from the Earliest Times to the Present Day*. New York: Simon and Schuster, 1945.

Ryle, Gilbert. "Exorcising Descartes' 'Ghost in the Machine.'" In vol. 3 of *Classics Of Philosophy: The Twentieth Century*, edited by Louis Pojman, 352–59. New York: Oxford University Press, 1999.

Silverstein, Harry. "'The Evil Of Death' Defended: Reply to Burley." *International Journal of Philosophical Studies* 16 (2008) 569–79.

———. "The Evil of Death Revisited." *Midwest Studies in Philosophy* 24 (2000) 116–34.

Suits, David B. "Why Death is Not Bad for the One Who Died," In *Life, Death, and Meaning: Key Philosophical Readings on the Big Questions*, edited by David Benatar, 265–84. New York: Rowman and Littlefield, 2004.

Swinburne, Richard. *Providence and the Problem of Evil*. Oxford: Oxford University Press, 1998.

Walls, Jerry. *Heaven: The Logic of Eternal Joy*. New York: Oxford University Press, 2002.

Zeller, Eduard. *Outlines of the History of Greek Philosophy*. New York: Henry Holt, 2007.

Index

absolute beauty, of God, 165
accidents, 23, 24
achievement-based account, 98
act of rebellion, of Adam and Eve, 110, 134, 141
action, running contrary to God's good nature, 79
Adam and Eve, 110, 131, 134, 141
Adams, Marilyn, 184–85, 187
adulterers, 145
advantages, conferred by death, 108–10
agnostics, on the existence of God, 40
agreeable impressions, arising from virtue, 21
alcohol, finding pleasure in, 50
Alston, William, 61, 117
An Enquiry Concerning the Principles of Morals (Hume), 22
annihilation, Epicurean doctrine of, 15
Anselm, 67, 81, 117, 187
appetitive part, of the human soul, 144
Aquinas, Thomas, 188
Aristotle, 38, 117, 188
Armstrong, D.M., 3–5
aspects, of the human soul, 144
assurance, notion of, 186
ataraxia (tranquility), life of, 38–39
atheistic probability theorist, on violations of God's will, 168
atheistic reading of the universe, why question and, 179

atheistic-materialistic perspective, on deeming evil synonymous with pain, 41
atheists
 confronted by an instance of suffering, 180–81
 on the existence of God, 40
 on God permitting pointless suffering, 10
 locating evil independent of religious overtones, 32
 universe having no overarching meaning and purpose, 188
 why question and, 178, 182–83
atheologians
 on pointless suffering, 159
 on the problem of evil, 32, 168
attendance-taking, different method of, 180
attributes. *See also* nature
 essential for a personal agent, 117–18
 forming an inconsistent set, 56
Augustine, 39, 79

bad, associated with sentience, 104
bad events, 97
badness, 7, 25, 90, 131
Basinger, David, 67
beauty of God, 164, 165, 166
behaviorism, 4, 5
being dead, 101, 102

beings, with the capacity for moral good, 40
belief in God, as properly basic, 67
believers. *See also* Christians
    choosing the good but failing to obtain, 166
    not thinking of God as morally reprehensible, 64
Bentham, Jeremy, 2, 25, 38
best interests, 59
best possible world (*BPW*), 156, 162, 185
betrayal, harming an individual posthumously, 99
BF *de dicto*, 91, 92
BF *de re*, 90, 91
Big Bang theory, 76, 77
blind forces of nature, 178
bodily pleasures, experiencing, 19
book of Hosea, God's feelings throughout, 124
Bradley, Ben, 96
Brandt, Richard B., 1–2
The Brothers Karamazov (Dostoyevsky), 169–70
Brueckner, Anthony, 88–92
"Brueckner and Fischer On the Evil of Death" (Feldman), 90–92

Campbell, Keith, 3
capacity, to feel pain, 131
Cartesian dualism, 4
categorical imperatives, 34
categorical propositions, 30, 31
category mistake, made by Swinburne, 139
causal entailment, as the relationship between evil and pain, 189–90
cause-and-effect relationship, between pain and evil, 134
character, 21–22, 58–59. *See also* nature
character building, 45, 59
character reformation, as painful, 149
character-building goals, evil having, 60
cheating, 34, 51
chief evil, pain as, 12, 17
chief good, pleasure as, 17

child of God, freely wanting to relate with God, 164
children
    deaths of innocent, 175–76
    God not rescuing dying, 60
    suffering of
        God allowing, 148, 170
        God not passive with regard to, 169
    innocent, 60
children of Israel, God's repeated attempts to love, 122
Chisholm, Roderick, 5
Christ, died of his own free will, 145
Christian belief, obstacles to undercutting, 176
Christian doctrine, presupposing the existence of God, 32
Christian essentialist reading of ethics. *See* essentialist reading of ethics
Christian ethics, 40, 41–42
Christian God, as one who must eliminate evil, 32
Christian theism, on God's love in the community of the Trinity, 117
Christian theology
    evil defined by, 68
    on a God capable of having feelings, 120
    on the origin of pain, 141
    presuppositions of, 129
Christianity, doctrines of as irrational, 57
Christians. *See also* believers
    not subscribing to the view that pleasure is the highest goal, 86
    troubled by the reality of suffering, 64, 186
    violating God's will at some point, 165
Cicero, 17–20
circumstances, determining good and evil, 23–24
circumstantial gladness, 62
coercion, 123
coercive power, God not exercising, 83
cognitive awareness, of God's hatred for sin, 164

Collins, Francis, 77, 190
communal being, God as, 117
conflict, possibility of, 189
conjunction, rule of, 55
conscious creatures, well-being of, 26
continued life, death depriving its
    victim of, 88
contradictions
    deriving explicit, 154
    as imperfections in knowledge, 130
    no evidence of in the Mackiean
        triad, 153
contrapositive claim, 79
converse inference, 30
Cornman, J. W., 156, 161–62
corrective measures, 174
cosmological argument, 67
Counselor, Holy Spirit as, 126
courage, reformers exemplifying, 73
course of action
    as both pain and pleasure, 55
    as evil and good, 53
    following if good and pleasurable,
        50
    as good and as pain, 52
    having evil, good, pleasure, and
        pain as attributes, 56
    if pleasurable must be good, 50
    as pleasure and evil, 55
    as pleasure but not good, 55
Craig, William Lane, 67
creatures. *See also* human beings;
        individuals
    with free will, 143
    predetermined to love God, 162
crime, framework for dealing with, 46
criticism, presupposing some form of
        objective standard, 72

Darwin, Charles, 178–79, 187
Dawkins, Richard, 178–79, 182
de dicto conception, 91, 92, 94
de re conception, 90, 91, 94–95
the dead
    having a zero-level of wellbeing, 99
    having sensations, 106
    no states of affairs bad for, 102
death
    badness of, 88, 90, 97
    conferring advantages, 108–10
    depriving
        of continued life, 100
        of good things, 99
        of some pleasant experiences,
            89
    as different from dying, 101
    as the end of one's existence, 99
    Epicurean view of, 16
    as essentially evil and painful, 87
    as evil, 37, 92, 93
    experience of, not always the
        experience of evil, 87
    frustrating desires, 98
    as God's way of accommodating
        the infamous rebellion in
        Genesis 3, 110
    as good, 9, 111
    harming an individual
        posthumously, 99
    as the highest form of pain, 9, 87
    implying the absence of sensation,
        16, 17
    as an instance of evil, 87
    keeping us from having the goods
        of life, 97
    located at the end of a person's
        dying process and at the
        beginning of a person's state of
        being dead, 101
    as a loss, 104, 105
    as neither good nor evil, 93
    as neither pleasurable nor painful,
        16
    as not always evil, 111
    not bad for us, 99
    not part of God's original plan for
        humans, 141
    as nothing to us, 17
    as the one thing humans fear most,
        87
    overriding God's metaphysical
        necessity, 80
    as painful, 107
    as a possible object of suffering, 94

death (*continued*)
    as really evil, 38
    reducing global value of a victim's life, 100
    remedy for our attitudes toward, 101
    as a result of human sin, 141
    Silverstein's comment on, 105
    as simply nothing, 107
death of Christ, 80, 145
deontological ethics
    of Immanuel Kant, 34
    problem of evil and, 86
depersonalized God, 128–29
deprivation, 88, 89, 91, 100
deprivationist objection, to the Epicurean argument, 99
Descartes, René, 5, 77
desire for survival, 76
the desire fulfillment account of wellbeing, 98
desires, God having, 117, 120
dialectical confusion, 97
Dialogues Concerning Natural Religion (Hume), 22
disaster, supreme sacrifice in the face of, 109
discipline, 43
disposition, to behave, 4–5
distance, between God and his creatures, 141
disturbance, as a variance of pain, 13
divine command theory, 42, 73
divine perfection, 184
divine system of justice, 46
divinity, human beings having a sense of, 67
Dostoyevsky, Fyodor, 60
dualism, 1
dying, 15, 101, 107, 108

earth, cursed, 141–42
economy of nature, 23
elimination, of pain and evil, 190
emotional constitution, of a personal entity, 128
emotional suffering, reduced to physical properties, 135

emotions, God having, 115, 118–19
entities
    contrary to God's essentially good nature but not evil, 67
    counting as evil, 86
    if evil then painful, 30
Epicurean account, of lack of sensation at death, 107
Epicurean argument on death, counterexample to, 96
Epicurean ethics, 16
Epicurean hedonism, 14–15
Epicurean reading of ethics, 86
Epicurean view of death (*EV*), 92–93
Epicureans, saying that death is neither an evil nor a pain, 37
Epicurus
    from the Christian vantage point, 107
    contended that death is nothing, 87
    on morality coming from pleasure, 38
    on pain and pleasure, 13–17
    Silverstein's interpretation of, 104
    subscribed to materialism, 12
equivocation, fallacy of, 36
Erickson, Millard J., 125–26
essentialist argument, on death as both painful and evil, 87
essentialist reading of ethics, 9
    adopting, 189
    as the correct one, 142
    on death as evil, 88
    on God's essentially good nature, 136
    on the problem of evil, 82
    on the understanding of evil, 86
essentialist reading of morality, 82
essentialist view
    of Christian ethics, 41–42
    of God, 45
eternal damnation, 113
eternal righteousness, 163, 165
eternal salvation, 80, 133. *See also* salvation
eternally self-sufficient being, God as, 117
ethical hedonism, 1

ethical relativism, 54, 70, 72–73
ethical theorists, on morality, 39, 57
ethical theory, 41, 44
Eudoxus of Cnidus, 12
EV (Epicurean view of death), 92–93
Eve. *See* Adam and Eve
events
    as bad in themselves, 97
    classes of, 105
    existing atemporally, 105
    occurring under God's jurisdiction, 183
"The Evidential Argument from Evil" (Rowe), 172
evidential argument from gratuitous evil, 159
evil
    as the antecedent cause of pain, 138
    brought about the facts and reality of pain in our world, 146
    cheating as, 34
    conflating with pain, 159
    contrary to God's essentially good nature, 42, 66
    death as, 108
    defined, 135, 160, 166
    definition of, 32, 42, 58, 78
    described, 48
    distinct from pain according to Socrates, 36
    elimination of, 190
    entailing the deepest form of suffering, 27
    equivocating with pain, 115
    as an ethical issue, 41
    example that is not an instance of pain, 31
    existence of, 142, 143, 161, 162
    as fully or nearly synonymous with pain, 29
    as fundamentally a moral problem, 138
    God allowed to occur permissively, 135–36
    God's reasons for permitting as hidden, 61
    having properties exactly identical to pain, 31
    instance of seeming painless, 34, 143
    lawbreaking as an example of, 35
    locating the precise nature of, 66
    as moral evil, 138, 139, 167
    more formal delineation of, 42
    not a sufficient condition for pain, 143
    not consciously experiencing, 103
    occurring
        externally to God, 136
        without the occurrence of pain, 144
    pain-reflecting qualities found in atheistic literature and, 41
    pointless instances of, 60
    problem of. *see* problem of evil
    reducing to pain, 21
    relation to pain, 134–51
    resultant effect of pain in the death of Christ, 145
    some attended by immediate pleasure, 44
    some times occurring unattended by pain, 34
    as a tag containing all instances of suffering and pain, 22
    unattended by pain, 31
    as violations of God's will, 167
evil actions
    may not be deemed painful as a possibility, 34
    running contrary to God's character, 67, 77
"Evil and Omnipotence" (Mackie), 11, 40, 57
evil and pain
    not necessarily entailing each other, 8
    relationship between, 146, 189
    as synonymous, 1, 52
    using interchangeably as incorrect, 36
evil choice, resultant effects of, 136
evil entities, running contrary to God's essentially good nature, 66

evil of death, standard argument for, 93
"The Evil of Death and the Lucretian Symmetry" (Fischer and Brueckner), 88–92
"The Evil of Death Revisited" (Silverstein), 92
"The Evil of Death" (Silverstein), 92
evil people, 47
evil things, 47, 53
evolutionary naturalism, 6
existence, of an event or state of affairs, 105
existence of evil, 40, 67, 142
existence of God
    arguments against, 35, 112, 174
    arguments for, 67
    objection to believing in, 11
    probability of, 167–68
existence of hell, as a good thing, 46–47
existential generalization, rule of, 53
existential instantiation, 53
experience
    having beyond death, 106
    Rosenbaum on, 102
experience argument (E), 96
experiential knowledge, of pain, 127
explicit contradiction, arriving at, 154
extreme materialism, 3

failing an exam, 52
failure, as intrinsically bad, 98
Fall of human beings, doctrine of, 147, 190
fallen world, living in, 147
false dichotomy, 37
falsity, establishing, 31
Father, Son, and the Holy Spirit, community of, 117
fear of God, instilled in the moral agent, 71
feelings
    David Hume on, 21–24
    determining good and evil, 14
    God having, 117
    morality and, 13
Feldman, Fred, 15, 89, 90–92

finite sets, considering, 30
first innate good, pleasure as, 14
Fischer, John Martin, 88–92, 97
"Fischer on Death and Unexperienced Evils" (Bradley), 96–100
Fischer/Nagel objection, 99
Flew, Anthony, 58
Ford, Lewis, 83
formally contradictory set of statements, 153–54
$4DF$ sense, existing in, 95
framework ($3DF$), Silverstein's three-dimensional, 95
framework ($4DF$), Silverstein's four-dimensional, 93
free creatures, used freedom to perform evil acts, 40
free will
    allowing the exercise of, 137
    choosing evil, 136
    creatures with, exercising their freedom, 130
    exercising free choice, 148
    existence of as a logical explanation for the existence of evil, 190
    explanation for the occurrence of, 167
    humans created with, 120–21
    necessary in heaven, 151
    in the New Heaven and the New Earth, 150
free will defense, 139–40, 161
"Free Will Defense" (Plantinga), 40
free-willed creatures, 122, 124, 143
future pleasures, caring about, 90
future world, 133

Garden of Eden, restoration of, 151
general laws, conducting the world, 23
generalization, rule of, 53n1
Genesis 3, 146
glad atheists, 63
glad materialistic naturalist, 63–64, 65
gladness, 62, 63
God
    absolute beauty of, 165
    all are guilty before, 168
    allowing

children to suffer, 148, 170
evil to occur, 148
horrendous evils, 64
pain, 68
pain and suffering, 39
suffering, 58, 65
violations of his will, 161
as all-powerful, 63, 67
awareness of his presence, 186
as a being who thinks, expresses emotions, wills, and relates, 116
bowing to a law, 84
capable of
    feeling pain, 9, 43–44, 120, 126, 127, 133, 155, 157–58
    grieving, 120
    having the full range of feelings, 119
    joyous and painful feelings, 118–19
    suffering, 57
as causal Mind of the Big Bang, 77
choosing
    to love or hate him, 123
    not to intervene, 59
    to remain passive, 168
could have prevented intense suffering, 173
created human beings as persons, 129
designed creatures with free will, 136–37
desires of, 120, 122
disciplining
    his children, 43, 45
    us for good, 59
divine perfection of, 78
eliminating all pain in the final apocalypse, 131
failure to act to alleviate pain, 58
feelings of, 124
feelings of approval over his passivity, 70
following a pointless course of action, 81
giving up on, 149–50
goodness of, 39, 42, 78
grieved by rejection, 121
guaranteeing that his free-willed creatures will always do what is right, 163
incapable of feeling pain, 126–27
infinitely superior to us in every way, 77
inflicting pain, 147
on Job remaining loyal, 64–65
knowing
    the course of action producing the greatest benefits, 81–82
    purposes and goals beyond our cognitive reach, 159
laboring to make us lovable, 45
living in the community of the Trinity, 117
not committing evil, 80
not justified in allowing the existence of pointless suffering, 65
not rescuing dying children, 60
not seeming to act, 58
not stepping in to stop his free-willed creatures from violating his rules, 168
not the originator of evil, 138
not violating himself pointlessly or purposelessly, 81
not willing happiness according to Philo, 22–23
obeying at least one law, 71
omnipotence of, 71
ordering the occurrence of all events, 183
pain and, 114–33
as perfect both structurally and morally, 78
permitting evils, 173–74
permitting suffering, 68
as a person, 115–16
as a pleasure-maximizer, 184
possessing supreme and infinite wisdom, 78
preempting the freedom of his creatures, 162
promoting his own interest, 81
providing a standard of morality, 79

God (continued)
   providing moral law, 137
   purpose for his own existence, 81
   reasons to believe in, 185
   refraining from alleviating pain, 59
   seeming to violate his own moral nature, 57, 64
   as the source of morality, 73
   standards for, 82
   suffering pain, 43–44
   taking the sins of the world upon himself, 80
   through Christ dying, 80
   trusting in the midst of suffering, 177
   violating his very own nature, 68, 80, 135
   wanting love for him to be free, 124
   warning Adam and Eve about death, 142
   wiping away all tears and doing away with all pain, 147–48
   working behind the scenes, 149
God's beauty, God's children freely choosing to preserve, 164
God's divine justice, hell carrying out, 113
God's image, being created in, 129
God's law, as an expression of his nature, 45
God's will, violations of, 45, 167
Gomer, 122
good
   described, 48
   existing without God, 33
   instance of, not be considered pleasure, 51
   instances of as pain, 52
   opposed to evil, 153
   reducing to pleasure, 21
   used synonymously with pleasure, 49
good action, consistent with God's good nature, 79
good and evil, 11, 147
good and pleasure, 21, 50, 56, 57, 65
Good Itself, 38

good things, 40, 51, 52, 137
goodness
   of the existence of hell, 46–47
   of God, 39
   understood as pleasure, 2
"Gorgias" (Plato), 36
gratification, 19, 26
gratuitous evil, 159
gratuitous pain, 158
"the greatest happiness principle," 25
Greek gods, morality of, 73
grieving individuals, 107
Grundem, Wayne, 125
guilty people, going unpunished, 47

happiness, 2, 25–26, 38
happiness and pleasure, 69
happiness and unhappiness, 25
hardship, 59, 158
Harris, Sam, 26–28
Hasker, William, 61, 64
healing, following grieving, 87
Heaven: God's Solution to Human Pain (Okello), 149, 164
hedonism, 8
hedonistic valuation, 6
hedonistic value, of a world, 15
hell
   doctrine of, 46, 111–13
   existence of, 46, 113, 145–46
   meant for evil people, 47
Hick, John, 60
highest good, 57
Hobbes, Thomas, 39
holiness in heaven, 150
Holy Spirit, 125, 126
"horrendous evils," 185
"Horrendous Evils and the Goodness of God" (Adams), 184n18
Hosea
   book of, 122
   commanded to love his wife as the Lord loves the Israelites, 123
"How to Be Dead and Not Care" (Rosenbaum), 101
human beings. *See also* creatures; individuals
   biased toward future pleasures, 89

created as persons, 129
disposition to behave, 4–5
glad for their existence, 61
God designing with robotic features, 163
love and appreciation for God, 132
natural bias toward future pleasures, 89
not rebelling against God in the afterlife, 150
as physical entities, 5
as rational animals, 116
saved by God's grace, 132
separated from God in hell, 112
human fall, doctrine of, 147, 190
human mind, 3, 4, 5
human reason, 77, 82, 144
human soul, 14, 144. *See also* soul
human systems of justice, 46
human values, determining, 26
humane aspect, of our personality, 170
humanity, law of, 71
humans and animals, not designed for the purpose of felicity, 23
Hume, David, 6, 20, 21–24, 39, 69–70
"Hume and Evil" (Pike), 22
hunger and thirst, considering the states of, 19

idea of God, 77
identity, law of, 30, 50
ignorance, of God's reasons for allowing horrendous evils, 186
immoral actions, reducing the chances of, 109
impotence on God's part, explaining why so much pain exists, 83
Inbody, Tyron, 125
individuals. *See also* creatures; human beings
as the aim of all action, 14
experiencing misfortune unknown to them, 96
having experience beyond death, 106
infant, lacking a concept of death, 92
information, Big Bang and, 76

informational attributes, of moral law, 74
innocent children
deaths of, 175–76
suffering of even one, 60
instantiation, rule of, 53n1
instrumental badness, versus intrinsic badness, 97
instrumentally desirable things, 2
intelligent design, 8
intelligent source, 33, 75
intentions, judging and punishing, 169
intrinsic badness, 27, 97
intrinsic evils, 99
intrinsic value, of a world, 15
irregularity, of nature, 24

Jesus
died to achieve a greater good, 80
as God incarnate suffering pain on the cross, 44
not tempted to abandon belief in God, 177
possessing a full range of emotions, 125
wept over the death of Lazarus, 127
Jezreel, 122
Job, 64–65, 176–77, 186
Judeo-Christian understanding of God, 116
just life (moral life), free from disturbance, 13
justice of God, facing, 47

Kalam cosmological argument, defense of, 67
Kant, Immanuel, 34, 39
Kantian deontological perspective, 69, 70
Kantian deontologist, 71
Kaufman, Frederik, 16–17
knowledge, as a perfection, 78

lawbreakers, 46
lawbreaking, 35
laws, 84
Lazarus, 127
Lehrer, Keith, 156, 161–62

Leibniz, 78
Leibniz's lapse, 156
Leibniz's Law, following, 30
"Letter to Menoeceus" (Epicurus), 13
Lewis, C. S.
    on Augustinian understanding of evil, 79
    on character reformation, 149
    on life having meaning, 183
    postulating that God made us to love us, 45
    on scientific integrity in understanding of Scripture, 190
    on this world as the only possible one, 166
lies, telling without painful consequences, 34
life
    becoming dispossessed of, 105
    denial of the meaningfulness of, 188
    full of pain as evil, 19
    giving up on prematurely, 150
    as meaningful without the existence of God, 187
    of pleasure as the ultimate good, 19
    questioning the meaningfulness of, 183
Little, Paul E., 125
Lo-Ammi, 123
Locke, as a supernaturalist, 1–2
logic, concerned with truth preservation, 129
logical problem of evil, stated, 160
logical problem of pain, 155
logically contradictory set, 160
Long, A. A., 20
Lo-Ruhammah, 122
loss, brought about by death, 103–4
loss of life, death as, 105
love, not reciprocating God's freely offered, 121
loved one, in a state of significant pain, 57–58
Lucretian symmetry argument, 100
Lucretius, 88
Luper, Steven, 15
lying, moral problem of, 35

Mackie, J. L., 115
    on classical doctrines of theology, 40
    on literature on the problem of evil, 29
    on physical evil, 11
    on the postulates of Christian doctrine as irrational, 140
    used evil and pain interchangeably, 153
Mackiean triad, revisiting, 57
Martin, Michael, 33, 183n16
material entities, trusting commands issued by, 76
material goods, dispossessions of, 105
materialism, 3, 8
materialist atheologian, on the problem of evil, 48
materialist persuasion, philosophers of religion of, 52
materialist reading of ethics, on death as an evil, 88
materialistic behaviorism, counterexamples to, 4
materialistic ethical hedonism, 8
materialistic hedonism, 1, 42
materialistic naturalists, 54, 65, 128
materialistic nature
    of Epicurean ethics, 16
    of Hume's view on ethics, 24
materialistic philosophers
    arguing that death is an evil, 87
    on pain and the existence of God, 114–15
    remaining consistent with hedonism, 2
    using the term evil, 29
materialistic thinkers, understanding of pain, 135
materialistic understanding, of evil, 17
materialistic view
    of good and evil, 11
    of human beings, 4
    upheld by Epicurus, 14
materialists
    on good and pleasure as synonymous, 49
    on the human mind, 3

INDEX

turning Christian theology on its own head, 42
matter, 75–76
maximum knowledge, God having, 118
McMahan, Jeff, 96
meaning
    theistic worldview and, 183
    theocentric worldview and, 189
meaningfulness, 188–89
meaninglessness, 81
mental pleasures, 14, 19
mental processes, 4
Mere Christianity (Lewis), 79, 137, 168
Metaphysics (Aristotle), 117
methodological naturalism, 27
Mill, James, 25
Mill, John Stuart, 2, 25–26, 38
Milne, Bruce, 125
Mind, 75, 76–77
Modern Square of Opposition, 31
modified experience requirement, 98
moral badness, 13
moral basis, for reproaching God, 63
moral choices, 143, 161
moral code, triggered by a nonintelligent explosion, 76
moral convictions, God creating us with, 81
moral evil, 29, 40, 138, 140, 156, 167
moral good, removing the possibility of, 40
moral goodness, informational in nature, 33
moral judgments, promoting the general wellbeing of others, 6
moral landscape, 26–27
The Moral Landscape (Harris), 26
moral law
    as binding, 70
    divine Mind promulgating, 33–34
    essential quality of, 74
    originating from Mind, 75, 76–77
moral perfection, of God, 77
moral phenomenon, evil as, 136
moral relativism, rejecting, 72
moral transformation, God's children realizing, 163
moral truth, 7
moralists, on the problem of evil, 39
morality
    as a branch of science, 26
    coming from God's essentially good nature, 9
    confined to feelings, 22
    as either objective, absolute, or subjective, 73
    emanating from God's own nature, 79
    God as the source of, 73
    as objective, 74
    reducing to feelings or pleasure and pain, 21
more intrinsic badness view, 97–98
murder, as evil and painful, 37

Nagel, Thomas, 5–8, 96, 103–4
natural causes, pain brought about by, 140
natural disasters, tracing back to God, 141
natural evil, 29
    existence of, 140
    God controlling the amount of, 156
    no such thing as, 167
    not existing, 138, 139
    as really moral evil, 41
natural selection, 179, 190
naturalistic account, of the origin of morality, 76
naturalistic biologists, 188
naturalistic reading of the universe, 176
naturalistic worldview, 180
naturalistic-cum-atheistic reading, denying that God created this universe, 176
naturalness, of judging pleasure to be good and pain bad, 20
nature, 24, 42, 141
near-death experiences, 106, 107–8
necessary falsehood, yielding, 154
necessary truth, 1, 87
neutral state, 19
New Earth, God's promises about, 150

New Heaven, God's promises about, 150
New Heaven and New Earth, as free of pain, 131
nonexistence, existing with zero well-being, 99
nonexistent things, attributing properties to, 99
nonlife, as inconsistent and contrary to God's attributes, 80
nonmoral pain, 37
nonobjective ethics, atheism implying, 33
nonreligious thinkers, disagreeing with materialistic ethical hedonism, 8
nontheistic objective morality, existence of, 33
nontheistic objectivists, contending that information has always existed, 75
nontheistic view of ethics, incapable of explaining evil, 74
noseeums, failing to see, 173
Nozick, Robert, 96

objective good, as possible without God, 33
objective laws, existing independently of God, 84
objective moral law, existence of, 74
objective morality, 71, 72, 74, 77
objective value, issuing from God's essentially good nature, 84
Old Testament, examples of pain and suffering, 176–77
omnipotence, questioning God's, 69
omnipotent being, making free creatures, 40
omnipotent God, 162
On Moral Ends (Cicero), 17
Outlines of the History of Greek Philosophy (Zeller), 14

pain
  aversion to, 7
  badness of, 7, 14, 17
  brought about by natural causes, 140
  as a category different and distinct from evil, 58
  as the consequence of human rebellion, 131
  contributing to the good of a person, 35–36
  described, 1
  as a direct consequence of sin, 189
  doing enough to stop the instances of, 148–49
  elimination of, 190
  as evidence against God's existence, 9, 114, 127, 133, 155, 189
  evil as the antecedent cause of, 138
  example of, that is also an example of evil, 86
  example unattended by evil, 32
  felt by God, 138
  following choices violating God's will, 137
  God and, 114–33
  God using, 69
  as good in itself, 7
  having the capacity for, 131
  highest form of earthly, 111
  implying an instance of evil, 29
  instance of compatible with the existence and character of God, 43
  as intrinsically undesirable, 18
  involving some kind of physical or emotional discomfort, 135
  in the life of creatures with personalistic attributes, 130
  materialistic understanding of, 15
  not avoiding every, 13
  not contrary to God's character, 43, 44, 57
  not evidence against God's existence, 120
  not fully eliminated in the future world, 132
  not synonymous with evil, 169
  as an object of aversion for all things, 12
  occurrence of, 60, 146, 155, 157
  as the only absolute evil, 14
  as part of God's emotions, 126

procuring some great pleasure, 18
of a psychological sort, 144
relation of evil to, 134–51
release from, 18–19
as the resultant effect of evil, 134, 140, 143
simultaneously an instance of evil, 111
some caused by God, 146–47
synonymous with evil, 69
synonyms of, 135
traceable to some occurrence of evil, 146
ultimate result of, 86–87
pain and evil, relationship between, 9, 21
pain and pleasure, 23, 36
pain and suffering, 140, 147, 176
pain or suffering, experiencing, 177–78
pain-free world, God cannot guarantee, 130
painful acts, 35, 45
painful course of action, 14
painful evil, 37, 38
painful physical activities, 35
painful things, that are also evil, 36
painless evil, 37
pains of hell, existing because evil exists, 146
parents, not blamed for the wrong choices of their adult children, 137
passive, God choosing to remain, 157, 168
passive state, God maintaining, 169
passivity, of God, 70, 168
pastoral care, for the sufferers, 170
Paul, 59, 107, 147
pedophilic act, 54
people, treating as ends and not as tools, 71
perceptions, located in impressions or ideas, 21
perfect being, God as, 77
"a perfection," test for being, 78
personal agent, idea of God as, 118
personalist interpretation, of the problem of evil, 156, 157, 167
personalistic predicates, 117
personhood, of God, 155
persuasive power, God exercising, 83
Peterson, Mike, 152, 158, 159
Philo, 22
physical behavior, human mind as part of, 4
physical fitness, involving considerable pain, 35
physical separation, of the dead, 107
physicochemical mechanism, humans no more than, 4
physicochemical terms, of the nature of mind, 3
Pike, Nelson, 22
plagiarism, 34
Plantinga, Alvin, 40–41
  on cognitive faculties and processes, 186
  critique of Rowe, 173
  on the flaw in the contention that this world is the best one possible, 162
  free will defense, 137, 138, 139–40
  on God's reasons for permitting evils, 61
  on how a good all-powerful God exists at the same time as evil, 140
  on humans having capacity for rejecting God, 121
  on the Mackiean triad, 153, 154
  on reasons for pain and suffering, 177–78
  restatement of Anselm's ontological argument, 67
Plato, 38
pleasant states, of mind, 1
pleasurable class of things, 50
pleasurable good, locating, 57
pleasure
  aiming at, 12
  as bad, 7
  as the chief good, 12
  described, 1
  as first innate good, 13
  happiness compared to, 2
  as intrinsically desirable, 18

pleasure (*continued*)
  materialistic understanding of, 15
  not synonymous with good, 49, 169
  as the only unconditional good, 14
  pain and, 6, 20, 49
  past, 89, 90
  resulting from the complete removal of pain, 18
  some types of, not good, 54
  sources of different for many people, 50
  as synonymous with good, 8, 49
pluralistic account, of Hick, 60
pointless evil, existence of, 175
pointless pain, God not allowing, 115
pointless suffering
  asking why God permits the occurrence of, 10
  example of, 172
  God allowing, 148, 181
  not counting as evidence against the existence of God, 190
  perhaps not pointless at all, 159–60
  seeking the point of, 182
  sophisticated unbeliever facing, 178
  theist on the occurrence of, 184
  thorny issue of, 174
Pojman, Louis, 72
Polkinghorne, 190
posthumous events and objects, 93
power, as a perfection, 78
premature death, adding some intrinsic badness, 98
prenatal nonexistence, 89, 90, 100, 101
"Principle Doctrines" (Epicurus), 13
principles of nature, inaccurate workmanship of, 24
probabilistic argument, strengthening, 166–67
probabilistic front, agnostics and atheists attacking from, 40–41
probabilistic problem of evil, versions of, 155–56
probabilistic problem of pain, 155, 158
probability, of God existing as very low, 156

probability theory, reliability of, 156–57
"pro-bias toward future pleasure," 88–89
problem of evil, 160–71
  comparing to pain, 2–3
  different from the problem of pain, 152, 160, 171, 190
  formed by the Epicurean quadrilemma, 27
  free will defense solving, 138–39
  locating, 169
  as a moral problem, 152
  of not a problem of pain, 8
  posed against Christian theology, 107
  redefining, 66, 67
  stating according to Hasker, 63
  theological postulates of the debate on, 68
  versions of, 152
problem of gratuitous pain, 158
problem of pain, 152–60
  different from the problem of evil, 111, 152
  failing to cast doubt on belief in the existence of God, 171
  logical version of, 152–53
process theodicy, 83
process theology, 83
proper basicality, 67
psychological healing, 170

rape, 38
rational being, God as, 118
rational creature, capable of exercising free will, 45
rational reflection, God capable of, 118
rationality, of attitudes, 90
real value, incompatible with materialism, 6
realism, value and, 6
realists, 6, 7
reason, 39, 77, 144
reasons, for suffering, 185–86
rebellion, God punishing, 169
rebellious person, experiencing eternal separation from God, 132

redeemed saints, choosing to live lives of absolute holiness, 164
reductio ad absurdum, form of, 31
reflexive definition, 42
relational being, God as, 117
relativism, 72, 188
relativistic meaning, assigning to life, 188
relativistic reading, of ethics, 70
reliability, of near-death experiences, 106
religious neutrality, issue of, 32
repentance, based on the painful death of Christ, 145
The Republic (Socrates), 144
requisite elements of personhood, 116, 120
righteousness, 165
robotic love, as not meaningful, 163
Rosenbaum, Stephen, 94, 101–5
Rowe, William, 172, 173, 175
rule, knowingly violating, 145
Russell, Bertrand, 14
Ryle, Gilbert, 5

salvation, 132, 133, 147. *See also* eternal salvation
science, 187
scriptural teaching, on God as good and evil existing, 41
second book of Kings, expressions of God's disappointment, 124
second death, 111–13
Sedley, D. N., 20
self-interest, 39
sensation, retained after death, 107
sense of experience, 103
sensus divinitatis, 67
sentience, bad associated with, 104
sentiments, 6, 39, 69–70
separation from God, as an instance of evil, 112
set theory, on identity, 30
sex outside marriage, 44, 45
sexual intimacy, in marriage, 57
sickness of the soul, 144
SIDS baby, 89–90, 91

Silverstein, Harry, 92, 93, 95, 104, 105
simplification, rule of, 53
sin
    awareness of the seriousness of, 164
    consequences of, 165
    as a morally sufficient reason for the occurrence of pain, 158
    punished by God, 144
    removal of, 151
    saved from the penalty of, 132
    separated us from God, 142
    suffering the consequences of, 148
sinful acts, punished by God, 145
sinful causes, of the occurrence of pain, 159
sinful creatures, having to experience pain, 149
sinning individuals, rendering God's existence impossible, 167
smoking, individuals finding pleasure in, 50
social contract, among humans, 39
Socrates, 36, 55, 144
Son of God, excruciating experience of, 129
sons, disciplining of, 59
soul, 16. *See also* human soul
soul-making, God's process of, 60
souls or spirits, existence of, 3
Spirit of God, 125, 126
spirited part, of the human soul, 144
spiritual immaturity, 165–66
spiritual maturity, 166
state of nonexistence, as "being dead," 102
states of affairs
    dead persons not experiencing, 102
    intrinsic desirability of given, 2
    as objects of fear and dread, 104
    posthumous existing, 93–94
subjectivism, 6
subjectivist grounds, problem of evil and, 70
subjectivists, on determining values, 6
substantially and morally perfect being, God as, 83–84
sufferer, 175, 176, 178

suffering
    as the causal result of human free choices, 148
    experiencing God's love and power during, 186
    fact and reality of intense human, 172
    God allowing, 68
    God preventing worse forms of, 149
    innocent, 170
    intense, 172, 173
    limiting the intensity of, 110
    nature of negating the existence of God, 41
    random instance of, 182
    reasons for, possibly available, 175
Suits, David B., 17
superhero, God as, 83
supreme generosity, making possible, 109
survival, natural desire for, 107
survivors of the deceased, as feeling pain, 38
Swinburne, Richard, 32–33, 108, 139, 174
symmetry argument, adumbrated by Lucretius, 100

temperance, as the chief virtue, 25
theist, 179, 184, 187
theistic reading of the universe, on the why question, 176
theistic sufferer, 179
thelo (to will), 117
theology, classical doctrines of, 40
thinking being, God as, 116
thinking capacity, of God, 117
thirst, pain of and pleasure of quenching, 55
thorn in the flesh, tormenting Paul, 59
thought, construing as lying behind behavior, 5
3DF sense, existing in, 95
time chart illustration, Silverstein appealing to, 95
timing argument, regarding Death's badness, 99
Torquartus, 17–20

Treatise of Human Nature (Hume), 21
Trinity, community of, 117
true love, coming freely from a person's heart, 121
trust, maintaining in God, 177, 187
truth-table method, 143

Ultimate Good, Torquartus on, 17
Ultimate Meaning, 81
unbeliever, understanding suffering, 140
uneasy impressions, arising from vice, 21
unexperienced intrinsic goods or evils, as not existing, 98–99
unhappiness, implying the privation of pleasure, 25
unintelligible law, as nonsensical, 74
universal instantiation, following the rules of, 53
universal law formulation, of Kant, 70
universe, 188
unpleasant states, of mind, 1
utilitarian grounds, raising the problem of evil on, 69
utilitarian reading of ethics, 32, 86
utilitarian writers, on mental pleasures, 26
utilitarianism, 20, 25
utility, 25, 69

valuation, realist understanding of, 6
value
    having a symbiotic relationship with feelings, 94
    hedonistic understanding of, 1
    reducing to mere sensations, 97
    scientific and materialistic understanding of, 6
value judgements, ground for the truth of, 7
values connect with feelings view (*VCF*), 93–96
vice, as misery, 22
victim's life, death diminishing the value of, 100
virtue, 21, 22, 25
virtue ethics, divine form of, 42

Walls, Jerry, 81
Watson, J. B., 4
well-being doctrine, 26–28
Wesley, John, 133
Whitehead, Alfred North, 83
why question (Q_w)
    atheist posing, 181
    commanding intellectual legitimacy on a theistic reading of the universe, 179
    on the occurrence of a specific instance of suffering, 175
    posing with regard to pointless suffering, 182, 183

Wilberforce, William, 72
world
    completely bereft of good, 112
    making better with less evil, 162
wrongdoing, decision to confess not pleasant, 51
Wykstra, Stephen, 61, 159

younger generation, inhibited by the aged, 109

Zeller, Eduard, 14
zero well-being, 99

www.ingramcontent.com/pod-product-compliance
Lightning Source LLC
Chambersburg PA
CBHW070317230426
43663CB00011B/2161